THE
AMATEUR'S
MIND

Other Siles Press books by Jeremy Silman

How to Reassess Your Chess—3rd Edition
The Complete Book of Chess Strategy

THE
AMATEUR'S
MIND

TURNING CHESS
MISCONCEPTIONS
INTO CHESS MASTERY

2ND EDITION/EXPANDED

by IM Jeremy Silman

SILES PRESS ☙ LOS ANGELES

First Edition

20 19

Library of Congress Cataloging-in-Publication Data

Silman, Jeremy.
The Amateur's mind : turning chess misconceptions into chess mastery
/ by Jeremy Silman. -- 2nd ed.
p.cm.
1. Chess.
2. Chess problems.
I. Title.
GV1449.5.S52   1999   794.1'2—dc21   99-32901

ISBN: *978-1-890085-0-25*

Cover design by Heidi Frieder

Printed and bound in the United States of America

Siles Press
a division of Silman-James Press
www.silmanjamespress.com

To Takako Abe, whose kindness allowed me to see shades of Tokyo that would normally have remained hidden,

and to Arrow and Deborah Chan, who turned a quick visit to Singapore into something very special.

CONTENTS

PREFACE

My desire in writing this new edition of *The Amateur's Mind* is to supply tools to the average player that will enable him or her to improve dramatically. Though the general base of the original book still exists, I've simplified the language when I deemed it necessary. The book's layout has been redesigned— now it's easier to pick out the key points and assimilate the material presented.

Most importantly, I've added twenty-six tests at the end of the book. The answers to these tests, all deep and instruction rich, add more than one hundred pages of highly useful information. The addition of a glossary allows the puzzled student quick and easy access to chess terms, strategies, and concepts.

I'm convinced that this original material, combined with the improvements outlined above, will turn any serious student of the game into a strong tournament player.

Jeremy Silman
April 1999

INTRODUCTION

Every chess student dreams of finding the perfect teacher—someone who magically knows what's going on in the student's mind and is able to surgically remove the flaws contained there. Unfortunately, this rarely happens in reality. The well-meaning master, not being a movie character or a psychic, thinks it sufficient to look at the student's games, ask questions and give pat answers to the problems that appear before his eyes.

While this is a good technique, I often wondered what would happen if a teacher could really get inside the student's head. To accomplish this, I played games with my students (always starting them off with a good position), had them talk out loud before they made a move and after I made mine, and wrote down their thoughts. To my amazement, I was soon seeing problems that I never imagined they possessed.

To add to this, I also had them annotate a series of Grandmaster games. Their responses to the Grandmaster's moves and plans showed me which concepts they were able to understand and which ones were absent from their make-up.

The Amateur's Mind is the result of these sessions. It is a road map of typical thinking errors that turn out to be reflections of *your* own thoughts as much as they are the thoughts of the people that originally shared them with me.

Within these pages you will find much of interest: easy-to-understand rules and recommendations, new strategies, surprising insights—all designed to help you eradicate the "chessic" doubts and fears that reside within you. Study this information carefully and spend some time thinking about it. Hopefully, it will be your first step in turning the chess misconceptions that you've owned for so long into the chess mastery that you have always dreamed of attaining.

IMBALANCES

The heart of my system of training is based on an understanding of the dynamic and static differences (known as imbalances) that exist in every position. By recognizing the different imbalances in a given situation, a player of virtually any strength can understand what his responsibilities are towards that position with relative ease.

Note that I used the word "responsibilities." A player *can't* do anything he wishes to do. For example, if you love to attack, you can't go after the enemy King in any and all situations. Instead, you have to learn to read the board and obey its dictates. If the board wants you to attack the King, then attack it. If the board wants you to play in a quiet positional vein, then you must follow that advice to the letter.

To illustrate this concept, let's take a look at the position in diagram 1.

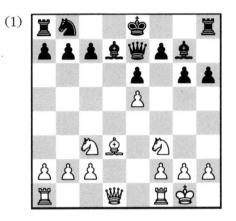

(1)

Dzindzichashvili-Yermolinsky, U.S. Championship 1993
White to play

What is going on here? Most players would either look at the position in a misty stupor or calculate move after move without really knowing what the respective plans are. However, an acquaintance with the list of imbalances would make things much easier.

List of Imbalances

➤ **Minor Pieces** — the interplay between Bishops and Knights (trying to make one superior to the other).

➤ **Pawn Structure** — a broad subject that encompasses doubled pawns, isolated pawns, backward pawns, passed pawns, etc.

➤ **Space** — the annexation of territory on a chess board.

➤ **Material** — owning pieces of greater value than the opponent's.

➤ **Files and squares** — files, ranks, and diagonals act as pathways for your pieces, while squares act as homes. Whole plans can center around the domination of a file, or the creation of a weak square in the ememy camp.

➤ **Development** — a lead in development gives you more force in a specific area of the board. This is a temporary imbalance because the opponent will eventually catch up.

> **Initiative** — dictating the tempo of a game. This is also a temporary imbalance.

A complete explanation of these factors (and a detailed system of planning) can be found in my book, *How to Reassess Your Chess—Third Edition*. However, a "planning shortcut" can be created by learning to recognize the imbalances for both sides. Once you can do this, simply list the imbalances you're hoping to utilize and strive to make them better than the imbalances your opponent will be using. This brings us back to the earlier discussion of "reading the board." Can you "read" the position in diagram 1?

Before you get carried away, let me remind you: DON'T look at individual moves! In fact, never calculate until you understand the basic components (imbalances) of the position. With this in mind, it's time for you to list all the imbalances you can find. Write this information down and then compare your work with the positional explanation that follows.

Imbalances in diagram 1

> **Minor Pieces**: Black owns two Bishops. The position is fairly open, and this makes us believe that the Bishops will prove superior to the White Knights.

> **Pawn Structure**: Black has no weaknesses in his pawn structure. The only pawn that can be looked upon as potentially weak is the unit on e5.

> **Space**: White has a spatial plus in the center thanks to his advanced e5-pawn.

> **Material**: Material is even.

> **Files and squares**: The d-file is open, but neither side has managed to occupy it with a Rook. The f6-square is potentially weak.

> **Development**: White has a lead in development.

> **Initiative**: It's not clear who, if anyone, has the initiative.

Did you find the imbalances? If you were a bit off, don't let it bother you. Like anything else, it takes practice. Keep searching for imbalances in every position you see and, in a very short time, you'll be adept at picking out every imbalance in any situation.

Now let's combine the imbalances from diagram 1 and see if a plan suggests itself. Black owns two Bishops and is also exerting some pressure against White's pawn on e5. Black would love to increase this pressure and make use of the fact that he owns a dark-squared Bishop while White doesn't.

White would like to make his Knights active (Knights need advanced posts if they are going to win a battle against Bishops). Two squares that call out to the horses are e4 and f6. White would like to place a Knight on e4 and then (somehow) bash it into the hole on f6. The problem for White is that using e4 as a post blocks the e-file and makes e5 harder to defend.

White's extra central space, given to him by the e5-pawn, won't prove very useful because he will be too busy defending e5. That leaves us contemplating White's lead in development (will it give him an initiative?). In the present situation Black will be able to castle quickly and the absence of any weakness will make it impossible for White to profit from this temporary plus.

The goals of both sides should now be clear: White must defend his e5-pawn and find a way to advance his Knights and make them active. Black will play to keep the enemy Knights at bay (Steinitz said that the way to beat Knights is to take away all their advanced support points) and to tie White's pieces down to the defense of e5. Since Black threatens to place his pieces on ideal squares by ...Bc6 (eyeing f3, one of the defenders of e5) followed by ...Nd7 (attacking e5), White lashes out in an effort to prevent Black from carrying out his ideas.

1.Nb5

This places the Knight on an active square and attacks c7. Now 1...Na6 would show that Black has lost sight of his goal (putting pressure on e5)—a Knight on a6 would no longer be able to go after the White pawn. Not wanting to be distracted from his desires against e5, Black simply takes the Knight (selling his two Bishops for a gain in time) and ends White's threats once and for all.

1...Bxb5!
2.Bxb5+ c6

This creates a hole on d6, but White's Knight will be so busy defending e5 that it will never be able to maneuver to this newly created hole.

3.Bc4 Nd7

White hasn't been able to make a dent in the Black position while the second player is still calmly following his original plan (taking aim at e5).

4.Qd4 Qc5!

Many people don't like to trade Queens too early; they feel it is a wimpy thing to do. However, Black realizes that his goal is not to attack the enemy King. Nor does it have anything to do with other things that might require the retention of the Queens. By swapping the ladies, Black insures the safety of his own King and gets rid of a White piece that could defend e5.

5.Qxc5 Nxc5
6.Rad1 Rd8
7.Rxd8+ Kxd8
8.Rd1+ Ke7
9.h4 Rd8

Another point of Black's 1...Bxb5 can now be seen. By creating Bishops of opposite colors, Black is able to attack e5 with his dark-squared Bishop while White is unable to use his light-squared Bishop for defense.

10.Re1

Trading on d8 would leave White helpless to prevent (after 10...Kxd8) ...Nd7 followed by the win of the e5-pawn.

10...a5
11.b3 a4
12.g4 Nd7
13.Kg2

Preparing to use the King as a defender of e5.

13...Nb6
14.Kg3

White would be happy to see Black trade off his Knight (which can attack e5) for White's Bishop (which can't play a part in the defense).

14...Ra8
15.Nd2 axb3
16.Bxb3 Rd8
17.Nf3 Nd7
18.Kf4 Ra8
19.Re2 Ra5 and White was completely tied down to the defense of his e-pawn. Black went on to score a long, tough victory.

I would like to end this chapter by discussing a letter I received in the April 1993 issue of *Chess Life* magazine. An irate subscriber accused me of offering inappropriate information to the readership. He complained that "weak" players in the "E" to "B" categories are not able to understand subtle things about minor pieces and weak pawns, adding that they can hardly see a mate in one!

I think this is completely untrue. After giving a student the basic mating patterns and strategies, you *must* begin feeding him advanced concepts. At first these ideas will not make sense; many players will have a vague idea of what you are talking about but nothing more. However, even a fragmented understanding of these concepts will prove useful, and eventually they will experience a marked increase in strength as these lessons are assimilated by repetition and example.

To prove this statement, let's allow a six-year old girl to open our eyes. When she was taking lessons from me, her rating was in the 900 range. I would go through her tournament games, offer advice, and occasionally throw her concepts that would seem to be for much older and more sophisticated players. One day we were looking at a game she had played when I noticed that she had reached a complicated Rook and pawn endgame. To my delight, she moved her Rook to the seventh rank and began taking her opponent's pawns. "Rooks are strong on the seventh rank!" she said.

A little while later she moved it away from the seventh. "Why did you retreat your Rook?" I asked.

Looking at me like I was an idiot, she answered, "I'm putting it behind my opponent's passed pawn before it becomes dangerous. Rooks should always be placed behind passed pawns!"

Let the gentleman who wrote me that letter take note. If a six-year old girl can make use of such advanced concepts, then why can't adults with much higher ratings do the same?

THE BATTLE BETWEEN BISHOPS AND KNIGHTS

The seemingly insignificant difference between Bishops and Knights is actually one of the most important imbalances on the chessboard. What gives the Bishop versus Knight battle even more weight is the fact that most players are entirely oblivious to it, thereby handing a student of the imbalances a huge advantage.

Rules of the Minor Pieces

Rules concerning the war between minor pieces are easy to understand and learn. In fact, you should thoroughly familiarize yourself with them:

RULE 1 — Bishops and Knights are both worth three points (as far as point count is concerned).

It's up to you to manipulate the position and make whatever piece you own more valuable.

Occasionally a book will assign a value of 3½ points for the Bishop and only 3 for the Knight. Don't buy into this! Either piece is capable of beating the other—it all depends on what you do with them and what you do with the other factors in the position that will influence them.

(2)

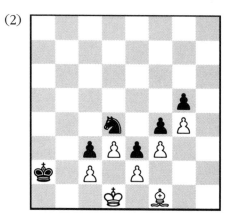

White to play

A book can claim that a Bishop is superior to a Knight until the cows come home, but a glance at the diagram will convince anyone of the Black Knight's vast superiority. Though White is a pawn up and has the move, he might as well resign:

1.Kc1 Ka1

2.Kd1 Kb2 and Black wins the c-pawn and quickly turns his own c-pawn into a Queen.

Once again: Bishops and Knights start out as equals. *You* are the one who will ultimately prove their true value.

RULE 2 — Bishops are best in open positions where pawns don't block their diagonals.

As a position opens up (i.e., the center pawns get traded), it becomes more and more likely that Bishops will be valued more highly than Knights. For example, the type of central situation that comes about after **1.e4 e5 2.d4 exd4 3.c3 dxc3 4.Bc4 cxb2 5.Bxb2** graphically illustrates the board-sweeping power that Bishops can possess. Those wide open diagonals allow the Bishops to reach their full potential.

> **RULE 3 — Bishops are very strong in endgames where both sides have passed pawns that are dashing to their respective queening squares. In such situations, the long-range capabilities of a Bishop make it far superior to the slow, short-range Knight.**

(3)

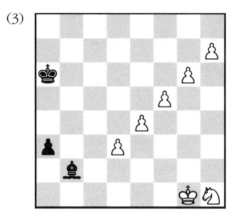

White to play

This position is way over the top but it illustrates Rule 3 extremely well. White is four pawns up, his h-pawn is more advanced than Black's a-pawn and, to top it off, White also gets to make the first move. Nevertheless, White is dead lost! Black's Bishop on b2, though far from the vicinity of White's pawns, shows its long-range mastery by stopping all of the enemy passers in their tracks. In the meantime, the lone Black pawn on a3 cannot be stopped because the ponderous Knight is unable to get over to the queenside in time.

> **RULE 4 — The term "bad Bishop" means that your Bishop is situated on the same color as your center pawns (which block it and limit its activity). If you have such a Bishop you usually want to do one of three things:**

➤ Trade It for a piece of equal value.

➤ Get the pawns off the color of your Bishop.

➤ Get the Bishop outside the pawn chain. It will still be bad by definition, but it will also be active. A bad Bishop can be a strong piece!

(4)

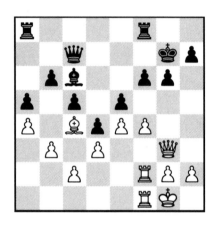

White's Bishop on c4 is "bad" but "active" since it resides outside the pawn chain. Even though it has the stigma of "bad" assigned to it, it is still a very strong piece. If it stood on e2 it would be very inactive and fully deserving of the name "bad." The Black Bishop on c6 is considered to be a "good" Bishop but it is not nearly as "active" as its White counterpart. This example shows us that the terms "good" and "bad" are useful for basic definition, but don't take them too literally! In general, if your Bishop is serving a useful function you can happily toss the "good" and "bad" terminology out the window.

RULE 5 — A Bishop's weakness is that it is stuck on one color for the whole game; anything resting on the other color is safe from its attention. Two Bishops work together very well because they control both colored diagonals, thereby negating this "one color" weakness.

(5)

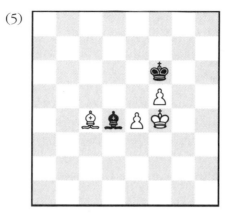

White to play

White is two pawns ahead in diagram 5 but he can't win because his Bishop is useless; it's not capable of chasing the Black King away from e5 or f6 and it can't help the White pawns advance. Give White another Bishop on e1 and Black another on d7 (creating a two Bishops versus two Bishops situation) and we will see a different result. Now both colors can be controlled and **1.Bh4+ Kg7 2.e5** sets the pawns in motion.

(6)

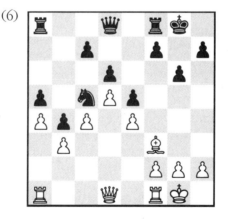

White to play, but Black's Knight dominates the game.

RULE 6 — Knights love closed positions with locked pawns. Their ability to jump over other pieces makes them very valuable in such situations.

In diagram 6, Black's Knight is strongly posted on c5 where it is safe from attack. It also eyes the enemy pawns on b3 and e4. White's Bishop is hampered by all the center pawns which block it and make it a passive piece.

> **RULE 7 — Knights usually stand better in the center of the board. One old chess adage goes: "A Knight on the rim is dim." There are two reasons for this: The first is that a Knight on one side's rim must make several moves to reach an endangered area on the other wing. A Knight in the middle can jump to either side at will. The other reason for this distrust of the rim is that a Knight simply controls fewer squares there.**

(7)

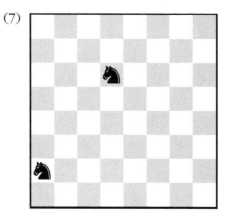

In diagram 7, the Knight on a2 only controls three squares (b4, c3, c1) and must make three moves to reach the kingside. The central Knight on d6 controls eight squares and can reach either wing in one hop.

> **RULE 8 — Since Knights are not long-range pieces, they need to have secure, advanced homes to be effective. These homes are called support points.**

In diagram 6, the Black Knight rested on the c5 support point. Other possible support points (if the Knight could reach them) would be c3 and d4. Note that a square like f4 is not a support point since White could easily chase an intruding Knight away by g2-g3. In general, a Knight would like to find itself as far up the board as possible. The following points could prove useful:

> Knights are not effective on the first rank. Here they act in a purely defensive role.

> A Knight stuck on the second rank is also defensive, and is considered to be inferior to a Bishop.

> A Knight on the third rank serves many defensive functions and is ready to jump further up the board at a moment's notice.

> A Knight securely placed on the fourth rank is considered to be fully equal to a Bishop.

> A Knight on the fifth is a powerful attacking unit and is usually stronger than a Bishop.

> A Knight reaches the zenith of its potential on the sixth rank. Here it eats most other pieces alive and the defender is often happy to sacrifice a Rook for the offending horse and the pawn that protected it.

> A Knight on the last two ranks offers diminishing returns since it does not control as many squares as it does on the sixth.

(8)

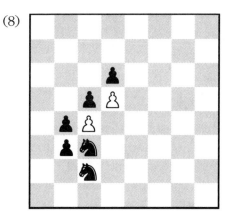

Knight on the 6th is better than a Knight on the 7th.

In diagram 8, the Knight on c3 attacks eight squares deep in the enemy camp. The Knight on c2 only controls six squares. This shows how a Knight loses some of its powers once it passes the sixth rank.

RULE 9 — Knights are superior to Bishops in an endgame if all the pawns are on one side of the board. This is because the Bishop's long-range powers no longer have meaning while the Knight's ability to go to either color square means that there is no safe haven for the enemy King or pawns. This is illustrated in diagram 9.

(9)

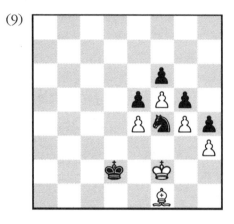

White to play, Black wins.

The White Bishop cannot come into contract with the Black King, Knight or pawns. In the meantime, the White pawns on e4 and h3 are vulnerable to the combined attack of the enemy King and Knight.

RULE 10 — The first official World Chess Champion, Wilhelm Steinitz, pioneered work on the minor pieces. He stated that the way to beat Knights was to deprive them of any advanced support points. Then they would be inactive and, as a result, inferior to Bishops. The reverse, of course, is that if you possess Knights, you must strive as hard as you can to create support points for them.

• • • • •

Now that we've examined the correct rules for a Bishop versus Knight battle, it's time to see how an amateur puts these bits of wisdom into actual practice. As will quickly become apparent, having access to this knowledge is one thing, actually using it in an over the board struggle is quite another!

The first position that we will consider in-depth came about after the moves **1.d4 Nf6 2.c4 e6 3.g3 d5 4.Bg2 dxc4 5.Qa4+ Bd7 6.Qxc4 Bc6 7.Nf3 Bd5 8.Qd3 Be4 9.Qd1 c5 10.Nc3 Bc6 11.0-0 Nbd7 12.Qc2 cxd4 13.Nxd4 Bxg2 14.Kxg2 Bc5 15.Rd1 0-0 16.e4 Qe7 17.Qe2 Bxd4 18.Rxd4 e5 19.Rd1 Nb6**. This led to the position in diagram 10.

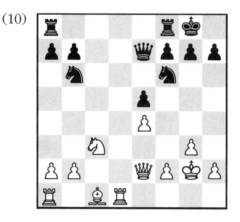

(10)

Silman-Gross, American Open 1992.
White to play.

What's going on in this seemingly boring position? The pawn structure is more or less symmetrical, nobody can lay claim to any space advantage, all the pieces are well-defended and neither King is in any trouble. Aside from the fact that White's pieces are more aggressively posted since they are trying to take control of d5 (while Black's Knights are passively trying to defend that square), the one major imbalance is a minor piece difference: White has a Bishop and Knight while Black is stuck with two Knights.

Due to the stated imbalances, White will use Steinitz's rule (to make Knights ineffective by taking away their advanced support points). He will do this by restricting the b6-Knight by b2-b3 (if necessary) followed by a2-a4-a5 (kicking it from its perch on b6). He will also place the Bishop on the flexible e3-square and move his Queen to b5 where it eyes the pawns on b7 and e5. All these things may seem small in themselves, but together they add up to unpleasant pressure on the Black position.

20.Be3 Rfd8

On 20...Qb4 White would have played the bothersome 21.Bg5.

21.Qb5!

Making each of his pieces better than their Black counterparts. White's Queen is obviously superior to Black's lady on e7, his c3-Knight (ready to leap into d5 at any moment) is more aggressively posted than either Black jumper, and his Bishop defends d4 and is constantly threatening to chop on b6.

21...Qe6
22.b3

Simply keeping the Knight out of c4.

22...h6

Black should have tried the more aggressive 22...h5!, intending to advance to h4 with some kingside threats.

23.a4 Rxd1
24.Rxd1 Rc8
25.Rd3 Qc6?

IM Jack Peters (chess columnist for the *Los Angeles Times*) recommended 25...Rc7 26.a5 Nc8. This holds on to his material for the time being, but Black's position still remains quite unpleasant.

26.Qxe5 Re8
27.Qd6 Nxe4

Now Black loses by force.

28.Qxc6 bxc6
29.a5! Nxc3

Black would also lose a pawn after 29...Nd5 30.Nxd5. Even worse is 29...Nc8 30.Nxe4 Rxe4 31.Rd8+ picking up a piece.

30.axb6 Nd5
31.bxa7, 1-0.

Black's case is hopeless. For example, 31...Ra8 32.Rxd5! cxd5 33.b4 followed by b5-b6-b7.

How would an amateur handle White's position from diagram 10? Would a student of mine, trained to recognize the imbalances that exist in any position, see and make use of them, or would he miss everything and just look at random moves? This question interested me, so I asked some of my students to take the White pieces and do their best to "show their stuff." They were told to think out loud, which enabled me to write down their thoughts and see just what, if anything, was wrong with their methods of thinking.

Of course, I didn't expect my students to play as I did in the Silman-Gross game. White's play was rather subtle and is not something that a class player would ordinarily come up with. However, I did hope that they would notice the Bishop versus Knight imbalance and try to make something of it. Instead, I found that my students (with one exception), after noting that this imbalance was present, refused to try to turn it into something significant. Why? Does the average tournament player think that a simple Bishop versus Knight difference is very little to work with? Do they think that such things are unimportant (even though I constantly tell them that Bishop versus Knight is extremely important)? Let's see if the following games can shed some light on these questions.

(11)

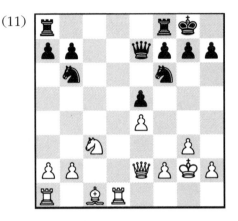

1000-Silman.
White to play.

1000: "White's King is a bit open so I prefer Black's position. Black's e-pawn is potentially weak, though. The main imbalance is Bishop versus Knight and, at the moment, I have control of a file. I would now like to develop my pieces. I'd like to get my Knight to d5, so Bg5 gives me more control of that post. However, his b6-Knight also controls d5 and I don't know if I really want to give up my dark-squared Bishop. Maybe a3 followed by b4 and Bb2 is good since that adds new pressure against e5."

In our next two games, both White players will not question giving up their Bishop for the enemy Knight. 1000 deserves praise for thinking that his Bishop should be retained. Unfortunately, the plan he does come up with is bad because it fails to use the Steinitz rule (take squares away from Knights). Instead, he gives the inactive b6-Knight a wonderful post on c4!

Also note his fear concerning the position of the White King. In fact, this fear was so pronounced that he immediately preferred his opponent's position! Amateurs tend to panic in the face of any hint of a kingside threat, and his comments show that he suffers from the same "King-safety" disease.

King safety *is* very important! But only worry if the enemy has some pieces aimed in your King's direction. In the present position, the only pieces Black has on the kingside are his f6-Knight and the e7-Queen; this can hardly be construed as a horde of attackers!

A little less worry about his King and a lot more interest in the Bishop versus Knight battle (in other words: pay attention to those imbalances!) would have served him much better.

1.a3

Though this was move 20 in the Silman-Gross game, 1000 was given this position cold turkey; for him, it was move one.

1...Rfd8

> 1000: "I'm not terribly worried about the trade so I'll keep going with my plan."

2.b4 Rxd1

> 1000: "I don't want to move my Knight backwards so my next move is forced."

3.Qxd1 Rc8

> 1000: "With Qf3 I advance and defend both e4 and c3."

He hasn't noticed that Black is jumping on the c4-square. A player should always avoid creating holes in his own position. If he put energy into the Bishop versus Knight battle (which he clearly didn't do) he would have, in theory, been aware of the potential of the enemy Knights. By thinking of other (less important) things, he failed to get the most out of his Bishop and he failed to restrain the enemy horses.

4.Qf3 Qc7

> 1000: "I will guard the Knight and free my Rook."

Something subtle and deadly has occurred. Did you notice it? Poor 1000 has ceased to think of his own ideas and is instead reacting to his opponent's. At first he noted the basic imbalances, and he even came up with a plan (not a good one, but a plan nonetheless). But he failed to ask what Black should try to do, and by failing to pose that important question, he failed to see the weaknesses in his own ideas. Thus his plan of placing the Bishop on b2 via a2-a3 and b2-b4 led to a hole on c4.

Simultaneously, after he followed his plan for a move or two he suddenly began (not consciously) to bow to the wishes of his opponent. Black makes a threat, White reacts. Black makes another threat, and once again White reacts. Soon, before he knows it, Black's ideas come to fruition while White's are nowhere to be seen.

5.Bd2 Nc4

1000: "I can't let you take on d2."

He tried 6.Qd3 but I pointed out that it loses a piece after 6...Nxd2.

6.Be1 Rd8

1000: "I can play 7.Nb5 to put pressure on his Queen and advance the Knight. It's dumb, though. He's much farther forward than me and I don't like his c4-Knight. I can go to c1 and get ready for a fork or a skewer. Unfortunately, that would hang my a3-pawn. I'll play h4 and hope to chase his Knight on f6 away with a later g4-g5. Then the d5-square might become available."

Unable to find a solution to his problems on the queenside, he lashes out on the other side of the board. Emotional decisions like this must be avoided, since they usually have very little to do with what's really happening in the position.

7.h4 Qc6

1000: "What is he up to? My e4-pawn is well defended. He's protecting f6 again, which means that he might be intending ...g7-g6. I can't move my Rook due to my a3-pawn so I'll play for more time."

Note how White is coming up with all kinds of esoteric rubbish to explain his opponent's moves. He should be able to figure out their true significance by working out their relationship to the positive imbalances in Black's position.

Here Black is simply defending the b5 and d5 squares and putting more pressure on the e4-pawn. I'm also giving my Queen the option of going to e6 in some circumstances. Amateurs often think that a good move must involve a direct threat. However, this is way off the mark. A move that tightens some key points while placing pressure on an enemy pawn deserves a lot more respect than White gave it.

8.b5

A one move attack that simply chases the Queen to a good post on e6.

8...Qe6

> 1000:" I'll get my a-pawn to safety by advancing it to a4."

9.a4 Rd4

> 1000: "Guarding his c4-Knight. I'll play Ne2 and attack his Rook."

10.Ne2??, and I stopped the game since White hung his e-pawn.

I hope the reader won't think me overly harsh for my comments in this game. I am not criticizing the man, just the player and his erroneous thinking processes. He does some things extremely well, but if he wants to advance in the rating system he will have to accept my literary lashings and iron out these problems.

Our next example features a player several hundred points higher rated than the previous one. Strangely enough, his break-down of the imbalances turns out to be worse than his lower rated predecessor, but his moves turn out to be better! How can this be? The main reason centers around the nature of White's moves: though he hasn't bothered to completely understand the position (by breaking down the imbalances), he still plays dynamic moves that always try to achieve some positive goal. In the previous example, White was aware of the Bishop versus Knight imbalance, but he never really made use of it. Simply put: dynamic moves based on ignorance tend to be better than passive moves based on fear.

(12)

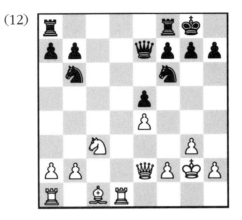

1600-Silman.
White to play.

1600: "I like 1.Nd5. If he takes, I get a strong passed pawn. I have to get my Bishop into play. So f2-f4 is a possibility and if he takes I go Bxf4. However, my King would then be open. I could also play Qb5 to support the d5-square and then Nd5. I could also pin by Bg5 to control d5 more."

I told him that he was not breaking the position down into imbalances. Instead he is just looking at a bunch of moves.

1.Bg5

1600: "This also connects my Rooks and develops my Bishop."

He never recognized his Bishop for Knight advantage so it's not possible for him to try and make use of it. However, he noticed the d5-square and he's trying to do everything in his power to grab it!

1...Rfd8
2.Rxd8+ Rxd8

1600: "Now Rd1 to trade Rooks allows me to continue my fight for the d5-square."

Though he hasn't followed the best plan, he's still sticking to a clear idea (domination of d5 or the creation of a passed pawn) with energy and admirable determination. White deserves a lot of credit for the way he's playing.

3.Rd1 h6
4.Rxd8+ Qxd8

> 1600: "I will exchange so I can have d5 and the center."

5.Bxf6 Qxf6

> 1600: "Now I'll try to get a passed pawn."

6.Nd5 Qd6

> 1600: "Now I will support my Knight and eye e8."

7.Qb5! Kf8
8.Nxb6

> 1600: "This gives him doubled pawns."

At the moment his Knight is superior to Black's, so why should he swap it without getting the passed pawn that he so desperately wanted? One must avoid dumping a plan for baubles lying on the side of the road.

8...axb6

> 1600: "Now I will trade Queens since he has a doubled pawn and my King is closer to the center."

I don't know why he thought that his King was closer to the center. It's clear that the opposite is true.

9.Qd5??

White has played a reasonable game and the correct result would have been a draw. Instead he rushes into a lost King and pawn endgame. He didn't realize that a passed pawn can be a target if it doesn't have support.

9...Qxd5
10.exd5 Ke7
11.Kf3 f5
12.g4 g6, and White lost the d5-pawn and the game.

(13)

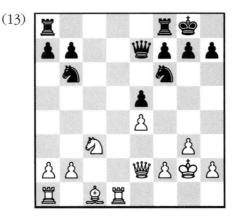

1200-Silman.
White to play.

> 1200: "At first glance I see that Black's Queen is unde-
> fended. White has Bishop and Knight versus two Knights.
> My Bishop has to move to complete development. So that
> would be one of my first considerations. I also control d5 so
> I could move my Knight to d5 attacking his Queen. This
> would also allow me to occupy both open files."

If we compare 1200 with the previous player (1600), we can
see that 1600 ignored the main imbalance but played purposeful
moves towards a secondary goal (which isn't so bad), while
1200 saw the main imbalance very clearly, but refused to make
use of it!

1.Bg5

> 1200: "I really like this move."

Why did he like it? True, it does pin the Knight, but trading
the Bishop instantly gets rid of your Bishop versus Knight
advantage. Don't like a move just because it appears to be
aggressive.

1...h6

> 1200: "Putting the question to my Bishop. If I take his Knight
> and play Rac1, I could grab both files. I think that this is a
> good idea. After Bxf6 he won't want to take with the pawn
> due to a check on g4."

He should have decided on capturing the Knight before he played Bg5. Don't stick your Bishops on b5 or g5 and act shocked if the opponent "tickles" it with …a6 or …h6. Only play a Bishop to those squares if the exchange is good for you or if the opponent can't break the pin. In the present case, Black can easily break the pin. Also, the exchange makes Black happy because he gets rid of White's Bishop versus Knight advantage.

2.Bxf6 Qxf6

1200: "Now I'll advance to d5 and attack his Queen."

Notice the word "attack." He's not too concerned with the state of the position after Black captures on d5. Instead, all he cares about is the obvious threat to Black's Queen, which apparently gives him an odd sense of power.

3.Nd5 Nxd5

1200: "Now I'll take with the Rook and double up on the open d-file."

Notice how he is jumping back and forth between a few ideas. One moment he's trying to control both the c- and d-files. Then he's hoping to control d5. Finally he is going to double on the d-file and try to dominate that. His thoughts are scattered and things only work out because he started with a solid position; trading a bunch of pieces can't hurt his game.

4.Rxd5 Qe6

1200: "Black is piling up on my Rook. Now I can place all three of my pieces on that d-file."

Black intentionally plays a planless, passive game (a suicidal act in a serious game, of course) so he can see how White will react.

5.Rad1 f6

1200: "Now he's lined up his Queen and King on the a2-g8 diagonal, which is alarming. If 6.Qc4 I don't have any threats. How can I get to that King? I can play Rd6 and chase the Queen; this will give me a check on c4 if the Queen moves off the diagonal. However, he has …Qf7 when the diagonal is still defended. My original plan was to place all my pieces on the file. He could challenge me with ...Rd8 while I do this. I'm looking at Qh5 followed by Rd6; he can't push the g-pawn so my Queen would be safe there. If 6.Qh5 Qf7 7.Qxf7+ Rxf7 I've only created an even exchange, but it does weaken his back rank."

White suffers from three illusions. The first is his desire to get at the Black King. Why do amateurs always try for mate? Why not continue to restrict Black's pieces and simply leave the opponent helpless? Yes, the win would take time, but a chessplayer is nothing without patience.

The second illusion is White's worry that Black will place a Rook on d8 and exchange some more pieces. It doesn't take a strong player to see that any Rook move to d8 would simply hang a Rook!

The final illusion is based on the a2-pawn. White seems unaware that any move of the d5-Rook would hang a pawn to ...Qxa2.

It seems clear to me that White's confusion is due to the lack of threats in the position. If he can't make a concrete threat, he feels that something must be going wrong. He won't be able to make any real chess advances if he doesn't mend this flaw in his thinking processes.

6.Qh5 Rac8

> 1200: "Now he's threatening to bring his Rook down to the seventh rank and attack my pawn. So, 7.Rd6 Qf7 8.Qxf7+ Rxf7. If I could only get his Rook off of f8 and my Rook on to d7."

We had just discussed double attacks so I was secretly creating a situation where the possibility for such an attack would exist.

7.Rd6 Qxa2

> 1200: "I saw that but I didn't think he would take it. I guess I thought he had to defend with ...Qf7. Now I have to worry about my b2-pawn. If I move my Rook to d7 then ...Qxb2 is met by Qg6 and I may mate him."

8.Rd7

1200: "This gives me a double attack on g7 and b7."

8...b6

1200: "Protecting his pawns. I'll follow through with my plan."

9.Qg6?

A quick move usually means a missed opportunity. He missed the winning 9.Qg4! with a double attack on g7 and c8. If 9...Rf7 10.Rxf7 picks up the c8-Rook. 9...g5 would also lose to 10.Qf5.

9...Rf7

1200: I'm in a bad endgame so Rxf7 is no help since his other Rook gets into play after 10.Rxf7 Qxf7 11.Qxf7+ Kxf7 12.Rd7+ Kg6 13.Rxa7 Rc2.

10.Rd8+ Rxd8
11.Rxd8+ Rf8

1200: "If 12.Rxf8+ Kxf8 then Black stands better. I've got a lost endgame but what can I do about it?"

12.Rxf8+??

What a strange move! He just said this was bad and then he does it anyway. I suspect this was due to too much respect for his opponent (or it could have been that he simply gave up due to depression). Natural, obvious, and best is 12.Rd7 Rf7 13.Rd8+ Rf8 14.Rd7 with a draw.

If his opponent were lower rated then he would almost certainly look for a better move. If you suffer from this "fear of the opponent" syndrome, you should refrain from looking at your opponent's rating until after the game.

12...Kxf8, and I stopped the game.

Tips

★ The imbalance of Bishop versus Knight is of vital importance. If you have the Bishop you must strive to take away all the advanced posts from the enemy Knight. If you have the Knight you must fight to create a good home for the horse and to create situations where the Bishop is not particularly useful.

★ Bishop versus Knight does not necessarily favor one piece or the other; you must plant the seeds which allow your piece to prosper. The same holds true for all the other imbalances. If you don't recognize and use it, you will find that this so-called advantage won't do you any good.

★ You must take your opponent's possibilities into account!

★ Don't ever play a quick, thoughtless move. That will usually turn out to be the move that ruins your game.

As interesting as I found the position that arose in Silman-Gross, I realize that some may find it dull. It *is* a quiet position and it *does* require a subtle understanding to make anything of White's chances. Perhaps this type of chess does not allow us to fairly assess the Bishop versus Knight acumen of the average class player. Perhaps a more dynamic situation would show other aspects of the amateur's mind that we have not yet seen.

(14)

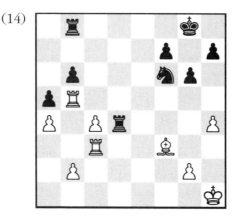

Fischer-Taimanov, Palma de Mallorca 1970.
White to play.

True, the position in the diagram is an endgame. However, White must react sharply if he is to prevent Black from achieving an ideal set-up with his Knight on the wonderful c5-square.

What are the imbalances? White has a queenside pawn majority while Black has a majority on the kingside. The main imbalance is the active White Bishop versus the rather unassuming Black Knight. Notice how White's two imbalances are working together—the Bishop's sphere of influence and the White pawn majority are both on the queenside.

All this seems nice for White but Black threatens to eat a free White pawn (on h4) with check. He also would like to play ...Ne4 (another way is ...Nf6-d7-c5), when White can either give up his strong Bishop or allow the Black Knight to reach its dream square on c5—a post that would stop the White pawns dead in their tracks. How can White stop all these threats? The answer is that he can't! If White wants to make use of his differences, he must give up the h4-pawn (not wasting time on its defense) and turn his queenside majority into a powerful passed pawn.

1.c5!

Making use of the pin on the b-file.

1...Rxh4+
2.Kg1 Rb4
3.Rxb4!

Sharon Burtman pointed out the interesting possibility of 3.Rb3!? Rxb3 4.Rxb3 Nd7 5.c6 Nc5 6.Rxb6! Rxb6 7.c7 and Black cannot stop the pawn from queening. I found this most enlightening. Her rating at the time was 2175 (she eventually made master and became the U.S. Women's Champion), but she saw the importance of time over material (i.e. giving up the h-pawn so her majority could make itself felt) and even found a pretty alternative to Fischer's method of play. Does this mean that most experts would find all these moves? No, I think that the majority would not come close. Sharon, though, had been well-versed in the imbalances (we had many sessions where I would yell, moan, and foam at the mouth. She quickly realized that the only way to shut me up was to learn these things!) and understood that her Bishop and majority had to take precedence over every other consideration.

3...axb4
4.Rc4 bxc5
5.Rxc5

The point of Fischer's play. The passed a-pawn is impossible to stop since the Bishop covers its Queening square.

5...Kg7
6.a5 Re8
7.Rc1!

Rooks belong behind passed pawns so White hastens to place his Rook on a1. Note that Black wanted to do the same thing—he threatened to play ...Re1+ followed by ...Ra1.

7...Re5
8.Ra1 Re7
9.Kf2 Ne8
10.a6 Ra7
11.Ke3 Nc7
12.Bb7

Now the Black Rook is permanently locked out of the game.

12...Ne6
13.Ra5 Kf6
14.Kd3 Ke7
15.Kc4 Kd6
16.Rd5+ Kc7
17.Kb5!, 1-0.

This example showed us how positional considerations (majority and Bishop versus Knight) often need to be supported by tactics.

When I gave this position to a 1700 student of mine, I hoped for nothing more from him than the realization that quiet play might allow my Knight to c5, when White's majority would be stopped and turned into a possible target (the c5-Knight would attack a4).

(15)

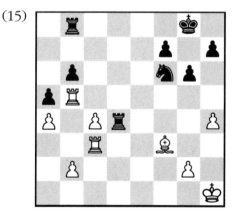

1700-Silman.
White to play.

> 1700: "My h4-pawn is hanging with check. The imbalances are three versus two majorities for both sides. The Bishop is better than the Knight. Black has a weakness on b6 while White has a hanging pawn on h4. What to do? What is my idea? King on g3, pawn on b3, and then the c4-c5 advance. What is the ideal square for the Black Knight so I can stop it from getting there? Where would it like to be? The hole on c5 seems best, blocking my c-pawn and attacking a4. I have to prevent this. My Bishop stops ...Rd1+, my c3-Rook must stay put and defend c4. All this must wait, though, since my h4-pawn needs to be attended to!"

1.g3?

He noted that the c4-c5 advance was important for him but he wanted to do it only after the preparatory moves g3 and b3. Why so slow to pull the trigger? He also pointed out that Black wanted to place his Knight on c5, and that he wanted to stop this from happening. Unfortunately, though he read the position well, he couldn't detach himself from the fact that his h4-pawn was hanging with check.

Yes, in a perfect world he would have liked to play b3, defending both c4 and a4. In a perfect world he would like to guard h4. But Black has ideas too, and sometimes it's a race between you and your opponent actualizing your respective concepts. When such a race for positional mastery appears, you must play quickly to achieve your goals, even if you have to make positional or even material sacrifices to do so!

1...Nd7

> 1700: "I will place my Bishop on d5 where it attacks f7 and defends c4. This frees my Rook."

Black could have played ...Ne4 but I wanted to see if he would try to punish me with 2.c5 bxc5 3.Rxb8+ Nxb8 4.Rxc5, though 4...Rb4 allows Black to put up a fight. As it turned out, White never even considered it.

2.Bd5

Played instantly. He was so concerned with making his Bishop good that he ignored the movements of the Black Knight.

Don't forget: you must not only follow your own plan, you must also take the opponent's ideas into serious consideration.

2...Nc5

> 1700: "He is attacking my a4-pawn. I will start a counterattack."

Why did White feel that this was the moment to start a counterattack? Why not earlier, when he could have made use of his advantages? The answer, I think, resides in wishful thinking. Earlier, White felt he could guard his h-pawn and still push through with his other plans (without seriously looking at what Black was going to do). Now he sees that his plans have ground to a halt, and with the dawning of reality comes a panic-sparked need for counterplay.

3.Rf3 Nxa4

> 1700: "I must take back on f7."

Notice how White is spending too much time with reactionary moves. First he defended his h4-pawn without regard to the other factors on the board (material takes precedence over positional considerations for most players. This is a big flaw, but it's very common). Then he let Black place his Knight on c5. Only at this point, when Black had made his Knight the equal of the Bishop (and the once-active b5-Rook had been turned into an out-of-play piece), did White see the need for counterplay.

This shows us that you *must* make use of what you have before its usefulness fades away. In other words, use it or lose it!

4.Bxf7+

> 1700:" I almost fell for 4.Rxf7?? Rxd5!."

4...Kg7

> 1700: "I will play Rf2 and guard b2 and my second rank.'

White is still playing a game of reaction and defense. Now this poor attitude turns fatal.

5.Rf2 Rf8, and here I stopped the game.

This game showed us that you must make use of your positive imbalances or they will turn into negatives. It also demonstrated what happens when you play a game of reaction: you end up playing defensive moves that do nothing but guard against the opponent's threats (but fail to stop his overall strategy). Such tactics inevitably lead to a deterioration in your position that results in a slow and painful death or an eventual game-stopping blunder.

In our next example of an amateur's approach to a Bishop versus Knight situation, I showed the moves from a game between "C" players to a student of mine who had a rating of about 1100. He was required to comment on these moves and tell me what was going on.

It would be beneficial to the student to play through these moves without looking at the notes. Make your own comments in a notebook. When you have completed this exercise, go over my notes and compare them to your own.

Kaletski-Samalii, Los Angeles 1993.

1.d4 Nf6
2.Nf3 e6
3.Bg5 c5
4.c3

> 1100: "This keeps a center pawn in the middle and lets the Queen out."

The other way to insure that White will retain a pawn on d4 is 4.e3, a move that frees the Bishop and, if Black captures on d4, allows White to recapture with exd4 and open the e-file.

4...Nc6
5.e4

> 1100: "Grabbing the center, but the pawn is not defended. It lets out the f1-Bishop. It looks all right. 5.e3 also lets the Bishop out but it defends the center better, though it doesn't grab as much territory. He could also have brought his Knight out with Nbd2."

White grabs some space in the center but lets Black grab the Bishop pair. Which are better in this position, the Knights or Bishops? At the moment that question has no clear answer, it is up to both players to shape the pawn structure to suit their individual minor pieces.

5...d5

> 1100: "Looks like a French Defense. This should be fine for Black."

A sharp but risky move. The simple 5...h6 forces White to give up his Bishop with 6.Bxf6 since 6.Bh4? g5 picks up the e4-pawn. After 5...h6 6.Bxf6 Qxf6 Black would attempt to show that his Bishops are superior to the White Knights. It is important to be on the lookout for ways to create imbalances right in the opening.

6.e5

> 1100: "That was the problem! Though I must admit to not seeing it. How about ...Qb6? Or, if you don't like that, then 6...h6 comes into consideration. If 7.Bh4 then 7...g5 might be playable."

Very interesting! 1100 was surprised by White's sixth move and panicked. Due to this panic, he was quite willing to give up a piece and hope that he gets enough after 6...Qb6 7.exf6 Qxb2 8.Nbd2. Instead of allowing this type of irrationality to consume him, a player must calm himself down after unexpected moves. Don't accept that you have made an error without a fight! An objective look at the position may show that you have a good reply.

6...h6

The only good move.

7.Bxf6?

And White makes an error. He should have played 7.Bh4 g5 8.Nxg5! with complications that are by no means bad for the first player. Notice how White played what he thought was a winning move (6.e5) but got flustered as soon as Black fought back

(6...h6). Instead of looking for a way to keep the pressure on his opponent (7.Bh4 g5 8.Nxg5!), he meekly accepted his fate and made the lame capture in the game.

7...gxf6
8.Bb5

> 1100: "White has knocked a hole in the kingside. Both are fighting for the center. Black can start taking in the middle and, at the moment, Black's Bishops are locked in. I like White's position since he has Knights and more space. If 8...c4 the center gets locked and Black does not want this to happen since he owns Bishops. 8...a6 is good since the trade is no big deal. I like 8...Bd7 best."

If both sides are fighting for the center (as 1100 wisely said) then why consider passive moves like ...Bd7 or ...a6? Black should take the fight to his opponent with 8...Qb6! with an immediate attack on b5 and pressure against b2 and d4. After 8...Qb6 9.Bxc6+ bxc6 Black has gained another center pawn (which he can use to hit the center with ...cxd4 followed by ...c6-c5). Also, after 9.Bxc6+ bxc6, Black's light-squared Bishop can come strongly into play via ...Ba6.

It's also interesting that 1100 likes the White position. This must surely come from the spatial plus offered by the pawn on e5 and, more importantly, from Black's cracked kingside. All this is illusion, though—Black is the one with the advantage! White's e-pawn and d-pawn are under pressure. As for the "cracked" kingside, Black enjoys an open g-file for his Rook and the potential lord of the dark-squares sitting on f8 (it cost White his dark-squared Bishop to rupture Black's kingside pawns. The price was too high).

Nevertheless, I understand 1100's trepidation. Most amateurs have an unholy dread of kingside attacks. This means that any opening up of the kingside structure tends to send them into a panic.

8...Bd7

This creates a little trap: 9.0-0 Nxe5! nets a pawn. This is a nice trap to know, and it occurs in many different situations. One might think that Black's move is good since it breaks the pin, develops a piece and sets a trap. But you must expect your opponent to see your threat: Don't fall in love with traps!

The main problem with 8...Bd7 is that it's basically a bit passive. It fails to put any pressure on White. This allows the first player to create a plan of his own (based on the imbalances): he will try to dominate the Black Bishops with his Knights!

9.Bxc6 Bxc6

> 1100: "I think White did Black a favor and I like Black's position more and more. Black can take on d4 and play his Bishop to b4, or ...Rg8 puts pressure on the g-file."

The Bishop doesn't do anything on c6. I would still prefer 9...bxc6 with an open b-file and one more pawn that can attack the White center and blow things open for the two Bishops.

To address 1100's previous comments, ...Rg8 puts a Rook on the file but such attacks need the support of several more pieces if they expect to draw success. Also lacking in sting is a later ...Bb4. What will the Bishop do on that square? Black's target should have been the White center (which restricts the Black Bishops), but he has not gone about this duty with sufficient energy.

10.0-0 Bg7

> 1100: "Putting more pressure on e5, but I don't see the value of it since e5 is easily defended."

Black has been floating for the last several moves and he continues to play without an active plan. Small wonder that the White Knights soon take over the game.

11.Re1

> 1100: "Adds another defender to e5 and seems to be a good move."

11...h5
12.Nbd2 f5

Really horrible. Aside from hanging a pawn, this completely closes the center and makes the Knights much stronger than either Black Bishop. Black lost the thread of the game when he didn't notice that the battle was one of Bishops versus Knights. As soon as that came about he should have tried to blast open the center and activate those Bishops.

13.dxc5 Rg8
14.Nd4 Qg5
15.N2f3 Qg6

> 1100: "I like Black's position. He has a lot of power on the g-file."

1100 likes the Black position because he has an "attack" on the g-file. This is very attractive to the amateur. However, a realistic look at this position would show that White can easily defend the g2-point, when he is left with an extra pawn and two strong Knights versus two poor Bishops. These factors add up to a winning position for White. For example, White can now simply defend with 16.g3 or he can switch over to a counterattack with 16.Nxc6 bxc6 17.Qa4 when Black's only hope is the mate on g2—something White will never allow!

Tips

★ If the integrity of your position is based on a one-mover like ...Qxg2 mate, then you are dead meat since such an obvious threat is usually easy to parry. Instead, you should nurture long-range plusses like material, superior minor pieces, etc.

★ When you find yourself crossing your fingers and hoping he won't see it, you know that you are in desperate trouble!

★ Once a minor piece imbalance is established, you must play with great energy to make that imbalance favor you.

(17)

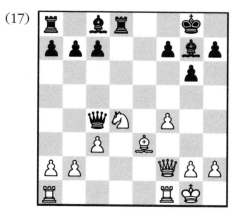

Rosenthal-Steinitz, Vienna 1873.
Black to play.

This position is one of the first games where someone demon-strated how to defeat Knights. Here Steinitz shows us that if you take away all their advanced squares, the horses become rather sickly creatures.

1...c5

Making the Knight move away from the fine post on d4.

2.Nf3 b6

Defending the very important c5-pawn. If this pawn were lost then the White Knight could return to d4.

3.Ne5

Trying to find another home.

3...Qe6
4.Qf3 Ba6

Defending the a8-Rook and attacking White's Rook at the same time.

5.Rfe1 f6

The poor Knight is deprived of yet another square!

6.Ng4

The active 6.Nc6 Rde8 7.Bf2 Qd7 8.Rad1 Qc7 leaves the poor beast trapped. Black will eventually play ...Bb7 and snap it off.

6...h5

Forcing it back to permanent inactivity on the second rank.

7.Nf2 Qf7

A multipurpose move. The Queen gets off the line of the Rook, defends g6 and covers b7. This allows the light-squared Bishop to rest on b7 and take control of the wonderful a8-h1 diagonal.

8.f5?

The pawn will be weak here.

8...g5
9.Rad1 Bb7

White has nothing to compare with the strength of this Bishop. The minor piece battle has clearly swung in Black's favor.

10.Qg3 Rd5!

Staying central and eyeing f5. 10...Qxa2 would give White counterplay after 11.Qc7.

11.Rxd5 Qxd5
12.Rd1 Qxf5

A pawn has been won and the central Black Queen will be able to deal with any temporary activity that White may get.

13.Qc7 Bd5
14.b3 Re8

Black doesn't worry about his a-pawn since he knows that White will never have the time to take it. Instead, the second player places all his pieces in the middle and starts his own counterattack.

15.c4 Bf7
16.Bc1 Re2
17.Rf1 Qc2

Threatening 18...Rxf2 19.Rxf2 Qxc1+ with two pieces for a Rook. Since two pieces are almost always better than a Rook (and usually superior to a Rook and pawn), White is compelled to retreat his Queen and accept the fact that he is doomed.

18.Qg3 Qxa2, and Black went on to win the game.

I am always raving about how a Knight must be deprived of advanced support points, so I was curious to see if two of my junior students (aged six with a 900 rating and nine with a 1200 rating) would catch on to this idea in the game we just looked at.

(18)

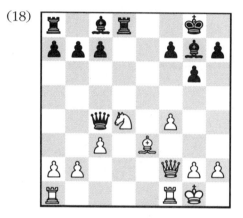

900 and 1200-Silman.
Black to play.

900: "White is better."

1200: "No, Black is better because he has the two Bishops."

900: "I still like White but I don't exactly know why."

1200: "I'd go 1...c5 to attack the Knight and chase it to a bad place."

I suppose 900 liked White since a glance gives the impression that White has the more active position; his Knight just looks better than everything else. However, a few pawn moves will show that this is just an illusion.

1...c5
2.Nf3

900: "Nothing is hanging."

1200: "No! The c5-pawn hangs, though f4 would hang too."

900: "Let's play 2...b6."

1200: "If the a-pawn did not hang then allowing Bxc5 would
be good for Black due to ...Qxf4."

1200 forgot that the c5-pawn was the only thing keeping
White out of d4. There is no way that Black should allow the
trade of his mighty c-pawn for the poor pawn on f4 (which just
blocks White's Bishop and Rook).

2...b6
3.Ne5

1200 & 900: "The Queen is attacked and we both like
3...Qe4."

3...Qe4

The first deviation from the Steinitz game! So far the kids have
played very well.

4.Rae1

1200 & 900: "Now our Queen is indirectly attacked."

1200: "I like ...Qd5."

900: "That's good."

4...Qd5
5.Qf3

900: "I like ...Bf5! with the idea of ...Be4."

1200: "I like ...Be6 to recapture with the Bishop and
threaten the a-pawn."

900 got her way on this one. Note how they are uncon-
sciously trying to make their Bishops better than the Knight,
though I would have been even happier if they had verbalized it
for me.

5...Bf5
6.Nc6

1200 & 900: "We both want to go …Be4. If he goes Nxd8 then …Bxf3 wins for us. It looks like White blundered!"

A very interesting moment, and one that demonstrates how many types of blunders are created. The attack on d8 made them focus their attention to that square. Thus the other threat, that of Ne7+, was completely missed. How does a player avoid this pitfall? One way is to write your move down first and then ask yourself, "After we play 6…Be4, can he take anything (yes, the Rook on d8 is hanging!)…does he have any checks?"

At this point you would notice Ne7+ and, if such a move were really a threat, you would erase your move and look for something else.

6…Be4
7.Ne7+

1200 & 900: "We didn't see this but it's still okay."

I like the fact that they didn't panic. Many older players would lose their composure when this oversight hit them in the face.

7…Kf8
8.Nxd5 Bxf3
9.Rxf3 Rxd5

The game was stopped. The kids did excellently!

The previous example showed us how important it is to deprive enemy Knights of advanced support points. It also showed us how a fixation on one threat or square can lead to an unfortunate oversight.

I should point out that any kind of fixation in chess is bad since it blinds you to other possibilities. No rule is correct all the time! For example, what if you have to make the following decision: You have two Bishops versus a Bishop and Knight. Should you take a square away from a Knight but close the position as you do so, or should you open the position and leave the Knight on its post?

The following position shows us such a quandary.

(19)

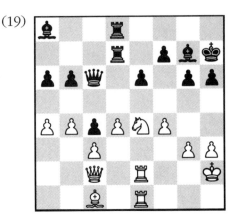

Longren-Silman, Santa Barbara 1989.
Black to play.

Black has the two Bishops and there is little doubt concerning the strength of the one on a8 which, combining with the Queen on the a8-h1 diagonal, creates mating threats against the White King. Unfortunately, the White Knight is blocking this line on e4 and the only way to chase it away is by ...f7-f5. Is this the right idea for Black? The answer is a resounding no! This pawn advance does chase the Knight away but it leaves Black with a backward pawn on e6 and a permanently weakened square on e5 (which White could eventually reach by Nd2, Rf2, Nf3 and Ne5).

Another reason to avoid ...f5 is that it makes the central situation stiff; it would be very difficult to open things up, and Black *does* want to open the position up since that would benefit his two Bishops.

After considerable thought, Black resisted the temptation to play the inflexible ...f7-f5 and instead played directly to rip open the middle of the board.

1...f6!

Now White cannot prevent the center-rending ...e6-e5.

2.h4 e5
3.dxe5 fxe5
4.h5 Rd3

The game is already decided. The opening of the center has led to the activation of both Black Bishops and the Rooks. It is true that the White Knight is still on e4, but the fact that it is stuck there and needs constant defense ties down all the White forces and gives Black a free hand everywhere else.

5.b5

Trying to draw the Black Queen off the a8-h1 diagonal.

5...axb5
6.axb5 Qe6!

Heading for the kingside. Now ...Qg4 is a threat.

7.Nf2 Qd5
8.hxg6+ Kg8
9.Ne4 exf4
10.Bxf4 Qh5+
11.Kg1 Qxg6

The combined action of the mighty Black Bishops and Rooks, plus the shaky state of the White King, make the result a foregone conclusion.

12.Qa2 Bd5

Black knows that the game is won so he defends his weak spots in an unhurried manner.

13.Qc2 Rf8!

This was the only Black piece that was not helping out. Now the threat is ...Rxf4.

14.Qc1 Bxc3!

Drawing the Knight away from its defensive location on e4. White resigned since 15.Rf1 hangs the Knight on e4 and 15.Nxc3 Rxg3+ 16.Kf1 Rg1+ 17.Kf2 Qg3 is mate.

Would an amateur be tempted by ...f7-f5 (from diagram 19 and 20)? I thought he might, especially if he recalled my insisting that you must chase enemy Knights from advanced support points. Let's see what transpired when I handed the ball to a 1700 student.

(20)

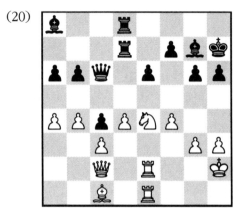

Silman-1700.
Black to play.

1700: "White has chances on the kingside since his Queen, Knight and Bishop are all pointing towards the Black King. White's King is exposed but well protected since the Queen and Rook defend the g2-square.

"What would Black's fantasy position be? He would like to make the Rook on e1 move off the first rank and mate on h1 with his Queen via ...Qh1 mate. Black would also like to get rid of his dark-squared Bishop and create weaknesses on that color complex. In terms of space, White is ahead. Since it is Black to move, how can he achieve his fantasy mate? At the moment, White's Bishop is better than Black's on g7—no doubt about it."

What to make of this? He did not go into detail about Bishop versus Knight and instead raved about a possible kingside attack for White (though he never told us how White was supposed to make this attack a reality) and a possible mate on h1 for Black (I suppose he sees both sides mating each other on the kingside!). He finally decided to chase the Knight away, but his reason for doing so had little to do with Steinitz's laws (take away advanced support points from enemy Knights) and more to do with a vision of a quick mate.

The question must be asked: will White allow such a mate on the light-squares? Can Black force it? Naturally, White will do everything in his power to prevent this one move knockout. 1700 must make the following adjustments in his thinking processes if he wants to improve his playing strength:

➤ Always expect the opponent to see your threat(s).

➤ Always expect him to make the best move! When you find yourself crossing your fingers and hoping that he won't see it, you are making a big mental mistake and are embracing very bad mental habits.

➤ Playing for a tactical shot (...Qh1 mate or ...Qg2 mate) is fine if you can force it. If not, take your time, keep your eyes on the tactics, get the rest of your army into the battle, and pay lots of attention to the positional features on the board! You're never going to go anywhere if you can't blend positional and tactical considerations together.

1...f5
2.Nd2

> 1700: "So I have forced the Knight back but now I must make an enemy Rook give up control of g2 or h1 since the White Queen is no longer defending g2. Unfortunately, I can't find a way to get his Rooks to move. If I could make his Knight move to f1, it's still mate (via ...Qh1). How can I accomplish this? How about 2...Bxd4 3.cxd4 and now 3...Rxd4 or 3...c3. Both give play but I can't see a clear continuation. It's interesting, though. I need to find some plan if there is no mate. I'll sacrifice with ...e5."

Lusting after a quick, violent conclusion (even though his two Bishops give Black a long-range plus), Black finally throws himself over a cliff. Why the hurry? Why the need to give up material? What is this guy doing?

2...e5??
3.fxe5

> 1700: "My idea is now to play ...Re7, ...Bxe5 and ...Rxe5. Then, if he takes my Rook on e5, it will be mate on g2."

Still living in the world of "He won't see it." I have tried hard to break 1700 of this habit but he clutches to it like life itself. By beating lots of lower rated players in this manner, he's convinced himself that he's doing something profound. That's why I recommend seeking players who are better than you. Yes, you might lose lots of games, but you will certainly get stronger and learn lots about chess that those weaker victims would never be able to show you.

3...Re7
4.Rf2

> 1700: "This allows me to continue with my idea after 4...Bxe5 5.dxe5 Rxe5 and he can't take due to ...Qh1 mate. Wait a moment! Aren't I down a Bishop if he doesn't take? My Rook does get to d3 with pressure for the piece so it deserves consideration. Let's calculate: 4...Bxe5 5.dxe5 Rxe5 and now he just moves his Rook and I lose—it doesn't work. I don't see how I can get his Rooks out of the way. I can also consider a different idea, namely 4...h5 and 5...Bh6. However, it's very slow since his Knight will come to f3 and block everything. I can't mate him! White is well protected here. I think that White had the better position all along; there is no question about it. I gave up a pawn to try to rip open the middle and fight it out but it was all in vain."

Notice that when reality hit him he began to blame the position. His problem is that he wants instant gratification. Trying to make use of one's advantages in a slow, controlled manner is an alien concept to him. He only speaks of kingside attacks and mate.

At this point I stopped the game in disgust.

Tips

★ Always expect the best move from the opponent. That way you will insist your moves accomplish some positive goal, no matter what the response might be.

★ If you have two Bishops, take note of that fact and try to open up the position! This takes precedence

over chasing an enemy Knight from an advanced
support point (you can do this at a later time).

★ Rules and guidelines are useful, but every rule was
made to be broken.

If you own the Bishop pair and they are already active (or the
position is already open), then you must concentrate on limiting
the range of the enemy Knight. Our next diagram shows a rather
exaggerated case.

(21)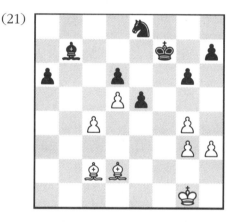

Hort-Ciocaltea, Budapest 1973.
White to play.

Hort saw that Black's Knight had no future on the queenside,
so all he had to do was deprive it of any kingside squares and it
would be a useless slab of meat. Once he killed the Knight, he
could take his time and torture his opponent, secure in the
knowledge that Black would be quite helpless.

1.g5!

Turning f6 into poison.

1...Bc8
2.g4!

The Knight can't go to f6, and now Black's pieces are also deprived of h5 and f5.

Grabbing my trusty old 1700 student, I set up the initial position from Hort-Ciocaltea (diagram 21) and had him give it a try (he took the White pieces).

> 1700: "First I must look for an imbalance for both sides. White has two Bishops but his pawns are doubled. However, g5 limits the Knight and h4 to follow up gets the pawns going. Black has a weak pawn on a6—it's not really passed since the White Bishop stops it. Black has backward pawns on d6 and h7. White's Bishops are active. White also has more space. As White, I must decide which side of the board to attack. I also want to limit his Knight and control f6. However, if he comes to f6 it's just a waste of time since e4 is not available. Black's plan is to get his Knight to c5, so I must prevent that."

He saw that Black wanted to get his Knight to c5 but he evidently overlooked that the way to that square was from f6-d7-c5. He also mentioned that White has two Bishops and that the scope of the Black Knight should be limited. However, once he said this he promptly forgot to do anything about it!

Because 1700 gave so many confusing messages in his initial statement, I feel it would be to the readers' benefit to examine some of them in greater depth:

➤ He said that g5 followed by h4 gets his pawns going. What does this mean? Does g5 followed by h4-h5 threaten anything at all? I'm not saying that the advance of the h-pawn is a bad idea, but I don't think he realized what this advance would really do.

➤ He said that Black has backward pawns on d6 and h7. Those are *not* backward pawns! A pawn is only backward if it stands on an open file (which these don't) and if it doesn't have a brother pawn behind it or directly to the side of it. The d6-pawn would be backward if White's d5-pawn were gone.

➤ He said that Black's a6-pawn wasn't really passed. Wrong again. The a6-pawn is indeed passed. It might not be going anywhere, but that doesn't mean that it's not a passed pawn.

1.Ba5

Missing his opportunity to restrict the enemy Knight. The concept of restriction seems a hard one for amateurs.

1...Nf6

> 1700: "He's going to d7 and c5 so I will attack d6 and slow him down."

2.Bb4

A purely reactionary move that just forces the Black King towards the center. Why play Bb4? Is the opponent going to hang the d6-pawn? I suspect not (especially when you're playing an International Master who is listening to your every thought!). Then why attack it in the first place? Remember: only attack something if the move improves your position even after he defends the attacked object.

2...Ke7

> 1700: "I must activate my King."

In an endgame it is always a good idea to bring one's King towards the center. However, he doesn't seem to have any clear plan in mind. One reason for this is that he missed his chance to come up with an easy plan (dominate the Knight) and now the increased difficulty has left him completely confused. If you are lazy or careless early, the chances are that matters will become much worse later on.

3.Kf2 Nd7

> 1700: "Black wants to go to b6 and attack c4. From there he can also jump into a4. If I play Bd3 I give up control of a4. I will bring my King closer."

Black had no intention of playing ...Nb6. The amateur often thinks that a move with a threat is something to covet, when in reality a simple threat is usually easy to parry. The real quest is to find a square where the piece is happy, active, and secure. Avoid squares where it makes a one move threat and then gets chased away.

4.Ke3 Nc5

> 1700: "This is a bad move. Now he has lots of weak points when I chop it off."

5.Bxc5 dxc5

White has gained a passed pawn and Black's pawns on a6, c5 and e5 are all isolated. However, these factors don't carry any weight at all. Why? First, to accomplish these things White had to give up his Bishop pair. Now he is left with a bad Bishop (his center pawns are on the same color as his Bishop) versus Black's good one. Though the pawns on a6, c5 and e5 are all isolated, none of them are in any danger—Black's King will block White's passed pawn (via ...Kd6) and defend both c5 and e5. The White King, however, will not be able to get close to the pawn on a6. We should also not forget that the pawns on e5 and a6 are also passed; that's two passed pawns for Black and only one for White.

6.g5

> 1700: "This takes away f6 from his King and fixes his pawns on white."

The best thing he's said all game! It is always good to fix enemy pawns on the same color as your Bishop since then they are vulnerable to the Bishop's later attentions.

6...Bc8
7.g4

> 1700: "Defends h3 and keep him out of f5."

7...Bd7

> 1700: "I will bring my King to the queenside and win his weak pawns."

White no longer has any advantage but he continues to speak as if I were lost! At least he has a positive attitude.

8.Kd3 Kd6
9.Kc3 e4??

> 1700: "What's the meaning of that? What's going on? Does he want to resign?"

Black could have drawn the game by doing nothing since the White King cannot penetrate into the queenside. However, I decided to add some life to the game and see how he would respond.

10.Bxe4 Ke5
11.Bc2 Kf4

> 1700: "He is coming into f4 and hoping to use the passed a-pawn. I don't care if he wins my doubled pawn."

12.Kb3

> 1700: "I'm going to trade Bishops with Ka3 and Ba4 and then promote my d-pawn."

Excellent! The way to make use of a passed pawn is to destroy the blockader (in this case my Bishop on d7 is the only thing blocking the White passer). White has suddenly begun to play good chess.

12...Ke3
13.Ka3 Kd4
14.Bb3

> 1700: "I don't want to lose both pawns, which would happen after 14.Ba4 Kxc4 15.Bxd7 Kxd5."

14...a5

> 1700: "Now I should have something good. 15.d6 is very tempting and it doesn't look like I can move anything else anyway. If I exchange too early I might even lose since he will get lots of pawns. After 15.d6 Ke5 16.Ba4 Kxd6 17.Bxd7 Kxd7 18.Ka4 I think I win!"

Wow! He appears to be on a hot streak. To complete his variation, 18.Ka4 Kd6 19.Kxa5 Ke5 20.Kb6 Kd4 21.Kb5 is indeed a win for White.

15.d6 Kc3

> 1700: "What is this? He's gone crazy again!"

16.Ba4 Kxc4

> 1700: "What did he do that for?"

17.Bxd7 Kd5

> 1700: "I'm up a Bishop for a pawn! This must be winning for me."

18.Kb3?

> 1700: "The idea is to stop his queenside pawns. Then I can sacrifice my Bishop for a kingside pawn and promote a pawn to a Queen over there."

This turns out to be a waste of time. Correct was 18.Be8 Kxd6 19.Bf7.

18...Kxd6
19.Be8 Ke5

> 1700: "He's lost."

20.Kc4 Kf4
21.Kxc5 Kxg5

> 1700: "I thought he was going to g3. If 22.Bf7 Kh4 draws."

22.Kb5

> 1700: "It looks like a draw."

Draw Agreed.

Tip

★ Create a plan right away or you may float without a goal for the rest of the game.

So far we have seen Bishops and Knights dominate each other in different ways. However, how easy is it to make the decision concerning which piece to retain and which to give up? Could a student recognize when a Bishop would beat a Knight or vice versa?

(22)

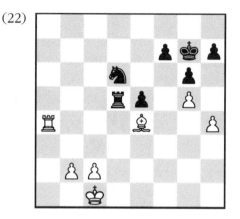

Silman-1850.
Black to play.

In this position (from the game Kavalek-Kaplan, Solingen 1974) Black has three possible scenarios: 1) He can play 1...Rc5 and play a Rook and Knight versus Rook and Bishop endgame. 2) He can play 1...Nxe4 and transpose into a pure Rook endgame. 3) He can play 1...Rd4 and go into a Bishop versus Knight endgame.

> 1850: "We have an endgame. I recall hearing that a Bishop is better than a Knight if passed pawns are on two sides. Here my King is in jail and my Rook is attacked. What would I like to do? What do I have? Where is his Bishop going? Do I exchange? What piece should I trade? I like 1..Rd4 because I can follow with ...f5 and get a passed pawn.

1...Rd4??

I find it amazing that he would recite the rule that states, "A Bishop is better than a Knight if passed pawns are on both sides of the board," and then play directly into the inferior side of such a situation! It sounds to me like he had too many choices and got hopelessly confused. However, when you have the luxury of knowing the previously stated rule then you might as well make use of it.

Instead of this, another rule (almost a joke rule actually, but there is still a lot of truth in it) says, "All Rook endgames are drawn." Following this, we can accept that 1...Nxe4 2.Rxe4 f5 gives Black good chances to hold the game. The swap of Knight for Bishop also makes a lot of sense; Black should see a pawn race coming and, knowing that Bishops are strong in such situations, he should hasten to hack the White Bishop off the board. Evidently, it is not enough to know the rules and guidelines—you must also make use of them!

2.Rxd4 exd4

So we now have a situation where the Black Knight will not be able to cope with the White passed pawn. On the other hand, the White Bishop will easily stop any passed pawn that Black can create.

3.Bd5

> 1850: "Why do this? He is losing the h-pawn!"

3...Nf5

I don't know why, but Kaplan also made the wrong decision in this game (and he was a very strong player who most definitely knew better!). That contest was decided after 3...h6 4.Kd2 hxg5 5.hxg5 f6 6.Kd3 Nf5 7.b4 fxg5 8.b5 Ne7 9.Bg2 Nc8 10.Kxd4 Kf6 11.Kc5 Ke5 12.c4, 1-0. Note how slow and ponderous the Knight was.

4.b4 Ne3

> 1850: "Uh oh. If I take that pawn I won't be able to stop the guy on the b-file."

5.Bb3

> 1850: "My Knight is dominated."

5...f5
6.b5 f4

7.Kd2 f3
8.Ke1

1850: "He stopped my pawn but I can't stop his."

We ended the game here.

Tip

★ Bishops really *are* better than Knights in pawn-race situations. It was demonstrated to Kaplan and then 1850 found out also. Don't let it happen to you!

Aquisition of the Center, Territory, and Space

Every chess player is attracted to beautiful combinations and razor-sharp kingside attacks. This attraction makes us want to emulate the great attacking masters and, as a result, we study games by Kasparov, Alekhine, and Tal.

Though this ability to calculate is invaluable—and at least a basic understanding of the mechanics of attack is imperative—the positional elements of chess tend to be ignored by the legions of amateurs that love the game. Why? Do amateur players think that subjects such as territory and the center are boring? Or could it be that the literature on these subjects simply presents the information in a dull manner?

Whatever the reason for this relative ignorance might be, most amateurs don't have a clue about the proper use of a space advantage or a full pawn center. Instead they constantly look for forcing continuations aimed at the enemy King and, once they give themselves the green light, they will start a completely unjustified attack or, even worse, just sit tight and do nothing at all.

Personally, I like nothing more than to create a large pawn center and squeeze my opponent to death in its space-gaining coils. After the game the poor victim often has a glazed look in his eyes; he knows he lost badly but he is not quite sure why.

Rules of the Center

Of the three areas of a chess board (kingside, center and queenside), the center is by far the most important. The reason for this is that your forces can move to either side with minimum effort and maximum speed. Thus, it is usually an excellent idea to play in the middle if you have the option to do so. Unfortunately, most amateurs seem to have "wing vision," they are always looking to play on one wing or the other.

The following rules concerning play in the center and on the wings may prove beneficial:

RULE 1 — A full pawn center gives its owner territory and control over key central squares.

(23)

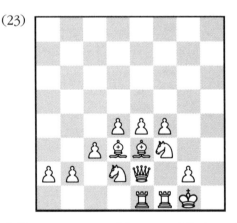

White's full pawn center (diagram 23) is well protected by other pawns and pieces. This center gives him strong control over c5, d5, e5 and f5. This will, in turn, assure White of an advantage in territory.

RULE 2 — Owning a full pawn center is a responsibility! Once you create it you must strive to make it indestructible. If you achieve this goal, then your center will cramp and restrict your opponent for the rest of the game.

RULE 3 — Don't advance the center too early! Every pawn move leaves weak squares in its wake.

(24)

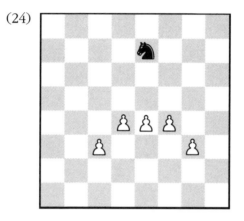

Advancing the e-pawn weakens both d5 and f5.

Notice (diagram 24) how the Black Knight cannot advance to the fourth rank due to the White center's influence. Even after ...Nc6 or ...Ng6, the Knight would still be unable to find an advanced central post. However, if White were to advance his center with e4-e5, then the d5 and f5-squares are suddenly available to the tormented horse.

RULE 4 — If your opponent has created a full pawn center, you must strive to attack it. This creates a battle of philosophies: He is telling you it is strong, you are telling him that it is a target. One of the most common cases of allowing a "strong" center in order to attack it comes about in the Alekhine's Defense.

1.e4 Nf6

Daring the e-pawn to advance.

2.e5 Nd5

3.d4 d6

Black immediately begins to chip away in the middle.

4.c4 Nb6
5.f4

White grabs all the central space he can!

5...dxe5
6.fxe5 Nc6

Developing and hitting d4.

7.Be3

The immediate 7.Nf3 would have allowed Black to intensify the pressure with 7...Bg4.

7...Bf5

Black wants to play ...e7-e6 but he doesn't want to block in his light-squared Bishop.

8.Nc3 e6
9.Nf3 Be7
10.Be2 0-0
11.0-0 f6

Striking at e5 and forcing White to trade off his most cramping pawn.

12.exf6 Bxf6

Training his sights on the d4-pawn. White claims this pawn is strong, Black claims that it's weak.

13.Qd2

Preparing to bring the Rook to d1 and give d4 more support.

13...Qe7

Preparing to place more pressure against d4 via ...Rad8.

14.Rad1 Rad8 with a certain status quo: White is doing everything he can to defend his center, Black is doing everything he can to attack it.

RULE 5 — If the center pawns get traded, then open files exist that make it easy to get one's Rooks into play.

After **1.e4 e6 2.d4 d5 3.exd5 exd5** it doesn't take a genius to see that the open e-file will be a nice place to stick a Rook (following the rule that Rooks belong on open files).

RULE 6 — If the center becomes locked, then the play switches to the wings.

After **1.d4 Nf6 2.c4 c5 3.d5 e5 4.Nc3 d6 5.e4** it's easy to see that the center is a dead zone. All the play will have to take place on the sides of the board.

RULE 7 — With a closed center, you know which wing to play on by noting the direction that your pawns point. The pawns point to the area where you have more space and that is the side that you want to control.

(25)

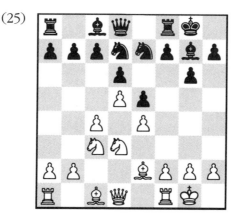

Where do the pawns point?

In diagram 25, Black's pawns point to the kingside (the c7-d6-e5 pawns are like a finger pointing in a specific direction). White's pawns can be construed as pointing in both directions the e4 and d5 pawns take aim at the queenside while the c4 and d5 pawns point in the opposite direction.

In general, you want to push the pawn that stands next to your most advanced pawn. This means that Black will try to achieve ...f7-f5 (gaining space and opening a file for his Rook. Black's most advanced pawn is his e5-pawn, and the ...f7-f5 push follows our rule nicely) while White will play to get a pawn side by side with his most advanced pawn: the guy on d5. This means that c4-c5 (White should avoid f2-f4 because, after ...exf4, Black would gain access to the e5-square, his g7-Bishop would become very active, and White's e-pawn would be backward) is our goal (gaining queenside space and preparing to rip open files on that side of the board).

> **RULE 8 — A wide open center allows you to attack with pieces. A closed center generally means that you must attack with pawns (this enables you to grab space and open files for your Rooks).**

Rules of Space

In general, having more territory is a very positive thing. You get more room for movement and your pieces experience superior coordination. However, as your pawns advance (your extra territory is mapped out by pawns in much the same way that a fence demonstrates the land you own) certain squares may become weak, and it is possible—like ancient Rome—to expand too far too quickly. For this reason, you must only annex extra space if you think you can control the territory behind your pawns. Also helpful are the following rules:

> **RULE 1 — When you have more space, it is usually a good idea to avoid exchanges.**

(26)

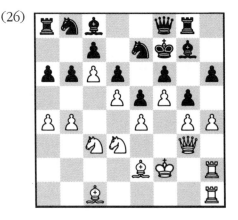

All cramped up with nowhere to go.

Black can quietly resign in diagram 26 because his minor pieces are so cramped that none of them have useful moves. However, if we were to remove all the pieces and only leave the pawns and Kings, Black would be fine simply because the cramping effect of the White pawns no longer has anything to cramp!

RULE 2 — If you have less space, an exchange or two will give the rest of your pieces more room to move about in.

RULE 3 — A spatial plus is a permanent, long-term advantage. You don't have to be in any hurry to utilize it. Take your time and let the opponent stew in his own juices.

• • • • •

In our first game, White comes out of the opening with an advantage in space but becomes worried about imaginary threats and ceases to think about an active plan for himself. Later, after some errors, White can still get some play in the center but he never even considers this and instead concentrates solely on the wings.

(27)

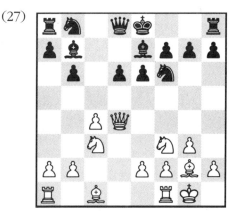

1750-Silman.
White to play.

The first moves were **1.c4 Nf6 2.Nc3 c5 3.Nf3 e6 4.g3 b6 5.Bg2 Bb7 6.0-0 Be7 7.d4 cxd4 8.Qxd4 d6**. 1750 had never faced a hedgehog formation before (he's an e2-e4 player) and so he was completely unfamiliar with the positions that result.

> 1750: "White has space and has more pieces out. The Black Bishop on e7 is temporarily bad but this is no big deal. Nobody has any real advantage. Since Black can attack my Queen by …Nc6, I would be wise to retreat it to a safer square."

I was happy that he noted the advantage in space and development, but was disappointed that he didn't make any effort to use these plusses. A lead in development (especially if the enemy King is still in the center) is most useful if the game can be opened up. In this case Black can castle immediately, so the development issue cannot be used in the traditional manner (e.g., attacking the King).

However, if White had noted Black's sole weakness on d6, he might have hit upon a plan that called for an immediate attack on this target by Rd1, b3 and Ba3. More fuel can be added to this fire by Ng5 and, after the trade of light-squared Bishops, Nge4. In this case the better developed side's attack is difficult to parry since Black is not fully mobilized yet and his pieces are not ready to rush to the d-pawn's aid. Theory has shown that Black can defend against these ideas, but I am always delighted to hear a student talk of "targets."

Remember that one doesn't just attack a King; you must also attack squares and pawns. If you have such a target, and also have an advantage in development, you must make instant use of this weapon before it disappears (a lead in development is temporary since the opponent will eventually catch up!).

Another plan White has is to make use of his space edge by increasing it whenever possible and playing to stifle Black's counterplay (based on the …b6-b5 and …d6-d5 advances).

Instead of dealing with these issues, White cops out and starts to worry about his Queen being attacked. Keep in mind that an attack on your Queen is no big deal since you can simply move it to safety. The opponent doesn't gain points for screaming, "Check to your Queen!" The moral is: **Don't fear checks or one**

**move attacks. Just make sure that they are ineffective in the
given position and go ahead with your own plans.**

9.Qd3?

This wastes a tempo and places the Queen on another vulnerable square since …Nbd7-c5 will be uncomfortable. Since he did
mention his edge in space, I would have been very happy if he
tried to increase that advantage by 9.e4. **Fearing every possible
threat that the opponent can throw at you turns you into a
timid player who reacts to ghosts.** Avoid this label and make
sure that every move you make does something positive!

9…0-0

> 1750: "Since I have more space, I want to increase it by
> moving up in the center with e2-e4."

That's more like it! To repeat: **Every move you make
should have a positive base and be geared to increasing the
advantages that you already possess.**

10.e4 Nbd7

> 1750: "He threatens to put a Knight on c5. If I stop that by b4
> then my c4-pawn is without potential support. So I'll stop it
> by Be3."

This illustrates a typical problem with the amateur's thinking.
Seeing a threat to win material (via …Nc5, hitting the Queen and
e4-pawn), White notes that he can protect himself and develop a
piece with 11.Be3. However, he fails to take into account the
resultant position after he loses his dark-squared Bishop for the
enemy Knight. **Don't make positional concessions to prevent a threat unless you have no other means of defense.**

11.Be3?

Better was 11.Nd4 (the immediate 11.Qe2 is also fine) which
allows the Bishop on g2 to help in the defense of the e-pawn. Then
11…Nc5 or 11…Ne5 can be met with 12.Qe2 followed by b2-b3,
when White would still have a solid position and a spatial plus.

It's clear that White didn't want to move his Queen again,
preferring to give up a permanent imbalance (the dark-squared

Bishop) in order to hold on to a temporary thing (the tempo that the Queen move would lose).

11...Nc5

> 1750: "He's attacking e4 with three pieces so I have to capture him."

The sins of his ninth move (9.Qd3) plus the laziness of his eleventh (11.Be3) have come back to haunt him. Note how he keeps making concessions. First 9.Qd3 to stop a Knight from making a harmless attack on his Queen (this cost him a tempo and placed the Queen on an even more vulnerable square), and then 11.Be3, a move that gives up the two Bishops and the dark squares.

12.Bxc5 bxc5

> 1750: "I was considering 13.h3 but I'm not worried about him going to g4 with his Knight. I'll move my Rook to e1 to give my pawn some added support."

Since the player with less territory should strive to exchange pieces (and thus relieve his cramp), Black can be happy with his acquisition of Bishop for Knight.

White is still making a big error by not formulating an active plan. Instead, he keeps guarding his e-pawn and worries about various harmless Knight jumps. Instead, something like 13.e5 dxe5 14.Nxe5 Qxd3 15.Nxd3 Bxg2 16.Kxg2 is sensible since it gets rid of Black's Bishop pair by swapping one off.

By isolating Black's c-pawn, White can now entertain thoughts of pressuring it with a later Na4. I'm not saying that this plan is good for White, but it would have shown a good mental attitude in that White would have been actively attempting to devalue Black's Bishops and trying to create a target on c5.

13.Rfe1 Qb6

> 1750: "He's attacking my b2-pawn. I'll simply defend it."

White doesn't realize it, but he has allowed Black to take the initiative. This is shown by White's readiness to keep making defensive moves.

14.b3 Rfd8

1750: "Defending d6 and perhaps threatening to play a ...d5 advance. If he pushes his pawn to d5 I'll go e4-e5 and attack his Knight. It's still basically even. I'll play Rad1 and strengthen my control of the center."

White is playing reasonable looking moves but he is slowly but surely running out of constructive ideas. By this I mean that he lacks a clear object of attack. It's not enough to just move your pieces into the center and hope that something good happens. It's your job to turn that amorphous "something" into a solid entity. To accomplish this, you must make all your pieces work towards a single goal. In our present game, White does not have a clear goal in mind. Note that the d6-pawn, though technically backward, is so solidly defended that White cannot hope to put any real pressure on it.

15.Rad1 Bc6

1750: "He's preventing me from attacking his Queen by Na4. He's also preparing to play ...Qb7 and increase the pressure in the center. If he does that I will play Nd2 and back that pawn up. Now I can play Qe3, which prepares to redirect it to the kingside via Qf4, etc."

Every time your opponent moves, you should ask, "Why did he do that?" It's very important to understand what the other side is trying to accomplish. Though White has paid attention to his opponent's plans throughout this game, he has not put enough energy into his own ideas. Now he seems to be leaning towards a kingside attack, but is this a realistic hope or a plan born out of the frustration caused by his earlier inactivity?

16.Qe3 a5

1750: "Starting a wing attack via ...a5-a4. I can move my Knight to d2 and defend both e4 and b3 now or later. Another idea is to play Rb1. I'll first move my Queen to the kingside, defend on the queenside as I need to, and start an attack by g3-g4-g5."

White finally realizes that he has to do something aggressive. However, a kingside attack is not a very realistic goal since Black has no weaknesses on that side of the board and White's army aims more at the center than at the kingside. White should have been playing for an e4-e5 advance.

17.Qf4 a4

> 1750: "Now I'll play Rb1, which makes his Queen a bit uncomfortable."

The Black Queen is not a bit uncomfortable since if White ever plays bxa4 Black would simply move his Queen to safety and start to chew up the weak White pawns on a4, a2 and c4. Unlike White's earlier display, Black has no fear of one-move attacks.

18.Rb1 e5

> 1750: "Forcing me to move my Queen. I can consider Qh4 but my Knight on c3 is undefended and my Queen is in a risky place. I'll move it back to the safe e3-square."

Black's last move (18...e5) fixes the center and takes away White's chances for counterplay based on a e4-e5 advance. Though some players might be horrified by the apparent weaknesses on d6 (backward pawn) and d5 (weak square), these turn out to be illusions. The d6-pawn is firmly defended and if a Knight jumps into d5 then Black would capture it. This would lead to a White pawn going to d5, which would cover up the hole and the backward pawn.

19.Qe3 axb3

> 1750: "If I play Rxb3 he has to move his Queen. If ...Qa6 is played, I can easily defend my attacked c4-pawn. It's still even."

White gets surge of confidence by attacking the Black Queen. Why? Does White really believe that Black will hang his Queen? I hope not. Then what makes an obvious one move attack so deadly (White fears such attacks from the opponent, and feels empowered when making them himself)? Nothing! They are not deadly in the least; in fact, they are more often than not completely useless.

In the present case, White will take on b3 with his Rook and attack Black's Queen. However, once the Queen moves to safety, White's pawns on a2 and c4 will be extremely weak.

20.Rxb3?

An "active" move that worsens his position. Correct was 20.axb3 (leaving himself with only one target on b3 to worry about instead of two—one on a2 and one on c4) followed by Nd2, when his position would still be very hard to crack.

White's statement claiming equality is way off the mark. He has no play and it's only a matter of time before White's two queenside targets lead to his demise.

20...Qa6

> 1750: "Attacking c4. I can protect my pawn by Qe2, Qd3 or Nd2. The Knight move seems best since it also defends e4."

21.Nd2 Rd7

> 1750: "He intends to double his Rooks. He can also play ...Rb7 but since he could have played this right away (...Rdb8) he must intend to double on the a-file.
> Now I could move my Knight to d5 when it's attacked by two pieces and defended by three. Unfortunately, I need this Knight on c3 to defend my a2-pawn so I can't do that. I can attack his d7-Rook by playing Bh3."

Still lacking a plan, White resorts to a series of one move attacks (20.Rxb3 and 22.Bh3). This is a typical amateur mistake. A one move attack is fine if it contributes to the overall improvement of your position. If it has no other point, then the move is simply a waste of time (your opponent will move his piece to safety!). If you look closely at White's next move, you'll see that he's just forcing Black to make a good move.

22.Bh3 Rda7

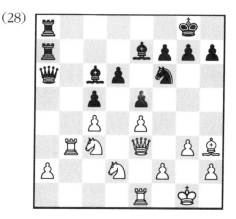

(28)

White to play.

> 1750: "Tripling on the a-file, but who cares? It doesn't do him any good at all. Now I can continue to attack his kingside by g4-g5 and chase his Knight away."

White is feeling pretty good right now but this is completely unjustified. Nevertheless, many people go into depressions and play badly when they get such poor positions so his positive attitude may serve him in the game. Actually, 1750 is quite a fighter and has saved many hopeless positions by refusing to acknowledge that all is lost. He always thinks there's a chance (this attitude is worth its weight in gold since even strong Grandmasters have been known to lose their vigilance and make bad errors in winning positions).

23.g4 Bd8

> 1750: "Intending ...Ba5, attacking c3 and a2 in turn. I can push up my pawn to a3 after ...Ba5 so I'm not worried about that. I'll continue my attack on the kingside."

The Knight on c3 eyes the d5- and b5-squares and also defends the a2- and e4-pawns. Black would be happy to trade his bad Bishop for such a useful Knight.

24.g5?

An unfortunate decision. White has weakened his King, the g-pawn and the f4-square. Now he allows the Black Knight to take up residence there. Don't create weaknesses in your own camp. When you see a hole like f4 being created, a danger signal should go off in your head!

24...Nh5

> 1750: "Heading for f4. Now I can move into d5 and protect the f4-point. Unfortunately, he will capture and move into f4 anyway. If 25.Nd5 Bxd5 26.exd5 Nf4 27.Bf5 and Qe4 still gives me an attack on h7 and his King. Whoops! I forgot that if I move my Knight I lose my pawn on a2. I must first guard my pawn and then Ne2 or Nd5 guards f4."

25.Rb2?

Much too passive (though a good recommendation is hard to find). He should have accepted the loss of the a-pawn and tried to find some way to bring his b3-Rook over to the kingside along the third rank. If you're getting positionally squashed and material loss is also looming, don't curl into a ball and wait to die. Give up some ballast (material) and attack the opponent for all you are worth. Put a scare into him and try to upset his equilibrium.

25...Nf4

1750: "Now he threatens to win my g5-pawn. I have to guard it. On Qg3 the e2- and d3-squares are covered."

26.Qg3 Bxg5

1750: "If 27.Qxg5 Nxh3+ wins my Queen by a fork. I better get my Bishop out of there."

Now Black has won material, enjoys a safe King and has retained the initiative. It's all over.

27.Bf1 Bd8

1750: "I've lost a pawn but I'm not lost since I'm still firm on the queenside. I have to get rid of his Knight."

He could admit he's lost and give up but instead he lies to himself and fights on. I can't criticize him for following the edict, "No one ever won a game by resigning."

28.Ne2 Ne6

1750: "Heading for d4 so I must maintain my Knight on e2. I'll attack his pawn on d6."

29.Qd3 Bc7

1750: "I'll head my passive d2-Knight to f3, h4 and f5. Also possible is Bh3, attacking the e6-Knight. Advancing f2-f4 can also be considered."

30.Bh3 Qc8

1750: "Now his Knight is pinned, but he's threatening my pawn on a2."

31.Ra1 Ra3

1750: "Attacking my Queen. I'd like to play Nc3 and head for d5 but it would be pinned. It's still good, though. I'd just have to move my Queen out of the way first."

32.Nc3 Nf4

Here the game was stopped since 33.Bxc8 Nxd3 leads to a further loss of material for White.

Tips

★ Try and appraise your position honestly.

★ Never give up hope! A positive fighter's attitude will bring you points even from the most hopeless-looking situation.

★ Look to the center for play. Chess is not just a bunch of battles on the wings.

★ Passive, planless play will lead to a loss every time.

★ Know what the opponent is planning at all times but don't allow yourself to become mesmerized by his ideas. Ultimately, your plans should prove to be stronger than his.

★ Don't make pointless one-move attacks. If you are crossing your fingers and hoping he doesn't see it, you are making the wrong move (you are also building bad mental habits). *Always* expect your opponent to see your threats! You want to play a move that improves your position no matter what he does. I tend to repeat this a lot, but I find it's a mistake that the amateur makes over and over again.

In our next three games we see Black allowing White to build up a very imposing center. Would the amateurs (all playing White) be able to make use of this central space advantage? Would they even notice that space was the advantage they possessed? These are important questions—if you can't ascertain what kind of imbalances exist, you won't be able to make use of them.

(29)

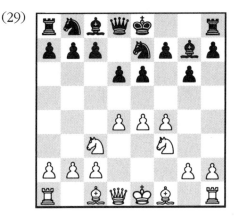

2000-Silman. Modern Defense.
White to play.

The first moves were **1.e4 d6 2.d4 g6 3.Nc3 Bg7 4.f4 e6 5.Nf3 Ne7**.

White reacted with scorn to Black's choice of opening. It's certainly ugly-looking, but it turns out to be a tough nut to crack!

> 2000: "6.Bd3 with the idea of eventually smashing him with f4-f5 is the obvious move."

His attitude shows some positive and negative features. The positive side is his confidence; he knows Black has played something fishy and he wants to punish his opponent for the insulting choice of opening.

The negative part of White's reaction is the speed taken for his decision and the fact that he ignored the imbalances. **When someone does something unusual, you must take extra time to measure its plusses and minuses.** This doesn't mean that there is anything wrong with 6.Bd3. I just expect the student to demonstrate a greater understanding of the position before a move is chosen!

6.Bd3 b6

> 2000: "Wow, he really seems to be asking for it! How can I take quick advantage of that move? Any targets? I'll just develop the rest of my army."

White is still refusing to take a calm look at the imbalances. The main factor in White's favor is the advantage in space that his big pawn center gives him. With this in mind, White should play to strengthen his center and prevent Black from undertaking any central counterattacking ideas (this is illustrated in the next game). By blindly developing his pieces, he breaks one of my big rules: **First develop a plan and then develop your pieces around that plan.** If you develop your pieces before you attain an understanding of the situation, you may ultimately find that your army is standing on the wrong squares!

7.0-0 0-0
8.Be3

> 2000: "Strengthening my center."

Finally mentioning his center, but not going any deeper into the position. While 8.Be3 is clearly a good move, this shouldn't disguise the fact that White is exhibiting signs of laziness. Instead of taking a long think and becoming master of this particular situation, he sits back, flicks out a developing move and hopes that positive things will just happen.

8...c5

> 2000: "I can consider 9.dxc5 but 9...dxc5 looks boring. So my options are 9.d5, 9.e5 and 9.Ne2. Pushing my d-pawn by 9.d5 seems bad because it leaves me with a weakness on d5. The Knight retreat to e2 looks too passive for my tastes. Though 9.e5 gives up the f5- and d5-squares, it opens things up and leads to a tactical battle that would suit my style."

9.e5?

A very poor move. Black has just initiated a central counterattack, so what does White do? He goes along with his opponent's plans by allowing his center to be ripped apart! I would have preferred either to maintain the center with 9.Ne2 Bb7 10.c3 or to start a central tussle (after all, White is ahead in development) with 9.dxc5 bxc5 (9...dxc5 leaves White with a space advantage, a solid pawn on e4 and a potential strong point on d6 after an e4-e5 advance) 10.e5!? (trying to leave Black with a weakness on c5 and also attempting to create a strong point on d6) 10...dxe5 11.fxe5 Nd7 12.Bf4 with Ne4 to follow.

9...cxd4
10.Bxd4

2000: "Otherwise I lose a pawn."

10...Nbc6

2000: "Now I'm considering Be4, which may be a tad slow. However, 11.exd6 is possible. Also, 11.Nb5 is a serious thought. So it's a choice between these two moves. Since Nb5 misplaces the Knight on the side, I'll go for exd6."

White is still playing without any kind of plan. He is not reasoning things out and he is not analyzing any variations. This type of "move by move" existence is often employed by players from the beginning level right up to the revered ranking of master. No matter what your rating may be, it is the wrong way to play chess!

11.exd6 Nxd4
12.dxe7 Qxe7

2000: "Now I have to make some decisions. I don't like his well-placed Knight, so 12.Be4 Nxf3+ 13.Qxf3 Rb8 14.Rad1 playing on the file looks good."

White has completely failed to evaluate the position. If he had taken some time to do so, he might have realized that opening up the center and giving Black two Bishops is not a logical course of action. He should have envisioned this several moves ago (before he allowed it to happen), since now all the trumps rest in Black's hands and it is too late for White to do anything about it.

13.Be4 Ba6!!

(30)

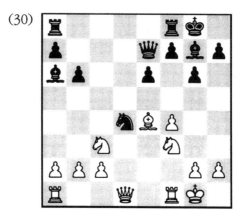

White to play.

2000: "An active move that may not be sound. I have to be careful not to exchange a bunch of pieces and end up in an inferior Bishop versus Knight endgame. Since 14.Nxd4 Rad8 runs into several pins (15.Nc6?? Qc5+ and 15.Nce2 Bxe2 are both bad for me) and 13.Rf2 Rad8 also looks terrible, I must challenge his idea and chop off his material!"

Shocked into action, 2000 finally looks at a few variations and takes the correct mental stand: **If you see a way to win material and don't see how your higher rated opponent can escape, you must go into the line and keep him honest.**

I have to point out that the variation he gave on his 12th move via 13...Nxf3+ (instead of Black's 13...Ba6!!) 14.Qxf3 Rb8 15.Rad1 also favors Black because the Bishop on g7 is better than any other minor piece on the board.

14.Bxa8 Rxa8?

The most accurate order was 14...Bxf1 15.Nxd4 Rxa8. The text was played to see how White would react to a greater range of choice.

> 2000: "I could keep the Exchange with 15.Rf2 but 15...Rd8 gives him tempos and is passive. The main move is 15.Nxd4, when 15...Bxf1 16.Kxf1 consolidates. So on 15.Nxd4 he will pin with ...Rd8 or ...Qc5 when 16.Ne2 Bxe2 17.Qxe2 Bxd4+ 18.Kh1 favors me."

15.Nxd4 Rd8?!

> 2000: "Since 15.Rf3 Bxd4+ and ...Bxc3 wins for him, I have to block with my c3-Knight."

More accurate was 15...Bxf1.

16.Nce2 Bxd4+
17.Nxd4 Bxf1

> 2000: "Now 18.Nc6 still loses to 18...Qc5+. What's wrong with the obvious 18.Kxf1? Am I falling for a trap; what am I missing? It looks like I'm winning."

18.Kxf1?

He had to play 18.c3 here (maintaining the powerful Knight on d4) or on the next move. His failure to do so leads to a speedy demise.

18...Qf6

> 2000: "Oh! He intends ...e6-e5; that's what he had in mind! Any smart ideas? If 19.Kg1 Rxd4 picks up my f4-pawn and 19.c3 e5 doesn't change anything. So I'll hold onto f4 with 19.g3."

Notice how White never started any ideas of his own. Instead, he just developed his pieces and reacted to Black's play. This type of descent into the opponent's world happens quickly and quietly and must be avoided at all costs. Naturally, the only way to avoid this is to impose your will on the game before the opponent does!

19.g3??

Missing his last chance: 19.c3! e5 20.Qd3! exd4 21.Rd1! Qxf4+ 22.Kg1 keeps White firmly in the game.

19...Rxd4

> 2000: "19.Qf3 allows 19...Rd2."

20.Qe2 Qd8

White's position is lost and we stopped the game at this point.

Tips

★ Even a seemingly bad opening will have some positive points. If you don't take what your opponent is doing seriously, then these positive points will end up beating you.

★ A plan comes before development.

★ When you accept laziness into your mental processes, it becomes a habit that's hard to break. Work
hard from the very first moves!

★ If you think you see a win, but are worried about
falling into a trap, you must be courageous and
make him prove his point. Never let fear talk you
out of a course of action.

Our next game arises from the identical opening. In this case, a
much lower rated player is able to come up with a reasonable
antidote.

1600-Silman. Modern Defense.

1.e4 d6 2.d4 g6 3.Nc3 Bg7 4.f4 e6 5.Nf3 Ne7 (see diagram 29)

> 1600: "I have good central control and a kingside space
> advantage. I want to continue my development and keep an
> eye aimed at the kingside. I would also like to maintain the
> e7-Knight's lack of mobility. Though this position looks
> good for me, Black is not just going to roll over; there is
> plenty of opportunity for him to get play in the center."

Not at all bad! He's making a determined effort to break down
the position. This effort was lacking in the previous game, even
though 1600 is much the weaker of the two. What nobody
mentions is that a kingside attack can only succeed if you control
the center or if the center is locked. Because of this, and his extra
central territory, White should strive to make his center indestructible and to restrict Black's counterplay. Once this is achieved,
White can turn his attention towards one of the wings.

6.Be2

> 1600: "Develops the Bishop and prepares to castle and
> activate the Rook."

Is the Bishop better on d3 or e2? Though d3 enables White to
envision an eventual f4-f5 break, I must ask how real this

possibility is. If it turns out to be just a pipe-dream, then e2 makes sense since it allows White to place a Rook on the d-file and discourage Black's ...c5 break.

6...b6

1600: "He's going to play ...Bb7 and put pressure on the e4-pawn."

7.0-0

1600: "Looking at it afterwards, I think my 0-0 was a poor move. If the center closes up, my white Bishop would be good and his is a bad one that he could exchange by ...Ba6. With my Rook on f1 this exchange would be forced."

This type of thinking just takes up time and makes a player paranoid. At the moment the center is not closed (meaning that White *does* want to be castled) and Black's light-squared Bishop is far from being bad. Besides, the first player can't really stop ...Ba6 anyway. If Black wants to take three moves (...b6, ...Ba6 and ...Bxe2) to trade a piece that's moved only once then White should rejoice. **Don't allow yourself to get in a state of mind where everything your opponent does has some lurking threat behind it.**

7...0-0

1600: "I'm looking at the center and whether it makes sense to close it up with 8.e5 when Black can take or play ...d5. If 8.e5 dxe5 9.fxe5 my f-file is opened and my dark-squared Bishop is freed but my d-pawn is weak. If he closes with ...d5 then a later ...c5 makes it like a French-type opening. It also gives him use of the f5-square. So I don't like the e5 advance. I'm also looking at a fantasy plan of Knight on g5 and Rook on h3 with a kingside attack but that's easily defended against. His threat is to attack d4 with ...c5 and ...Nbc6 with pressure so Be3 looks good."

It must be kept in mind that pawns on e4 and d4 control all the critical central squares. As soon as you push one of them you give up some of this control! After 8.e5? Black would not activate White's f1-Rook and c1-Bishop with 8...dxe5?. Instead, he would simply play 8...Bb7 when White has given up control of the f5- and d5-squares. Then an eventual ...c7-c5 would blast the once-proud center apart. **Don't think that moving forward means that you are automatically improving your position!**

8.Be3

The game was stopped because the student's time had expired. Black's position is not easy. White intends to play Qd2 and Rad1 when a ...c7-c5 advance would allow White the opportunity to rip open the d-file whenever it was favorable to do so (White would only play dxc5 in answer to ...c5 after he got his heavy pieces on the d-file). Also note that ...c7-c5 followed by ...cxd4 leaves Black with a backward pawn on d6. Because of this potential weakness along the d-file, Black's plan of ...c7-c5 is not very effective. Unfortunately, Black doesn't have any other methods of counterplay and White can lay claim to an advantage. All this comes from White's extra space and Black's lack of active play.

Tips

★ If you're going to worry about something, make sure it is worth worrying about!

★ Games are often won by simply taking space and restricting the opponent's options. You don't have to attack like a wild man to score a point.

In our final example with this favorable White opening, the first player (a man with a solid A rating) tries hard to defend his center right from the start.

1950-Silman. Modern Defense.

The first moves were: **1.d4 g6 2.e4 Bg7 3.Nc3 d6 4.f4 e6 5.Nf3 Ne7**.

> 1950: "White has a broad center. The Silman school says that White has an obligation to maintain the center and, once this is done, he can switch to some sort of action on the wings. So how to develop and maintain the center?

"I can find moves that protect my center, but is that enough? I'm looking at Bc4. 6.Bd3 doesn't seem bad either. Also reasonable is 6.e5, gaining space, but I can do that at any time. That's why Bd3 is all right since e5 frees it.

"Black must attack the center. He can do this with any one of four pawns but the most likely is the c-pawn. There is something to be said for placing the c3-Knight on e2 and bolstering my center with c3. I'll go for Bd3."

I was very happy that he seemed to remember the content of our lesson on the center. I looked forward to him defending his center with everything he had.

The fact that some of his moves were incorrect didn't bother me (for example, his idea of 6.Bc4 is poor since it walks into a ...d6-d5 advance). Far more important than moves are ideas, and his first big think showed that he was trying hard to use every idea he had been exposed to.

6.Bd3 b6

1950: "Preparing to fianchetto."

7.Ne2

1950: "The troubling thing about my move is that I'm moving a piece twice in the opening but, since it's a semi-closed game, this is not terribly important. At least, I hope it's not!"

7...Bb7

1950: "There is no reason to rush the center-guarding c2-c3—I can do this whenever I need to. There are more important moves to play. Ordinarily you don't want to castle where a fianchettoed Bishop is bearing down but, in this case, he has fianchettoes on both sides! However, my pawn center is blunting both of them.

"I can't help but be tempted to play g4 with the idea of Ng3 but it leaves my King open. Kingside castling also looks natural since it placed the Rook on the someday-to-be-opened f-file. I'll go for the restrained approach."

What's this about not castling in the direction of a fianchettoed Bishop? Is this some sort of chessic urban legend? Just because a Bishop aims at your King doesn't mean it's mate!

8.0-0 0-0

> 1950: "Now I feel that his King is stuck on the kingside and I'd like to play there. I'll try either c3 or Be3. By defending d4 with c2-c3, my e2-Knight is free to move to g3 and threaten f4-f5. To stop this Black will be tempted to play ...f7-f5. Then exf5 ...gxf5 opens his King. However, if he answers 9.c3 f5 10.exf5 with 10...exf5 then I feel that I have given up my good central pawn. So perhaps the immediate 9.g4 is the right way to go.

He was so careful to defend his center and then he suddenly abandoned the idea and went charging the kingside. Why? The simple 9.c3 (or 9.Be3 with c3 to come) would give him a fine game with no weaknesses. Only after making his center indestructible should he entertain ideas concerning attacks against my King.

9.g4

Here we ran out of time and the game was stopped. His play was logical and impressive up to his 9th turn. Then he tossed all his lessons out the window and gave in to emotion and desire.

Tips

- ★ Once you start a plan, make sure you finish it. Don't allow yourself to get sidetracked.

- ★ If you own the center and are killing all the opponent's counterplay, there is no hurry to start an attack on the wing. Continue to take your time, gain more space and take away the enemy's options.

The next example is a fine game played by Fischer against the Romanian Grandmaster Florin Gheorghiu. I showed this to a student who owned a 1600 rating (though he was 1900 in postal) and asked him to annotate it as we went.

Fischer-Gheorghiu, Buenos Aires 1970.
Petroff Defense.

1.e4 e5
2.Nf3 Nf6
3.Nxe5 d6
4.Nf3 Nxe4
5.d4 Be7

> 1600: "I like 6.Bc4. It attacks f7, threatens Ng5 and allows me to castle. He could push to d5 but then I play Bb3 followed by Nc3 when it's equal. Another interesting move is 6.c4 when 6...d5 7.cxd5 Nxd5 8.Bc4 Be6 9.Nc3 is promising."

This incoherent litany really shows why he doesn't do so well in tournaments. He never tried to figure out what he had that his opponent didn't. Due to this, he began to look at moves in a complete state of ignorance. Not seeing (or caring) that he had a slight advantage in space, he first looked at 6.Bc4, saying that 7.Ng5 would then be a threat. Why? Would Black just sit around and allow White to capture on f7? At the moment, the g5-square is covered by three Black pieces, making Ng5 impossible. However, even if White did manage to play Ng5, Black could toss in ...d6-d5 and end White's one-move threat instantly.

He also mentioned 6.Bc4 d5 7.Bb3 followed by Nc3 (he proudly claimed equality for White. Why is early equality desirable for the White pieces?). However, 7...c6 leaves the Bishop on b3 hitting granite while the c3-Knight would also find itself doing nothing (can't go to e4 and is putting no pressure on the well-defended d5-square).

Finally, his claim that 6.c4 d5 7.cxd5 Nxd5 8.Bc4 Be6 9.Nc3 is promising falls on its face after 9...Nxc3 when Black has won a piece!

It's clear that he is just trying to develop his pieces, but you must only develop pieces to posts where they do something, preferably in relation to the imbalances (in this case, space).

6.Bd3

> 1600: "Logical, but it doesn't seem very aggressive to me. It's solid but rather boring. Black should play ...Nf6."

Why let the Black Knight remain on the active e4-square? With 6.Bd3 White develops the Bishop to a safe but important post and gains time by hitting the enemy Knight.

6...Nf6

> 1600: "White is slightly better because he has space and his dark-squared Bishop is better than Black's. White should gain more space. How to do this? 7.c4, 7.0-0 and 7.Bg5 are all good. Even 7.h3 is possible which keeps Black's Bishop back. I'd go for 7.h3."

He finally began to take note of White's spatial plus and, as a result, he got one right. 7.h3 is an excellent move because it restricts the enemy pieces—the player with an edge in space should be choking the opponent's army at every opportunity.

7.h3! 0-0
8.0-0 Re8

> 1600: "White can play 9.Bf4, 9.Bg5, 9.Re1, 9.Nc3 and 9.c4. I'd probably play 9.Re1."

9.c4

White's plan consists of increasing his advantage in space and, at the same time, in taking away squares from the enemy pieces. The advance of the c-pawn fits in nicely with these ideas: White grabs more space and takes the d5-square away from the Black pieces.

9...Nc6

> 1600: "Fighting for the squares on d5 and e4 by 10.Nc3 is correct. This also keep a flexible position."

The Knight-move to c3 is very natural and good. Some of my students have recommended 10.a3, preventing ...Nb4. However, this Knight sally is nothing to fear since Bb1 saves the Bishop. Then White, by a2-a3, could chase the Knight back to where it came from. **Don't go out of your way to prevent things that cause no real harm!**

10.Nc3 h6

> 1600: "I like 11.Qc2 when a later Bxh6 may be possible. Another idea after 11.Qc2 is Ne4, getting rid of a kingside defender. I don't like 11.Bf4 but 11.Re1 looks good."

White's pieces *do* aim at the kingside, but I don't see how Qc2 helps make Bxh6 a threat.

11.Re1 Bf8

> 1600: "12.Be3!? is best, since I don't like exchanges."

While I don't like his 12.Be3, which just clogs up the White army, I do like his statement that exchanges are not what White wants. It appears that 1600 is well aware that the side with more territory should avoid unnecessary exchanges since that just helps to relieve Black's cramp.

12.Rxe8

The trade of one Rook won't do any harm to White's cause.

12...Qxe8

> 1600: "Now 13.Bd2 followed by Qc2 and Re1 is indicated. It's still just a bit better for White because Black is very solid."

13.Bf4

The Bishop is obviously more active here than it would be on d2.

13...Bd7

Note how the lack of space prevents Black from posting his pieces on active squares.

> 1600: "I don't like Qc2 anymore. 14.Qd2 gives potential for sacrifices and a kingside attack."

So he finally realizes that his Qc2 had no real point (aside from allowing potential forks by ...Nb4). This is why one should make the Queen one of the last pieces to be moved; you often don't know where it belongs until most of the other pieces are out.

14.Qd2

(31)

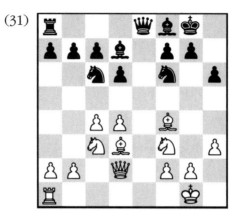

Black has trouble finding a plan.

1600: "Black can't attack White in the center. 14...Ne7 with the idea of ...Ng6 makes sense."

14...Qc8

1600: "Does this threaten to sacrifice? Looks scary since 15...Bxh3 16.gxh3 Qxh3 and, if Black can get rid of the Bishop on f4, ...Ng4 would create a strong threat of ...Qh2+. Perhaps 15.Nd5!? which threatens Nxf6+ and ties his Queen to the defense of c7 is worth trying. If ...Bxh3 wasn't a threat, I'd love to play 15.Re1."

When someone makes a threat, it is very important to determine if this threat is real or imagined. In the present case, White thinks that Black is threatening to sacrifice on h3. If Black's sacrifice ultimately fails, then why would you go out of your way to prevent it? In this case Fischer sees that ...Bxh3 is nothing to worry about so he happily continues with his space-eating ways.

15.d5

1600: "This cramps Black's game more and forces him back. White is attacking on the kingside while Black should play ...Ne7 and play for a queenside attack."

How does ...Ne7 help Black create a queenside attack?

15...Nb4

1600: "White could play 16.Be4 when 16...Nxe4 17.Nxe4 is fine for White."

White does not wish to give up the two Bishops here. He also sees that 16.Bb1 allows soothing exchanges after 16...Bf5.

16.Ne4!

1600: "Black must play ...Nxd3 but then 17.Nxf6+ is strong."

Why *must* Black allow his pawns to be shattered by Nxf6+? If 1600 was Black, would he actually play ...Nxd3 and let this happen? Clearly, 1600 is suffering from some kind of panic reaction, though what that might be is anyone's guess.

16...Nxe4
17.Bxe4 Na6

1600: "Were is the killer? 18.Bxh6 fails. White probably has to start a pawn attack via 18.Kh2, g4 and g5. Another way is 18.h4-h5, Kh2, Rg1 and g4-g5. Here Black would have big problems. Another idea is Nh2 and Ng4."

Why the crazed wing attack? It seems that most amateurs suffer from a lack of patience. They probably think that if you don't do something forcing, then your advantage will disappear. In this case White sees that ...Bf5 is still a threat so he centralizes his Knight and prevents this move once and for all.

Fischer's actual choice makes a much better impression than 1600's suggestions, which all weaken the position of his King.

18.Nd4 Nc5
19.Bc2 a5

1600: "White is still better but has no big attack. White must get his Rook into the attack. I like 20.Kh2 with the idea of g4. White *must* play for a kingside attack. 20.a3 with b4 to follow doesn't work, and 20.a4 is horrible. 20.Re1 is not as strong as a g4 and Rg1 idea."

First 1600 says that White doesn't have any real attack. Then he says that White *must* attack. What's going on here? It's clear to me that quiet play in the middle and slow build-ups are alien to 1600. In his mind, you must attack even if your chances for success are not good.

Ultimately, a simple question must be asked: why weaken one's King when you can play quietly in the middle with no risk?

20.Re1

1600: "Going to e3 and g3."

20...Qd8
21.Re3 b6
22.Rg3

This threatens the simple Bxh6. Notice how White's chosen method of attack has left his kingside pawns safe and sound.

22...Kh8

> 1600: "White should have something crushing since he has too much over on the kingside. 23.Qc3 Qf6 24.Rf3 Re8 is not so clear but I know that something good is hiding from me."

23.Nf3!

White does not want to allow Black to defend with ...Qf6. Now Qd4 is a huge threat and 23...Qf6 is met by 24.Be3! followed by 25.Bd4.

23...Qe7
24.Qd4

Here we ran out of time and stopped the game. White threatens Bxh6 and the only way to stop this is by 24...f6 (which weakens the light-squares and allows Nh4 followed by Ng6) or by 24...Qf6 (this was played in the game) 25.Qxf6 gxf6 26.Nd4 (heading for the hole on f5) 26...Re8 27.Re3 (White feels that his superior pawn structure is enough to win so he carefully prevents Black from gaining any counterplay) 27...Rb8 28.b3 b5 29.cxb5 Bxb5 30.Nf5 Bd7 31.Nxh6 with material gain and a win on the 35th move.

Tips

★ You can win games just by increasing your edge in territory bit by bit.

★ If you own a space advantage, play to restrict the enemy pieces.

★ The side with more space should not trade too many pieces.

★ The side with less space should strive to exchange whenever possible.

★ Don't be in a rush to force things. A slow squeeze is quite enough to torture the opponent and force his eventual capitulation.

Our next example shows a position where the center is dead and the space advantage lies on the kingside.

(32)

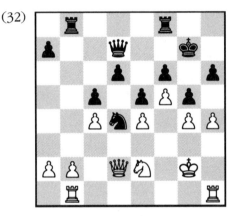

Reti-Carls, Baden-Baden 1925.
White to play.

Reti won this position in instructive fashion. He first avoided unnecessary exchanges and then made use of the h-file—a file that White can open whenever he desires to do so.

1.Nc3!

Avoiding exchanges and bringing the Knight to the active d5-post.

1...Rh8
2.Rh3!

Of course, since White has a space advantage on the kingside, that is where he directs his play. The text follows an instructive but common idea. White will play on the h-file but, seeing that

2.hxg5 hxg5 allows exchanges, he will only open it when he triples by Rh3, Rbh1 and Qh2. Since Black has far less territory on that file, he will be unable to copy White's movements there.

2...Rbg8
3.Rbh1 Qd8
4.Nd5!

Threatening Kg3, Qh2, hxg5 and Rh7+.

4...gxh4
5.Rxh4 Kf7
6.Kf2 Qf8
7.Rxh6 Rxh6
8.Rxh6 Qg7
9.Qa5!, 1-0.

Mate follows 10.Qc7+. Reti made this look easy, but good things happen if you play where your favorable imbalances reside.

Could an amateur with a 1700 rating handle things so well? Would he recognize his chances on the h-file? I decided to allow my student the chance to walk in Reti's shoes.

(33)

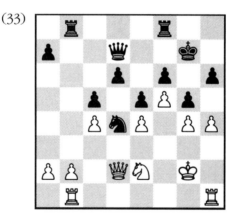

1700-Silman
White to play.

1700: "First we must look at the imbalances. Black has an imbalance on the queenside and on d5, e6, g6, and h5.

Black's position is a big hole...it's bad.

"White doesn't have any imbalances. Well, that's not quite true, he has one on f4 (though it's guarded by the Knight). White has space everywhere while the open file for Black means nothing. The best place for the White Knight is e6. White does not want to trade Knights because his is more mobile than the Black one. White can also cramp Black some more by h5."

This is just terrible! After several weeks of lessons, 1700 thinks that imbalances are weaknesses. I must have failed badly to let him believe this, but let's stop you, the reader, from thinking the same thing!

Imbalances are differences in the position! One person can have a Knight and the other a Bishop. *That* is an imbalance! One can have space while the other player has the superior pawn structure. *That* is also an imbalance (note that it's sometimes not clear who the imbalances will ultimately favor). While imbalances can be weak pawns or weak squares, they can also be many other things (and can be positive, negative or neutral).

For the most part, everything 1700 said was off the deep end. In fact, if this is how he actually thinks, I'm amazed that he keeps a rating as high as 1700!

1.h5??

I almost had a heart attack when he played this positional blunder! In many ways, this move is far worse than hanging a piece. Why? Because everyone, even Grandmasters, hangs pieces from time to time. Hanging a piece is a moment of blindness. But playing a move like 1.h5 shows a horrible lack of understanding about chess. Clearly, this is far more serious.

When you have an spatial advantage in some area of the board (and White's resides on the kingside), it won't mean anything if you can't find a way to break into the enemy position. White had a clear route into the kingside via the h-file, but closing it by 1.h5 permanently closes that road. White has gone from a clear advantage to a disadvantage in only one move!

1...Rb4

2.b3 Rfb8

The center is closed and the kingside is also locked up. This means that Black is free to devote his full attention to the queenside.

> 1700: "Black is trying to pile up on the queenside; he's hoping to take the pawn on c4 (by ...R8b6, ...Qb7 and ...Rxc4) and pick off the Rook on b1. This is permanently prevented by Nc3."

3.Nc3 Qb7

> 1700: "He's pinning my e-pawn to my King. What happens if I play Nd5 and attack his Rook?"

Black is targeting all of White's potential weaknesses. These are the pawns on b2, c4 and e4. It's clear that Black has all the play.

4.Nd5 Qc6

> 1700: "Why does he want to give me a Rook for a Knight? I don't understand this. Do I take his Rook or do I double on the b-file? Ahhh...if 5.Nxb4 Qxe4+. What does that do? It does not look so bad for me. For example, 5.Nxb4 Qxe4+ 6.Kh3 when White's not winning, but Black might have a draw.
> "Actually, he might get my Knight and two pawns for that Rook. This is good for him so I can't do that. I'm also worried about 5...Nxb3 6.axb3 Rxb3 but that's not so dangerous. I better protect my e-pawn."

He doesn't realize it yet, but White's no longer following a plan of his own. Instead, he's just reacting to Black's ideas (in other words, Black has the initiative).

5.Re1 R4b7

> 1700: "Black has queenside space but his pieces are inactive. How good is space if your pieces are not doing anything? So I must take the fight to him even if I lose a pawn: 6.b4 cxb4 7.Nxb4. However, then 7...Qxc4 is possible. I'm not worried because I will take with the Rook."

1700 is a frisky guy, but if you have less space than your opponent you should not go out of your way to open things up. 1700's desire to win at all costs often clouds his judgment.

Remember: desire mixed with the cold light of reason is something you want to nurture in chess. But emotion and wishful thinking are enemies of every player.

6.b4??

You should always be able to list the great things your moves do for your position. In the present case, 6.b4 only helps Black's cause. Notice how this move opens the b-file for Black's Rooks and creates a self-inflicted weak pawn on c4.

6...cxb4
7.Rxb4 Rxb4
8.Nxb4 Qxc4

> 1700: "If 9.Rc1 Qxb4 then I win his Queen by 10.Rc7+ Kg8 11.Rc8+! The other move is 9.a3, but what do I do about 9...a5? So 9.Rc1 looks very good."

9.Rc1 Qxb4

There's nothing sweeter than "falling" for the opponent's (unsound) trap. In doing so, you break his confidence and allow him to use his own errors to beat himself.

10.Rc7+ Kf8
11.Rc8+ Ke7

> 1700:" So my sacrifices didn't work."

We stopped the game and discussed the horrible 1.h5. To this day the sight of 1.h5 raises my blood pressure and makes me cringe with horror.

Tips

★ A space advantage means little if there is no way to penetrate into the enemy position.

★ Open files are precious things. Don't close off the very roads that you so desperately need!

(34)

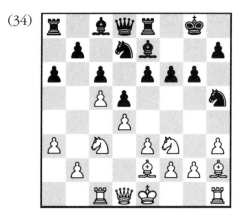

Silman-Barkan, U.S. Open 1981.
White to play.

White enjoys a clear space advantage on the queenside in diagram 34. Normally the first player might try to add to this by b2-b4 and a3-a4, followed by an eventual b4-b5.

However, it is not enough to look at your own plans to the exclusion of the opponent's. Just what *is* Black going to do? Apparently, he will attempt to advance in the center with ...Bf8 and ...e6-e5 (thus annexing territory of his own). Why should White allow this? Why not take space everywhere and leave Black with little or no counterplay? This is the reasoning White employed when deciding on his next move.

1.e4!

Grabbing a spatial plus in the center. Now White would welcome 1...dxe4 since 2.Nxe4 would allow him to make use of the d6-square and, once White castles and places a Rook on e1, the backward pawn on e6. This move shows us that it is not enough to simply recognize a space advantage. You must also be able to *create* extra territory; don't expect it to magically appear.

1...Bf8
2.0-0 Bh6
3.Rc2 Kh8
4.Re1 Nf4
5.Bf1 Rg8
6.b4

White's last few moves are easy to understand. He has gotten his King to safety, placed a Rook on the e-file (which can be opened whenever White decides to play exd5), and solidified his position on the queenside.

6...Nf8
7.a4 g5

Since Black is clearly worse on the queenside and in the center, he goes for his last shot on the kingside. Normally central play (which White has) will prove to be more valuable than this type of desperado attack on the wing. However, White comes up with a very greedy idea: he decides to take control of the kingside also! If successful, White will gain an advantage in all three areas of the board.

8.Bxf4 gxf4
9.Nh2!

Preparing to bring the Queen over to h5. Black can't prevent this by 9...Qe8? since 10.exd5 cxd5 11.Nxd5 would prove to be more than bothersome.

9...Ng6
10.Qh5 Bf8
11.exd5 cxd5
12.Bd3

White has an enormous advantage. His pieces aim at the kingside and dominate the center. White also has a powerful queenside pawn majority that gives him excellent chances in any endgame.

12...f5
13.Nf3 Be7
14.Rce2 Bf6

Trying to cover the weakened e5- and g5-squares.

15.Rxe6!

Decisive. The White army bursts into the Black position, picking up pawns as it goes.

15...Bxe6
16.Rxe6 Be7

Stopping Rd6.

17.Bxf5 Nf8
18.Ne5! Qe8
19.Nf7+ Kg7
20.Nxd5!

(35)

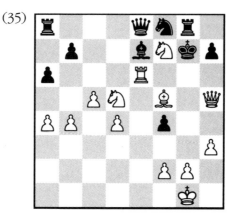

Black is doomed.

20...Nxe6

Or 20...Qxf7 21.Rxe7.

21.Qh6+ Kxf7
22.Bxe6 mate.

Though White started with his space advantage on the queenside, he went out of his way to conquer territory in other areas also. Can the amateur copy this mind-set and create a space advantage where none seems to initially exist? This is the problem that I set before a couple of my students.

(36)

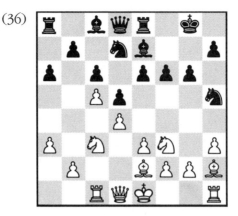

1500-Silman

White to play.

1500: "Material is even. White's pawn structure is better than Black's. His pawns are aiming at the queenside and he has a space advantage there. My Bishops are superior. The h2-Bishop is bad but it's outside the pawn chain. Black has a slight space edge on the kingside. Black's d6-square is weak. White definitely has the better game here. Due to the nature of the position (closed center) I can get more space on the queenside with b4."

He did a good job in recognizing what White had. Unfortunately, he didn't pay attention to his opponent's plans.

1.b4 Bf8

1500: "Black's trying to get his Bishop active by playing it to h6. Another possibility is to play it to g7 and go for a push in the center. I would like to get to his backward pawn on b7 if I can. I am debating whether to castle or not to castle right now."

He's doing reasonably well. This time he noticed some Black ideas, but he didn't bother trying to prevent them. In fact, it never occurred to him to strike in the center first. Why make it a battle between one person's queenside attack versus another person's center or kingside attack when you can have it all?

2.0-0 e5

1500: "He's playing to open up the center and activate his Bishops. His options are to take or push. I eventually need to play a4 and b5 but I'm not quite sure where to place my pieces on that side. I'll forge ahead."

3.a4 e4

1500: "Grabbing more space in the center. I'll move my Knight over to the queenside."

All of a sudden Black has a space advantage in the center that aims at the kingside. This translates to active kingside play for Black, compared to the passive stance that Black was forced to endure in the Silman-Barkan game.

4.Nd2 Ng7

1500: "Black is playing for a kingside pawn storm by pushing his pawns there. So I should push on with what I want to do since it's now a race."

He wisely states that you should play quickly on your respective side in an race situation. However, why did 1500 let Black map out central and kingside space in the first place?

5.b5 f5

1500: "He is continuing to put pressure over there. I don't think Black has any immediate threat so I must make my attack faster."

6.bxc6 bxc6
7.Rb1 Ne6

1500: "Black's trying to get his pieces over to the queenside so he can defend. I will push my a-pawn so I can sink something into b6."

I played ...Qxa5 (after he played 8.a5??) so he took it back.

1500: "I will play Na2-b4 and put pressure on c6 and a6."

8.Na2 a5

1500: "I'm starting to panic. Every entry point is defended by his minor pieces and pawns."

9.Qc2 Bh6
10.Bd6

1500: "The point of Qc2 was to play Bd6 even if his Bishop was on f8. Then, if he took, I could open the c-file with cxd4. Unfortunately, with my wandering, your attack has gotten more serious."

10...f4
11.Rb3 Qh4

1500: "My Bishops are still better but I think Black's position is now superior since it's easier for his pieces to get through to me."

The game was stopped at this point.

(37)

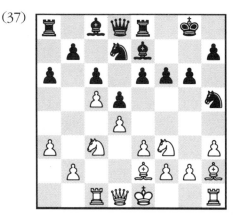

1650-Silman.
White to play.

1650: "White has more space on the queenside. He also has two developed Bishops. White's Knights have better central positions. Black should be breaking in the center with ...e5 which frees his Bishops and other pieces. White should prevent Black from attacking the center."

Excellent! White not only notes his own queenside play but also sees that he should prevent Black from getting his own stuff in the middle.

1.e4 Bf8

1650: "I don't want to capture since it opens the e-file. I will build pressure on e4 with Qc2."

2.Qc2

Not a terrible move, but pretty much unnecessary. The e4-pawn was already well defended so an extra defender is sort of pointless. Instead, he should have castled since you don't want your King sitting in the middle when the center is opening up.

2...Bh6
3.Rb1

> 1650: "Bring it to b1 so I can play b4 and gain more space on the queenside."

3...Bf4

> 1650: "I have a space advantage so I don't want to trade since that will give him more room. Instead I will force him to retreat."

4.g3?

Absolutely terrible. It is good that he knew that exchanges should be avoided if you have a space advantage, but don't prevent trades if it results in an entombed, useless piece.

4...Bc7

> 1650: "Now I will try to gain an attack on the kingside since his pawns are kind of weak. First I will activate my e2-Bishop by getting my Knight out of the way."

5.Nh4

1650 has sort of lost his mind around here. First he plays the excellent e3-e4, but then he kills off one of his own pieces with g2-g3 and next he sticks his Knight away from the center on h4.

5...Ng7

> 1650: "Now I will gain more space."

6.f4

It's wonderful that he wants to gain more space, but why weaken his kingside and leave the poor King stuck in the center?

6...dxe4
7.Nxe4 Nf5

1650: "I don't want to trade since I have the space edge."

He's stuck on that rule. In this case, he doesn't want to trade since it allows Black to open the e-file to the White centralized King.

8.Nf3 Ne3

1650: "My Queen is being attacked but I want to keep her as close to the center as possible by Qd3. If he checks me on g2, his Knight is trapped."

9.Qd3 Nd5

1650: "Now your Knight is in the center on a strong square. I will continue to eye his kingside and activate my Bishop."

I don't know why White wants to avoid castling so badly (not to mention the fact that he keeps sticking his Knight on the rim). Evidently he doesn't realize that a centralized King stops the Rooks from connecting and will come under attack if the enemy can open up the center.

10.Nh4 f5

Threatening ...Nxf4.

1650: "I will bring my Knight to the nice g5-square."

11.Ng5 e5!

Taking advantage of the fact that White's Knight on g5 is only defended by the pawn on f4.

1650: "He is trying to open up the file for the Rook. I have to capture it."

12.dxe5 Nxe5

1650: "He is giving up a piece to get an attack on my King with his Rook."

13.fxe5

1650: "Oh, he's getting a piece back! I've really blown it."

13...Qxg5. Here the game was stopped.

Tips

★ Feel free to grab lots of space as long as you aren't creating serious weaknesses in your position.

★ Don't allow a race (both sides attacking on opposite wings) if you don't have to.

★ It is rarely good to leave your King in the middle of the board.

THE
CONFUSING
SUBJECT OF
PAWN
STRUCTURE

If you ask an amateur player what he thinks of when you say hanging, doubled, backward, or isolated pawns, the most likely response will be "a weakness." Unfortunately, most amateurs don't really know how to go after pawn weaknesses, much preferring the thrill of a King-hunt. The other side of the story follows the same pattern. If the amateur gets these so called weaknesses, he usually panics because he is not aware of the dynamic potential inherent in all these structures. The simple truth is, it's impossible to label anything in chess as always being weak. The examples that follow show when to punish the existence of these pawns, and when to welcome them into your own position.

Doubled Pawns

(38)

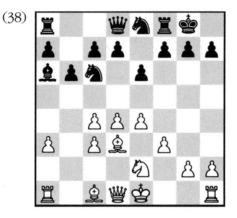

White to play.

NEGATIVE — The doubling of pawns reduces their flexibility and, at times, leaves one or both of them vulnerable to attack (though it's usually the lead pawn that is the weaker).

White's c-pawns are doubled in diagram 38. Though the pawn on c3 is very safe, the guy on c4 is further advanced and thus vulnerable to attack by the enemy pieces. Black will torment this pawn by ...Nc6-a5 (when his Bishop and Knight both attack it) followed by ...c7-c5, ...Rc8 and, if necessary, ...Ne8-d6.

POSITIVE — The doubling of pawns leads to extra open files for your Rooks and increased square control.

After **1.e4 e5 2.Nf3 Nc6 3.Nc3 Nf6 4.Bc4 Bc5 5.0-0 0-0 6.d3 d6** White can play the silly-looking **7.Be3** (see diagram 39).

Is it wise for White to allow his pawns to be doubled? Actually, White would love Black to capture on e3! After 7....Bxe3 8.fxe3 White gets increased control of the d4- and f4-squares and immediately creates a fine open f-file for his Rooks. Since e4 is solidly guarded by a pawn, and since the e3-pawn is quite safe (Qe2 defends it), White suffers no negative consequences at all from this doubling.

(39)

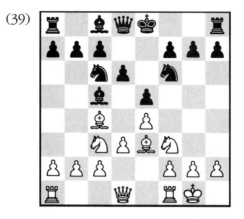

Black to play.

Since White has shown his desire to get some "mighty" doubled pawns, Black should refuse and try for some doubled guys of his own! After 7.Be3 Black does best to either play 7...Bb6, when 8.Bxb6 axb6 gives Black a firm pawn structure and use of the open a-file, or 7...Bg4 when 8.Bxc5 dxc5 gives Black use of the half open d-file and powerful control of the d4-square. Note that the doubled pawn on c5 is easily defended by ...b7-b6.

Isolated Pawns

(40)

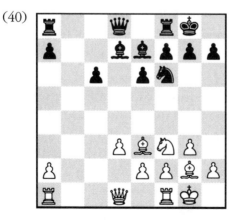

White to play.

1ˢᵗ NEGATIVE — An isolated pawn cannot be defended by another pawn and is very vulnerable to attack if it stands on an open file.

In diagram 40, White can bring his whole army to bear on the poor c6-pawn by Rac1, Nd4 or Ne5 and, if necessary, Qa4 or Qc2.

1ˢᵗ POSITIVE — The creation of an isolated pawn may bestow upon its owner the use of a half-open file.

(41)

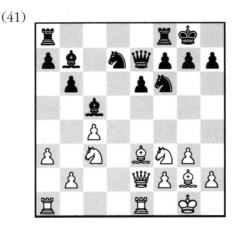

White to play.

After 1.Bxc5 (diagram 41) Black could safely play 1...Qxc5 or 1...Nxc5. However, 1...bxc5!? also deserves serious consideration. True, this pawn is now isolated. However, it is not very weak since it doesn't stand on an open file, it keeps the White pieces out of d4, and Black is able to generate pressure down the newly opened b-file against White's pawn on b2.

2ⁿᵈ NEGATIVE — The formula to beat an isolated pawn calls for control of the weak square in front of the pawn so it can't move, the trade of all minor pieces (which ends all attacking chances for the owner of the isolated pawn), the retention of a Queen (this stops the enemy King from taking part in the defense of the pawn) and one or two Rooks (which will be used to attack the pawn), the doubling of these pieces against the pawn and the use of a friendly pawn to attack the pinned isolated target.

(42)

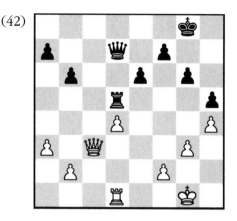

Black to play.

In diagram 42, Black wins the fixed, isolated d-pawn by playing 1...e5.

(43)

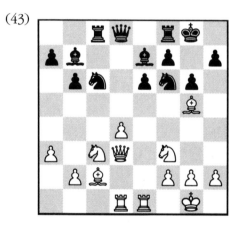

White has good attacking chances.

2nd POSITIVE: An isolated d-pawn at d4 (for White. The pawn would stand on d5 if Black owned the isolated d-pawn) gives its owner plenty of space for his pieces and open files for his Rooks. The person that possesses this pawn should play for dynamic play with his pieces.

White's d-pawn (diagram 43) gives him extra space, use of the e5-square (a nice home for his Knight) and possibilities of a kingside attack or a central advance with d4-d5.

If you own the isolated pawn and your opponent has managed to trade off most of the minor pieces (ending its dynamic potential and turning it into a pure weakness), you still have one final line of defense: Exchange all the Rooks and the enemy won't have enough force left to seriously threaten your pawn.

(44)

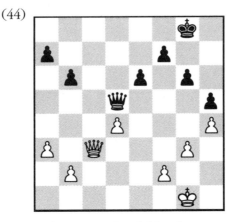

The game should be drawn.

In diagram 44, Black is unable to apply more pressure to the pawn and White can easily hold the position.

Backward Pawns

(45)

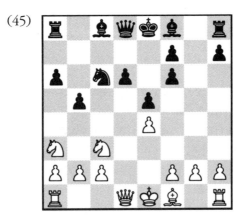

White to play and fight for d5.

NEGATIVE — A backward pawn is only weak if it is sitting on an open file and if it is unable to advance. The side playing against the backward pawn should strive to control the square directly in front of it (turning it into an immobile target), since this square cannot be defended by a pawn. One way to do this is to exchange all the pieces that defend this square.

In diagram 45, White will play to increase his control over the d5-square by Nd5, c2-c3, Na3-c2-e3 and, if necessary, g2-g3 followed by Bg2. If White could exchange off Black's c8-Bishop and Knight (the only two pieces with potential influence on d5), the first player would have permanent control over d5.

POSITIVE — A backward pawn acts as a guard to a more advanced pawn to the side of it. This advanced pawn can block enemy pieces and control important squares. The backward pawn cannot be considered a bad thing if the square in front of it is well-defended.

(46)

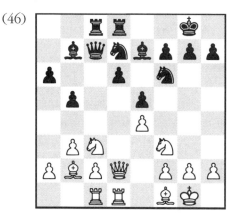

White to play has nothing.

In diagram 46, White can play 1.Nd5 but after 1...Nxd5 2.exd5 the d5-square is covered up by a pawn. In this position the d6-pawn (which defends the important e5-pawn) is well-defended and is not really a weakness at all. In fact, Black's active pieces and pressure on e4 give the second player the advantage.

Hanging Pawns

NEGATIVE — This kind of structure can be weak if the other side is able to circumvent any dynamic advance of the pawn duo and, since the pawns would then be immobile, train the power of all his pieces against them.

(47)

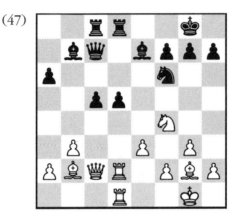

In diagram 47, White has created strong pressure against the d5-pawn and there is nothing Black can do to save it. **1...Ne4** fails to **2.Nxd5! Bxd5 3.Bxe4**.

POSITIVE — The traditional hanging pawns on c5 and d5 (or c4 and d4 if White has them) control many important central squares, give their owner an advantage in territory and also offer play on the half-open b-file and e-file.

(48)

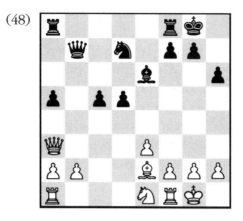

Bertok-Fischer, Stockholm 1962.
White to play.

In diagram 48, Black's hanging pawns are well defended and give him extra space, control of the center and strong play down the b-file. Since Black threatens to play 1...Qb4, White takes steps to prevent this.

1.Nd3

This covers b4, threatens the pawn on c5 and prepares for Nf4 with pressure on d5.

1...c4!

This creates a weakness on d4 that White will not have time to use. With 1...c4!, Black fixes the enemy pawn on b2 and turns it into an immobile target.

2.Nf4 Rfb8 and White was in great difficulties. After **3.Rab1? Bf5 4.Rbd1 Nf6 5.Rd2 g5!** White gave up a piece and the game with **6.Nxd5? Nxd5** rather than face 6.Nh5 Ne4 7.Rc2 Qb4.

Passed Pawns

NEGATIVE — A protected passed pawn is not always an advantage, though most players think it is. If the square in front of the pawn can be controlled by the other side, then the pawn is stopped in its tracks and becomes a non-factor for a long time. Even worse, if this square falls to a Knight, then the horse will radiate power on the neighboring squares and pawns.

(49)

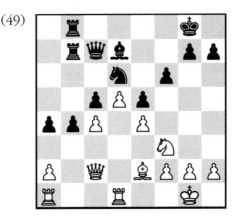

White to play has a bad position.

In diagram 49, Black's Knight on d6 prevents the enemy passer from going anywhere. It also eyes b5, b7, c8, e8, f7 and f5, aside from attacking the White pawns on c4 and e4. Under normal circumstances, Black's Knight wouldn't be able to stay on d6 since White's pressure on the d-file would make it run away. However, in this case the d5-pawn is acting like a traitor by blocking it's own pieces.

With White's pawn stopped, the active Black queenside majority shows itself to be more valuable.

POSITIVE — A passed pawn is very strong if its owner has play elsewhere. Then it can be used as endgame insurance. A passed pawn is also strong if the square in front of it is cleared for the pawn's advance.

As can be seen, when a passed pawn exists, the square in front of it becomes the most important square on the board. Whoever owns this square dominates the game, so great energy and imagination must be demonstrated by both sides if they want to wrest control of this critical point.

(50)

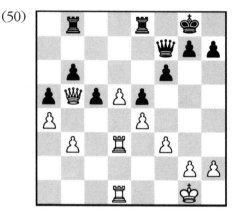

White to play.

In diagram 50, Black is in big trouble since he does not have control of the square in front of the passed pawn. White plays 1.d6 followed by 2.d7 and the whole Black army will be forced to run before the pawn's might.

Remember: **So-called weak pawns are only weak if you can seriously attack them or make use of the weak squares that may come with them.**

After giving my students several lessons concerning strong and weak pawns, I usually wait a few weeks and then give them the chance to show me what they remember about our discussions. The first game revolves around the proper use of hanging pawns.

1600-Silman. Queen's Indian Defense.

1.d4 Nf6 2.c4 e6 3.Nf3 b6 4.e3 Bb7 5.Bd3 d5 6.b3 Nbd7 7.0-0 Be7 8.Nbd2 0-0 9.Bb2 c5 10.Qe2 cxd4 11.exd4 dxc4 12.bxc4 Rc8.

(51)

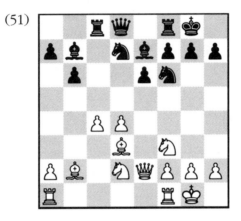

White to play.

1600: "I will back up my pawns with Rooks."

Not delving deeply into the position at all but still coming up with a reasonable method of development. White must realize that, aside from the well-known potential weakness of his pawns, this structure also has its good sides. The pawns on d4 and c4 control all the important central squares (e5, d5 and c5) and give White more space. If White can make his pawns safe from attack (putting his Rooks behind them strives to do this) then this advantage in territory will give him a promising position. He will then have tactical chances based on a timely d4-d5 advance or, if this should never prove effective, the simple Ne5 followed by Nd2-f3 will enable White to annex even more squares.

13.Rac1 Re8

> 1600: "There is a possible discovered attack on my Queen on the e-file. But there are two pieces in the way at the moment so I will continue to back up my pawns with my Rooks, which also gives my Queen more room to move."

There is an old saying that goes: "When in doubt, place your Rook opposite the opponent's Queen, it's bound to prove useful."

Though this is partly said in jest, the truth is that a quick d4-d5 advance can now be thrown out the window since it opens up the e-file and brings the dormant Rook to life. However, even if Black's Rook did not stand on e8, this advance, which does activate the b2-Bishop, also gives Black's Knights access to c5 and is usually only played if there is some sort of tactical justification to back it up.

Of course, it turns out that ...Re8 has a more substantial purpose than some hazy hope of a future attack against White's Queen. That purpose will become clear after Black's next move.

14.Rfd1 Bf8

> 1600: "If I go back to f1 with my Queen then ...Bb4 might be good for him. There is also a possibility that he will play an ...e5 advance. I don't need to worry about ...Bb4 because I can defend by Bc3."

White was showing signs of early laziness in placing his Rooks behind the pawns without a detailed plan of action. Now that he has moved his Rooks, he becomes hopelessly passive and doesn't even try to find further ways to improve his position.

The problem White is facing is the very common *fear of ghosts*—a fear of things that may or may not be real. It is the job of the player to decide whether a threat is real or not, but you can't ever decide one way or the other without proof. This means you must analyze and come to a final and clear assessment of the situation. Is the White Queen really in enough danger to warrant its retreat to the passive f1-square? No, of course it isn't. Is ...e5-e5 a threat? No again. So it seems that White went out of his way to place his Queen on a bad square for absolutely no reason at all.

If you find yourself in this kind of mind-set, you will never come up with dynamic ways to put pressure on your adversary.

More aggressive (and constructive) ideas are 15.Ne5 Nxe5 (if Black does not do this then White will follow up with 16.Ndf3 with a very nice game) 16.dxe5 Nd7 17.Ne4 and though White has a weak pawn on c4 his control of d6, pressure down the newly opened d-file and chances of attack against the Black King give him many attractive possibilities.

15.Qf1?

> 1600: "So my Queen is safe if he plays ...e5."

Black never came close to threatening ...e6-e5 so White has found himself in a frame of mind that will come up often in this book—the overwhelming desire to respond to every possible threat (real or imagined). This is the bane of most amateurs and must be avoided at all costs. In this case, White has used a precious tempo to move his Queen from a fine square to a poor one.

15...g6

> 1600: "He's going to put his Bishop on g7. I can move my Bishop back to b1 and then swing my Knight over to b3."

This shows the main idea behind Black's 13th move. The Bishop will go to g7 where it will defend the King and eye the target on d4. Notice how Black is improving his position with every move while White is floundering about in a panic.

16.Bb1 Bg7

> 1600: "I can now swing over to b3...wait! He'll go ...Bxf3 and open me up on the kingside. I can move my Queen to d3 before I play Nb3, then f3 is defended."

White is still reacting to every Black possibility. At least he realizes that his Queen was not participating in the game on f1, but the original e2-square is where it really belongs.

17.Qd3 Qc7

> 1600: "Putting more pressure on c4. I can put pressure on the e-file by Re1 followed by Ne5. At the moment, my Knight is not doing much."

White continues to flit about from one idea to another, but at least his ideas are becoming more aggressive! The intended 18.Nb3 would have been well met by 18...Ba6.

18.Re1 Red8

> 1600: "Now he's putting pressure on d4. I'll play Nb3 and guard it."

19.Nb3 Qf4

Tempting was 19...Ba6 while 19...Ng4! with the threat of 20...Bxf3 was extremely strong. However, I wanted to give him a bit more room to come up with his own ideas.

> 1600: "Now he's attacking my f3-Knight and also threatening to move his Bishop to e4. If I move my Knight to e5 he still can play ...Be4. It's better to move my Knight back to d2."

20.Nfd2?

He's so sure that everything is going to be bad for him that he miscalculates. Black doesn't threaten 20...Be4 because 21.Rxe4 would win two pieces for a Rook. Also 20...Bxf3 21.Qxf3 Qxf3 22.gxf3 is not necessarily the end of the world for White. Finally, 20.Ne5?? would have lost to 20...Nxe5 21.Rxe5 Ng4. A bad or lazy attitude will always lead to the worst possible results. Never give up hope and even if things have not been going well you must fight to the bitter end. You will be surprised how often you can turn a game around!

Instead of this passive and useless retreat (remember: 20...Be4 didn't work. Don't take time out to stop your opponent from blundering!), White should have remained calm and played the simple 20.Qe3.

20...Ng4

> 1600: "Threatens to check me. I have to move my Queen to g3."

21.Qg3 Qxg3

> 1600: "I will capture towards the center."

Still defending and following the basic rules (always capture towards the center). This is simply not good enough! You must strive to come up with creative ideas that challenge your opponent! Putting your arms up, closing your eyes and fending off blows isn't going to get the job done.

22.hxg3 Nb8

This Knight is coming to c6 where it will chew on the d4-pawn.

> 1600: "He has two pieces against d4 and one Rook against c4. I must chase his Knight away."

23.f3 Nf6

> 1600: "I want to keep his Knight from moving to h5."

Why? A Black Knight on h5 would not have helped the second player in his battle against the weak pawns on d4 and c4. Since ...Nh5 could always be answered by Kf2, White should have taken the opportunity to play a more useful move. Superior was either 24.Kf2 or the more assertive 24.a4! (intending to create a weakness on b6 by a4-a5xb6) 24...a5 25.c5! when the Black pawns are also turning out to be in need of defense.

Remember: Be aggressive—create pawn weaknesses, fight for squares and space, do something positive! Just because you have some weak pawns doesn't mean you can't create some in the opponent's camp as well.

24.g4?! Ne8

Eyeing d4 with the g7-Bishop and giving himself the possibility of ...Nd6 with more pressure against c4.

> 1600: "c4 is adequately guarded by the c1-Rook so I'll centralize my Knight."

25.Ne4 a5

> 1600: "He's threatening ...a4 and a capture on d4 so I have to guard d4."

26.Red1

Black would now meet 26.a4 with 26...Bc6 27.c5 Bxa4 and the Knight on b3 is no longer defended by its twin.

26...a4
27.Na1 Nc6

> 1600: "Putting another piece on d4. I have to defend it."

28.Nc2 Na5

> 1600: "Now he has two attacking c4. I can still defend, though."

29.Ne3

The game was stopped here since both 29...Bh6 30.g5 Bxe4 and 29...Bxe4 followed by 30...Bh6 would win material.

So the pawns eventually fell (a case of use them or lose them!). This occurred, however, due to inactivity on White's part. If he had made use of his advantages in space and piece activity then the hanging pawns might well have been heroes instead of goats.

Tips

★ Always play to improve your position. Don't panic and retreat from good squares.

★ Owning hanging pawns means that you must play dynamically. Passive play will lead to your hanging pawns turning into weaknesses.

★ If you are playing against hanging pawns, you must attack them with everything you've got.

In the next example, we see hanging pawns in a better light. Black is able to advance them and demonstrate their dynamic potential.

The starting moves were **1.d4 d5 2.c4 e6 3.Nc3 c5 4.cxd5 exd5 5.Nf3 Nc6 6.g3 Nf6 7.Bg2 Be7 8.0-0 0-0 9.Bg5 cxd4 10.Nxd4 h6 11.Be3 Re8 12.Rc1 Bf8 13.Nxc6 bxc6.**

(52)

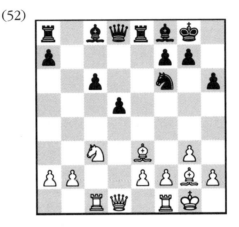

1800-Silman. Queen's Gambit Declined, Tarrasch Defense.
White to play.

1800: "My center pawns are gone and my Bishop is blocking my e-pawn. His c-pawn is weak. He can't move it because his d-pawn would fall. He has more pawn islands and his a-pawn is isolated and weak and my Bishop on e3 ties his pieces down to its defense. I could attack his c6-pawn by Qa4 but this pawn is easily defended. His pieces are passive right now and are sitting on the back rank. What's the nastiest move to attack his pawns? Wait a minute…14.Qa4 almost wins a pawn outright! If 14…Qc7 then 15.Nb5! is very strong."

White is looking at Black's pawns as weaknesses without any good points whatsoever. This is not a correct view. The trick to battling potentially weak pawns is to first contain them (fix them on vulnerable squares) and only then to attack them (14.Na4 is the best move). Instead, White goes right for the throat but forgets that they can move forward and annex some space.

14.Qa4

Note that 14...Qc7 *is* bad, but White's idea of 15.Nb5?? is not the reason because 15...cxb5 wins a piece. Instead, 14...Qc7 fails to 15.Nxd5.

14...c5

> 1800: "Now his d-pawn is extremely weak. I don't see how he can defend everything."

He has a positive attitude but it's somewhat lacking in realism. Note that White did not fall for 15.Nxd5 Nxd5 16.Bxd5 Qxd5 17.Qxe8 Bb7.

Now the question is raised: Are Black's pawns wimpy targets or towers of strength? They *do* control the e4-, d4-, c4- and b4-squares so they can't be all bad! The battle lines are drawn: White will try to either win a pawn or force one to advance which will (hopefully) create a weak square on c4 or d4. Black will defend his dynamic duo and try to create counterplay on the half-open b-file and e-file.

15.Rfd1 Be6
16.Nb5?

> 1800: "Attacking a7 and c5 simultaneously."

This move does uncover an attack on c5 but White seems unaware that Black is allowed to play a move too! Don't get so full of your own plans that you forget that you have an opponent. Much better was 16.Bf4 which takes away the b8-square from Black's Rook, threatens Be5 in many situations and creates the possibility of e2-e4.

16...Qb6

> 1800: "Now both his pawns are pinned. There must be a way to pounce on them!"

Black was easily able to defend his c-pawn and now threatens something that White misses entirely. However, Black's position was already very good since the White Knight can be chased back, the hanging pawns can be solidly defended by ...Red8 and ...Rac8, and White must constantly worry about threats along the b-file and pawn advances like ...d5-d4.

17.b4?? Bd7

1800: "My Knight's in a little trouble."

The game ended at this point. We went back to the starting position in the previous diagram and I made him play the correct 14.Na4 (instead of the previously tried 14.Qa4).

(53)

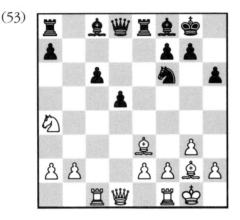

Black to play.

14...Qa5

1800: "If my Rook eats on c6 then ...Bd7 wins, so I'll play Bd2 and attack his Queen, which also gets it off the poor post on e3."

White shows that he still doesn't understand the position. The Bishop on e3 was not badly placed at all. Indeed, it helped control the critical c5-point in an effort to fix the pawns on static and passive squares. Black's 14...Qa5 is an active attempt to counter White's control of c5 and put pressure on the a2- and e2-pawns. If Black did not do this, White would have gotten a fine game by Bc5 followed by the exchange of dark-squared Bishops and Nc5 with a bind on the d4- and c5-squares. In that case, the Black hanging pawns would play no active part in the game.

As it turns out, 15.Rxc6! was correct after all since the complications that follow 15...Bd7 16.Rxf6! have been shown to favor White. I could not expect 1800 to know this but I did have hopes that he would understand the need to block the Black pawns. Something like 15.Bc5 would have made me happy (though 15...Ba6 is a good reply) because his heart would have been in the right place. Even 15.a3 followed by 16.b4 would have shown that he wanted to control c5.

15.Bd2? Qb5

> 1800: "He's attacking e2 but this is no big deal; I can push it or guard it with my Rook."

White is looking at direct threats and moves but is not looking at a long-range plan. Because of this, he soon ends up in a passive position.

16.e3

Black also gets active play after 16.Re1 Bg4.

16...Bf5

Here we stopped the game due to lack of time. Black's well-placed pieces clearly outgun their passive counterparts.

Tips

★ Any kind of weak pawn must first be contained (blocked) before it is attacked.

★ No pawn structure is always good or bad. Look for the potential plusses in any given structure and make sure the opponent doesn't achieve them.

★ Though I repeat this in every chapter, I will take time to do so again: Don't just react to the opponent's plans. Find an active idea and follow it with as much energy as you can muster. On the other hand, don't get carried away with your own ideas and forget that you have an opponent. Take his plans into account and make adjustments when necessary.

The game that follows, played in a weekend tournament by a student of mine, made a deep impression on me. It takes one of the most maligned of structures, the dreaded tripled pawns, and shows that they are not necessarily bad—even in an endgame!

(54)

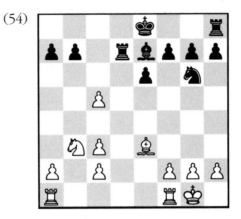

Black to play.

The position in the diagram was reached after 15 moves. Black, though a pawn down, undoubtedly thought that he stood well; after all, White's pawns hardly inspire confidence. However, Harold (my student) realized that these pawns gained space, tied up the enemy pieces and allowed him to generate play against the opponent's remaining queenside pawns by moves like Rb1 and Na5.

16.Rad1

Harold challenges the d-file and tells the opponent that he can only castle if he is willing to give that file up.

16...Rc7
17.f4!

Following Steinitz's important rule: The way to beat Knights is to take away all their support points.

17...0-0
18.Rd3 Rd8
19.Rxd8+ Bxd8
20.Rd1 Bf6
21.Rd3

White is playing this game in a remarkably calm manner. Since

Black has no real counterplay, White is able to slowly strengthen his position.

21...Nf8
22.Bd4 Be7
23.Be5 Rd7
24.Bd6

The White Bishop has taken up a powerful post. I love the way he methodically brought his Bishop to this nice square.

24...h6
25.g3 g6
26.Bxe7

Harold sees that his exchange will allow his Rook to penetrate into the hostile position.

26...Rxe7
27.Rd8 Rd7

And now, instead of the hasty 28.Rxd7?? (which trades a very active Rook for its passive counterpart), White could have achieved a winning position with 28.Ra8! a6 29.c6 bxc6 30.Rxa6.

I suspected that most amateurs would take one look at those tripled pawns and proclaim their dislike of the White position. Is this view correct or was I giving the chess playing masses less credit then they deserve? I set the same position up and gave a student the chance to prove me wrong.

(55)

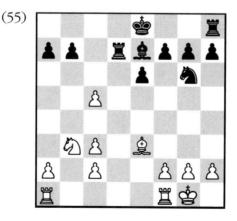

1500-Silman
White to play.

1500: "Three isolated pawns on one file is bad, but on the other hand White is better developed, has an open b-file and is a pawn up. Also Black has no pressure on White's game. White has the chance to sacrifice one of his isolated pawns with c6 and isolate Black's pawns, but first I would like to play my Knight to a5. I like this move but I want to concentrate on my development—I must use this before it goes away. I will play 1.Rfd1 and activate my Rooks."

So I stand humbled—1500 also liked the White position! Is this because isolated pawns don't bother the average amateur, or are my students so well-schooled that they are able to see beyond typical forms of chess bigotry that color most people's perception?

I was delighted when 1500 pointed out that he had to play fast if he was going to take advantage of his lead in development. Actually, just about all of 1500's comments were right on the money. Perhaps I am breeding a race of super-players!

1.Rfd1 Rc7

1500: "So I have taken control of the d-file. Now the Knight can go to a5."

White's lead in development will soon be gone but he has managed to convert it into a long-lasting control of the important d-file.

2.Na5

The b7-pawn is an excellent target but he is now rushing his position a bit. Harold's treatment, which held onto the c5-pawn and took squares away from the enemy pieces, was much better.

2...0-0

1500: "I want to concentrate on the b-file and the b7-pawn."

3.Rab1 Bxc5
4.Bxc5?

White thinks he is getting good value by trading off two of his tripled pawns for the healthy one on b7. This is quite wrong. Instead, White has freed the Black pieces from their prison and from the necessity of defending b7. The patience that I praised Harold for is quite lacking in this game.

4...Rxc5
5.Nxb7 Rxc3

> 1500: "I would like to play Rd7 and take the seventh rank but I don't want to sacrifice my passed pawn. On the other hand, I don't want to play too defensively. I would like to trade one Rook, defend c2, and bring my Knight back so it can defend my pawns. The b4-square is good for this and can be reached via c6 or a6. White was better at the beginning and he still is. I should place a Rook behind my passed pawn."

6.Rdc1

> 1500: "This Rook was chosen so I can follow up with Rb3."

6...Rb8

Here I stopped the game since White's advantage has completely disappeared.

Tips

★ A so-called weak pawn is only weak if it can be attacked! Each individual pawn has its own plusses and minuses and must be judged accordingly.

★ Patience is a real virtue in chess. If your opponent has little or no counterplay, then why should you feel compelled to force the issue? It is much better to take your time and add a host of little advantages to the plusses you already possess.

A backward pawn is a potential weakness because no other pawn an defend it, but its main problem is not so much the pawn itself but the square in front of it. The game that follows shows what happens if you ignore this simple fact.

(56)

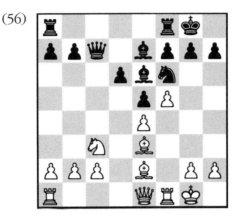

Smyslov-Rudakovsky, Moscow 1945.
Black to play.

Black must move his threatened Bishop. Since 1...Bc8 seems wrong, that only leaves 1...Bd7 or 1...Bc4. Most players don't like having to retreat and prefer the more aggressive 1...Bc4. Indeed, that is what Black chose in the actual game.

1...Bc4??

Would you believe that this natural move leads to a postionally lost game? It does! As hard as it is to accept, 1...Bc4 is a positional blunder. To understand the position, we have to look at the backward pawn on d6. Is this pawn weak or in danger? No, it is well defended. However, the square in front of it (d5) only has two defenders—the light-squared Bishop and the Knight. Black's error with 1...Bc4 was that he traded one of the critical defenders of d5 for a piece that had virtually nothing to do with that square. Smyslov was quick to jump on this mistake.

2.Bxc4 Qxc4
3.Bg5!

Immediately chopping off d5's final defender.

3...Rfe8
4.Bxf6 Bxf6
5.Nd5! Bd8

Black would lose the Exchange after 5...Qxc2 6.Rf2 Qc5 7.Rc1 followed by Nc7.

6.c3 and White's domination of d5 (and the superior minor piece that came with it) gave him a huge advantage that was confidently converted into a win after **6..b5 7.b3 Qc5+ 8.Kh1 Rc8 9.Rf3 Kh8 10.f6 gxf6 11.Qh4 Rg8 12.Nxf6 Rg7 13.Rg3 Bxf6 14.Qxf6 Rcg8 15.Rd1 d5 16.Rxg7**, 1-0, since 16...Rxg7 17.Rxd5 leaves Black with no answer to Rd8+.

All right, Smyslov played well, but could a student of mine do the same? I gave this task to 1330. First I gave him a lecture on strong and weak pawns. Then we spent a few weeks on other topics. Once I was sure that he'd forgotten everything we had spoken about earlier, I threw this position at him.

(57)

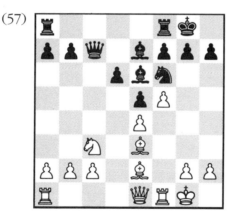

Silman-1330.
Black to play.

1330: "Well, I have to move my Bishop to either c8, d7 or c4. At the moment White's Bishop is better than mine. I could force a trade on c4 but he would chase my Queen all over the board. Possible is ...Bd7 but I hate to retreat, and c8 is even worse. I like d7 since my Queen is safe and I keep pressure on f5."

I began to search for the cattle prod. He didn't even mention the fact that Black was saddled with a backward d-pawn! As for his comment about his Queen being chased around, is this reality or laziness? Let's take a look: 1...Bc4 2.Bxc4 Qxc4 3.b3? Qc6 and the c3-square has been weakened (which in turn weakens c2) by White's thoughtless one-move attack (b2-b3).

From White's point of view, we must ask if Black would leave his Queen on c4 after b2-b3? It's clear that a sane person wouldn't. So White is left with the following question: "Did b2-b3 improve White's game in other ways?" Not at all. It just weakened squares and had no purpose other than the obvious attack on the Queen.

This shows us that White shouldn't even consider b2-b3 after 1...Bc4 2.Bxc4 Qxc4, and Black shouldn't fear it (in fact, he would happily pay White to play it!).

Don't make moves that have no purpose other than some obvious threat that can easily be parried.

1...Bd7!

So 1330 played the right move for the wrong reason. 1...Bd7 is correct since it will go to c6 where it attacks White's e4-pawn and defends the delicate d5-square. Then Black can play ...a6, ...b5, ...Qb7 and ...b5-b4, undermining both d5 and e4.

2.g4

> 1330: "He is starting a horrifying kingside attack. I'm concerned about g4-g5 when my Knight has no good squares. I could block that by ...h6 but this would weaken my kingside. However, I like my Knight's position since it attacks e4 and defends d5."

He mentioned the d5-square and the e4-pawn! Thank goodness for that. I would have been even happier if he had first played 2...Bc6 (bringing another piece to bear against d5 and e4), since I was sure that he was not aware of the proper followup to 2...h6.

2...h6
3.h4

> 1330: "He still has the same threat. Is this the time for 3...d5? I lose a pawn. I could go to h7 and defend g5."

3...Nh7

Better was 3...Bc6, attacking e4 and guarding d5, and only then ...Nh7.

4.Qg3?

4.Nd5 was stronger (a move that could have been prevented by an earlier ...Bc6) but I wanted to give him the chance to find an all-star defensive idea.

4...Bc6??

Too late. If White can successfully get g4-g5 in, he will have a winning attack. Black could have punished White for his last move by the retreating 4...Qd8!, a move that attacks h4 and covers g5. If White answered this by 5.h5 then Black would be free from the worry of g4-g5. If White played 5.Bf2, then the g5-square would still be in Black's hands and 5...Bc6 would be an intelligent move.

Just because a piece moves backwards doesn't mean that it's retreating.

5.g5 hxg5
6.hxg5

> 1330: "What is the threat? My Bishop is practically worthless. I might be able to hole it up with 6...f6. If 7.g6 Ng5 8.Bxg5 fxg5."

Driving a stake through his own heart. However, his game was already very bad. If you keep playing on the side where your opponent dominates, then you will almost certainly lose.

6...f6??
7.g6 Ng5
8.Bxg5 fxg5
9.Bc4+ and Black wisely resigned. Of course, 9.Qh3 was also promising.

Black lost this game because he reacted to the White attack and he never got his own play started.

Tips

★ The weak square in front of a backward pawn is
often a greater problem than the pawn itself.

★ You can play to win a square by trading off its
defenders.

Our final example takes us away from weak pawns and into the
world of pawn structure as it relates to the plans for both sides.
Deciding whether you want to keep the center open or allow it to
be closed is an important decision in chess, and must only be
made with a firm knowledge of the other imbalances.

(58)

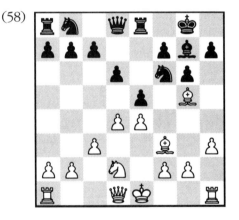

1650-Silman, Torre Attack.
White to play.

The starting moves were **1.d4 Nf6 2.Nf3 g6 3.Bg5 Bg7
4.Nbd2 0-0 5.e4 d6 6.c3 Bg4 7.Be2 Re8 8.h3 Bxf3 9.Bxf3 e5**.

> 1650: "Though the Black pawns point towards the kingside,
> I should still castle on that side of the board. Black's Bishop
> is hitting granite and his b7-pawn might hang if he's not
> careful. After 10.0-0, if he plays 10...Nc6 then 11.d5 gains
> time and drives the Knight away. After I castle, White will
> continue Re1 and Nc4 and then he can initiate the capture

on e5. If Black takes the time to play ...h6, then White will take on f6. However, after 10.0-0 Nc6 11.d5 Ne7 he breaks the pin on the h4-d8 diagonal, so closing the center with d5 may not be very good. Back to my plan of 0-0, Re1 and Nc4. I'm not sure where my Queen goes, but after an eventual Rd1 his center will fall."

When 1650 refers to the pawns pointing in a certain direction, he is trying to make use of my rule of pointing pawns: **In closed or semi-closed positions you will usually attack in the direction where your pawns point.** In other words, the pawns on c7, d6 and e5 are aiming at the kingside—they act as a finger pointing the way.

Why does this work? Because that is the direction where you have the most space, and you should usually play where you own more territory. Though it's a good sign to see 1650 thinking about this rule, he's forgetting that the center is still in a state of flux and the pawn-pointing rule only applies to a closed or semi-closed position. If you keep the center open and play in that sector, then the pawn-pointing rule has less validity. This is because the center is the most important place to play on the board and play there usually take precedence over play on the wings.

Another interesting but incorrect statement is that "10...Nc6 can be answered by 11.d5 with a gain of time." I often notice that amateurs love to attack enemy pieces with a pawn. The reasons for this are: 1) They are attacking something and this threatening gesture gives them a certain sense of security. 2) They think that they are gaining time.

Let's look at the flaws in this reasoning. Keep in mind that when you attack something it *will* move to safety (I am constantly surprised by the amount of players who harbor secret hopes that the attacked piece will stay put and die!). It is also important to understand that a pawn move only gains time if it chases a piece to an inferior square or places the pawn on a better post than where it started. In the present case, 10...Nc6 11.d5 Ne7 does not gain time for White because he's closing the position (something that favors the person with Knights), making his f3-Bishop a poor piece and taking away his central play. White should not crow about any of these accomplishments.

Other things that were stated or ignored by 1650: 1) He's ignoring the important imbalance of the two Bishops. Since Bishop like open positions, an acknowledgment of this imbalance would tell him that closing the center with d4-d5 might not be a good idea. 2) Black's Bishop is not hitting granite! It's a good piece and can easily become active after an eventual ...exd4. Admittedly, the center-closing d4-d5 makes Black's Bishop bad but this would also devalue White's two Bishops. 3) He says that after a certain series of moves, Black's center will fall. Why should this be true? After a move like ...Nbd7 or ...Nc6 Black has a firm grip on his e5-pawn.

What is *really* going on? At some point Black can pressure White's e4 and d4 pawns with ...exd4 (this also frees the g7-Bishop). White should try to kill off this counterplay and activate his two Bishops with 10.dxe5! dxe5 (10...Rxe5 11.Bf4) 11.0-0. White would then gain space on the queenside with a4 and b4 and get his light-squared Bishop into the game with Bf3-e2-c4. This plan would give the first player a small but safe edge because Black would have no points of attack and the Black Knights would have no advanced support points. On the other hand, White's Bishops would take up active posts on e3 and c4.

10.0-0 Nc6

> 1650: "If I play 11.d5, then 11...Na5 is bad since b3 takes away all his squares. After 11.d5, the center is locked with his pawns pointing towards the kingside while mine aim at the queenside. I don't want to play d5 but I'm tempted because it drives the Knight and gains time. If I do that, where does my Knight go then? My light-squared Bishop also seems poor. I'll tour my Knight to d5 via c4 and e3 instead of closing things."

The comment about 11.d5 Na5 12.b3 (he's missing 12.b4, which picks up the poor beast) taking away all the Knight's squares is based on the lesson that the best way to deal with Knights is to take away all their advanced support points. However, why would Black want to place his Knight on the side where it is cut off from the rest of its army? Since he states that d5 leads to queenside chances for White and kingside play for Black, wouldn't it be more logical to bring the Knight to the side where Black intends to pursue his play? Thus 11.d5 Ne7 is much more sensible. Always make the pieces and pawn structures work together, whether you're looking at your moves or your opponent's possible replies.

11.Nc4 h6

1650: "If I go to h4 then 12...g5 13.Bg3 gives me pressure on e5."

He tried to go to h4 but I warned him that something was wrong with the move. After a few moments he noticed that he would lose his e4-pawn to 11...exd4 12.cxd4 g5 so he panicked and blitzed out a few moves.

Let's devote a few lines to the subject of panic. Everyone has been unpleasantly surprised or has had the experience of noticing—usually at the last moment—that their intended move is bad. If this happens, you must not make any hasty decisions. Instead, forget about the game and take a few moments to calm yourself down. Once this is done, you can reassess the situation and avoid making a decision based solely on emotion.

12.Bxf6 Qxf6
13.d5

Still riding high on emotion, White has ceased to think about his moves. The quiet 13.dxe5 keeps a very safe position.

13...Ne7

Now that the center is closed, the pawn-pointing rule comes into effect. Black will play for a kingside attack with ...f7-f5 while White should try to create a breakthrough on the opposite wing. Why? The center is closed so the wings are the only places where play can be initiated. Since most of Black's space is located on the kingside (his most advanced pawn is on e5), he should try to add to this with ...f7-f5 when his space advantage in that area is more apparent.

In closed situations, you must play on the side where you have more freedom of movement and try to annex as much space as possible. Note that this is done with pawns advances since that allows files to be opened and the Rooks to enter the fray.

14.a4

1650: "This stops him from chasing my Knight with ...b5."

At the beginning of this game, White did what he was taught and tried to break the position down into its component parts. Unfortunately, he failed to correctly assess matters because his thinking was vague and disjointed. After the shock of hanging material (see the note on the 11th move), he played a few hasty moves and from now to the end of the game he does nothing but play one-move attacks or defend against specific threats. In other words, he has been reduced to a purely reactionary role. To be fair, the move that 1650 played (14.a4) is actually quite a good one. My criticism is that he only played it for a defensive purpose (to keep his Knight on c4). He should have been thinking in a more aggressive vein about gaining space on the queenside and trying to drum up an initiative there.

14...Qh4
15.Ne3

1650: "I don't like his Queen being there so I'll harass her."

Very interesting! A moment ago White was intent about keeping his Knight on c4. However, Black's move upset him—his King is being attacked and he feels the need to defend. Sadly, his statement about harassing Black's Queen is not based on accurate calculation. Instead, he's bringing some pieces to the vicinity of the kingside and hoping that something positive happens for him. **Never play moves with your fingers crossed! Never hope that he misses your threat or that things will somehow work out.**

All chess players should get rid of words like maybe and somehow. Clarify what's going on to the best of your ability; perhaps you won't get it right but at least you will be creating some good habits. 1650 has gotten lazy and is no longer putting his full energy into the game.

15...f5
16.exf5

1650: "I like his pawn structure but I feel my King is safer than his."

Another lazy and erroneous thought. Don't think that a King without a full pawn cover is necessarily in danger. A King is only in danger if the enemy pieces can get to it. I don't mind incorrect analysis or incorrect thinking—people can only perform at whatever level they have reached. Laziness, though, is a preventable disease that makes improvement impossible.

The capture on f5 is bad because it opens the g-file for Black's Rooks and makes Black's pawns on e5 and f5 mobile.

16...gxf5
17.a5

> 1650: "A trap. I intend 18.Ra4."

Why is this a trap? The one-move attack White gets on Black's Queen is hardly fatal. Notice how White is going more and more towards the reactionary role I discussed earlier?

17...Kh8
18.Ra4 Qf6
19.Bh5

White's last two moves have been simple one-move attacks (please keep in mind that my criticisms usually refer to the thought behind the moves rather than the moves themselves). He is playing without any kind of plan.

19...Rg8

> 1650: "We are both building up. I want to weaken the f5-pawn and put pressure on him."

Finally some words of wisdom. White has identified a target. Now he should play 20.f4! when he holds back Black's pawns and threatens to initiate an attack on f5 with fxe5 at some point.

The comment about "building up" is less astute:**You must first identify a target and only then build up your forces to attack it.**

20.Qf3?

Rather than stopping the advance of Black's central pawns, White places his Queen in a vulnerable position and makes the advance of the e-pawn all the more tempting.

20...Raf8

> 1650: "He has a pretty good buildup. I'm not sure how to respond. I like Black's game now. It looks like the tables have turned."

This new bout of depression comes with the realization that the f5-pawn is solidly defended. The rest of White's moves are all on the kingside. This is something that the attacker loves to see because that means White is reacting to what you are doing. Instead of this, he should have been creating counterthreats on the opposite wing (the b7- and c7-pawns are undefended).

21.g3 e4

> 1650: "I need to find a good location for my Queen. I would like to play it to g2 for defense but e2 is also tempting because it guards my Bishop on h5."

All thoughts of a counterattack are gone. White is only thinking about ways to hold things together.

22.Qg2 Qg5

> 1650: "I made the wrong choice. The e2-square was superior."

23.Be2 Be5

> 1650: "I'm busted."

24.Kh1 f4

Black, who is dominating the game on the kingside (note that White never got his queenside counterplay going), easily won. White's position is a real mess after 25.gxf4 Qh4.

Tips

★ The pawn-pointing rule is useful to know in closed or semi-closed positions. If the center is locked, you must attack on the wings with pawns. This increases your control of space and opens files for your Rooks. The pawn-pointing rule enables you to tell which wing you are supposed to play on by "point-ing" the way. See the note to Black's 9th move for a more detailed explanation.

★ Don't attack something for no reason! Attacking an enemy piece has no value in itself. You must always expect your opponent to play the best move, so he *will* (and you have to believe this!) see the transparent attack and move away to safety. If you have gained something valuable, even if he sees your threat, then the attack is useful. If there is nothing to be gained after his best reply, then restrain yourself and leave his pieces alone! Remember: you are trying to follow a plan that benefits your whole army and takes advantage of the weaknesses in his camp. One-move attacks are only useful if they do something to benefit your plan.

★ Avoid vague thoughts. Concentrate on one or two important features of the position and go as far with them as you can. This will enable you to stay on track. If you find yourself saying things like, "I'll somehow attack his King," you are being too vague. You must only attack the King (or anything else, for that matter) for a specific reason and you must be very clear with yourself on how you intend to go about doing it.

★ Don't allow surprise or depression to influence your moves. If something unexpected or bad happens, you must sit on your hands until you regain your equilibrium. When this is done, reassess the situation as if the game were starting over again and calmly figure out what the position needs.

★ Don't just react to the opponent's threats. At times, defensive moves are called for. However, if you find that you have lost track of your own plans and are just reacting to your opponent's blows, you must realize that you are on the road to defeat. Chess is a game where the opponent tries to impose his will on yours. He wants you to do what he tells you to do. Fight like a madman and refuse to go along with his agenda!

MATERIAL

Of all the imbalances in chess, a material plus carries more weight than anything else. An extra Bishop, or—in top-flight events—even an extra pawn, is often more than enough to give you a victory. For this reason, you must be very careful not to give away your units without just cause. Unfortunately, holding on to your pieces is not always so easy. I have noticed that the vast majority of games between amateurs are decided by some gross blunder of material. This means that if you can simply not give anything away (no deep strategy here!) you will see hundreds of points pad your rating.

How can we avoid this type of gross blunder? One useful method is to write your move down before you play it. Don't just scribble it, make the written move a work of art! The reason for this is that, as we look deeply into a position, our mind goes off on tangents that often take us far afield of the reality of the moment. Writing the move down in this fashion brings us back to the here and now.

Once you have written the move down, you should ask, "When I play this move, does my opponent have any checks? Can he capture or threaten any of my pieces?" You will be surprised how often you will suddenly notice that your intended move, the move you placed so much hope in, is in reality a game-losing mistake. Instead of losing the game, though, you can now scratch out or erase your blunder and think of something new.

Even though so much importance is placed on material, we must remember that it is an imbalance, just like any other imbalance. Don't win a pawn if it gives the opponent an advantage in development, space, pawn structure or several other things. Remember that a material plus is a static advantage; don't allow yourself to be beaten by the enemy's dynamics or by a combination of other static factors.

If you're lucky enough to find yourself with an advantage in material, you should follow these rules:

RULE 1 — Material beats the initiative if you can neutralize the opponent's plusses and equalize the game (this might take quite a few moves to achieve, so you have to ask if you have the time). Then your extra material will, slowly but surely, bring him down.

RULE 2 — Material gives you an extra unit of force. If you make this unit an active participant in the game, you will have your opponent outnumbered.

RULE 3 — Material edges like the Exchange (Bishop or Knight for a Rook—three points for five) are only useful if you can give the Rook an open file to fly on. An advanced, centralized Knight can easily beat an inactive, useless Rook. This means that you must be careful not to allow simple point count

(the pieces' numerical value) to influence you more than the particular position.

(59)

Black suffers even if he has the move.

If we were to judge the position in diagram 59 on point count alone, we would have to say that Black seems to be an easy winner—he has a pawn and a Rook for a Knight (six points to three). However, his Rooks are completely helpless and his extra pawn on d7 is immobile. On the other hand, the White Knight on d6 dominates the board. Black cannot prevent White from playing Rc7 with a winning bind.

> **RULE 4 — When you win material you may find your pieces are off balance and without purpose. That is because they have fulfilled their mission and now need a new goal. If they are off balance, don't keep lashing out. Instead, bring your pieces back together, make everything tight and safe, and then prepare a new plan based on your material edge. Remember: extra material gives you a long-term advantage. You don't have to be in a rush to use it.**

• • • • •

We will begin our look at material advantages with a seemingly simple position in which White is an Exchange up for a pawn.

(60)
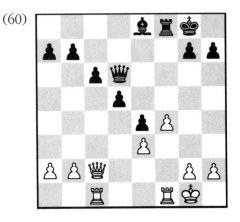

Kramer-Thomas, Utrecht 1949.
White to play.

In the position shown in diagram 60, Black enjoys more space due to his strong pawn chain on b7-e4. The things that White can crow about are his kingside pawn majority and his material advantage.

I have stated over and over again: when you try to find a plan, you must base it on the advantages (positive imbalances) in your position. You probably wouldn't wish to rush White's kingside pawns (one of your two advantages) forward (in an attempt to make use of your majority) since that would place your King in peril. This leaves you with that extra Exchange; how can White make use of it?

Rooks only reach their full potential on open files. Unfortunately for White, no completely open file exists. Still, if you want to make use of that extra Rook, you will have to find a way to create a file for it.

Before we go further, we must ask what Black's advantages are. As stated before, he has that mass of pawns in the center. He also has to address the difference of Bishop for Rook. Rooks are better than Bishops, but that doesn't mean that you must accept their inferiority and just wait to lose. Instead, you should play to make your Bishop as strong as possible. Black's plan is this: he will attempt to advance his pawns to b6 and c5 and then he will swing his Bishop around to the powerful d3 post via b5.

Armed with this knowledge, White's plan should be easier to find since you must always strive to prevent the opponent from succeeding in his plans at the same time as you fight to bring your own to fruition.

1.Qc3!

A simple, but very fine move. White prepares to centralize his Queen on d4 and also covers b4 so that he can continue with b2-b4. This advance stops Black from advancing his own pawn to c5 and also prepares to force a file open with an eventual b5.

1...Bd7
2.b4 a6
3.Qd4 h6
4.Rfd1

Threatening to win a pawn with 5.Qxe4.

4...Qe7
5.a4 Kh7
6.b5!

White is happy to sacrifice a pawn if that allows his Rooks to break into the enemy position.

6...axb5
7.axb5 Ra8
8.bxc6 Bxc6
9.Ra1

White lays claim to the open a-file.

9...Ra3
10.Rxa3 Qxa3
11.Ra1 Qb3
12.h3

White has succeeded in most of his aims and now takes a moment to see to the safety of his King.

12...Qd3
13.Qc5

White sees no reason to give Black a passed pawn on d3 with 13.Qxd3 exd3. Besides, the combined attack of White's Queen and Rook will soon lay waste to the Black King.

13...Kg6
14.Ra8 Kh5
15.Kh2!

This allows the White Queen to move without having to fear a check on e3.

15...Qe2
16.Rg8, 1-0.

(61)

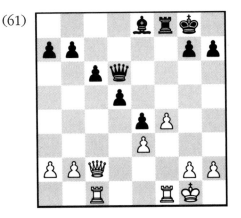

1000-Silman.
White to play.

It's now clear that White is winning in our beginning position. However, that takes a high caliber of play, so I set it up again to see how my students would handle this type of technically winning situation.

> 1000: "I'm a Rook for Bishop ahead but there are no open files for my Rooks. Black has one extra pawn and is more advanced than me. The pawns on a2, b7 and a7 are undefended but I don't see any way either side can take advantage of this. His pawns are blocking his Bishop so that means his Bishop is bad. This is in my favor. Black can boast that he has more space. So how do I use these advantages? There is a possibility of pinning the d-pawn and attacking

the one on e4. I must open a file for my Rooks and keep a close eye on my undefended pawns. One plan is Qb3, Rd1-d4 and Rxe4 winning a pawn due to the pin on the a2-g8 diagonal. Another similar idea is to place a Rook on d1 and play Qxe4 but that's no big deal since he should be able to defend against this type of thing. His e4-pawn stops my Rooks from going to f3 or d3. I'm inclined to advance my f-pawn and open a file. I'll do this by doubling Rooks on f2 and f1 and then advance the f-pawn by f5 and f6."

He did an excellent job of picking the position apart; far beyond what one would expect from a 1000 player (we had just finished talking about good and bad Bishops so he was very much aware of that idea). Also impressive is the fact that he noticed some hidden tactical possibilities based on Rd1 and Qxe4. Unfortunately, his reasoning falls apart when it comes to the actual plan chosen. He notices that no open file exists and makes a plan that tries to create one. This is excellent. However, he completely fails to take into account his opponent's moves. **Just because you have a superior or even winning position doesn't mean there is nothing for your opponent to do!**

1.Rf2? b6

Now White didn't ask why I played my move! You must always settle down and try to figure out what your opponent is up to. Instead, White forges ahead with his own (erroneous) ideas and completely ignores his opponent.

2.Rcf1?

Played instantly. Better was 2.Rd2 with the threat of 3.Qxe4. White could then have put pressure on Black's central pawns and tried to discourage Black from advancing them. Of course, White could not expect Black to miss this threat (after 2.Rd2), but placing your pieces on centralized posts is rarely bad, and at the worst serves to make it hard for Black to make use of his center pawns.

2...c5

1000: "I don't like the way your pawns are coming forward. I'll stop them with 3.b3."

All of a sudden White starts to pay attention to Black's moves and now he forgets his own plans and begins to focus on his opponent's! You can't ignore your opponent's ideas but you also must avoid getting to a mental place where you do nothing but react to his moves and ideas.

3.b3?

Now Black's Bishop gets outside the pawn chain (one of the most important things you can do with bad Bishops) and takes up an excellent post on d3. Black no longer has any problems whatsoever.

3...Bb5

> 1000: "I'm not going to give you my Rook! I'll go to d1 and pin the d-pawn."

Notice how everything White does is just a reaction to Black's moves.

4.Rd1 Bd3

> 1000: "You have no threat other than the Queen so I'll go to c3 with activity."

White has lost his grip on reality and thinks he stands better just because he's up an Exchange. This is not true. **Rooks are no better than Bishops if you can't make use of them.** Don't get trapped in the world of point count and ignore what's happening on the board.

5.Qc3 d4

> 1000: "I think I'm going to get my open file. After 6.exd4 Qxd4, I'd be happy to trade Queens."

6.exd4

During the last few moves, White should have begun damage control operations and given the Exchange back by Rxd3.

6...cxd4

> 1000: "I'll retreat to c1 which keeps me dominant on the file."

7.Qc1? e3

> 1000: "I like that. It's easy to defend my Rook, and his Bishop is hanging. His Queen is also stuck defending his d-pawn so I'm not unhappy about his move."

Amazing! White is so possessed by the newly opened file that he ignores all the plusses that Black has created for himself (active Bishop, two powerful passed pawns and pressure against the White f-pawn).

8.Rb2

Here 1000 tried 8.Rf3 but took it back when I pointed out the possibility of 8...Be2.

8...Ba6

> 1000: "I'll play 9.a4 and try to kick his Bishop off the a6-f1 diagonal with b4-b5. Wait a minute! I just missed the excellent 9.Qxe3! Fortunately I noticed it before I did anything else."

I give him credit for noticing this tactical shot (made possible by the undefended position of Black's Queen). It's just bad luck that it doesn't work out.

9.Qxe3 dxe3
10.Rxd6 e2??

This turns out to be a serious mistake that allows White to escape with a draw. However, the first player doesn't see it because he becomes depressed. This leads to a sense of hopelessness, and this again leads to an inability to see what's really going on in the position. Black should have played 10...Rxf4! when the threat of mate on f1 gives Black an important tempo. This would have led to the win of a White Rook (much as in the actual game).

> 1000: "I must retreat to b1. 11.Kf2 loses to 11...Rxf4+."

> Notice the comment, "I must." Saying this almost guarantees that you will miss the reality of what's going on. "I must" is a chain around one's brain, and must be permanently exorcised from your chess vocabulary!

11.Rb1??

Trapped by the hypnotic tone of "I must," White fails to see 11.Re6! Rxf4 12.Rbxe2 with a drawn position.

11...Rxf4
12.Re1

There was no defense.

12...Rf1+, 0-1.

It's clear that White will become a much stronger player if he starts to pay attention to his opponent's possibilities as well as his own.

Our next try at this same position shows the amateur doing much better.

(62)

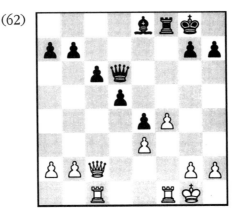

1550-Silman.
White to play.

1550: "Black has a pawn majority on the queenside and in the center. White has pressure on the c-file. Black is down the Exchange. His pawns are on the same color as his Bishop so he will want to do something about that. Even though Black is down the Exchange, if he can keep the game closed and not allow the Rooks to be activated, he will have a good position. If Black can get his Bishop to d3, he will stand very well and White may have to sacrifice a Rook to get rid of it. White, on his end, will use his kingside majority by trading Queens. He will also prevent Black from activating his Bishop. If he can open up files for his Rooks, he will win."

Another excellent breakdown of the position. Notice how White considered some of Black's ideas too.

1.Qc5

1550: "Centralizing my Queen and challenging his. Since Black's Queen is his most active piece, it's a good idea for me to trade it."

I like his logic. In general, it is always good to trade off the opponent's superior pieces. However, in this case White could

have used his Rooks in conjunction with his Queen to eventually
create an attack against the enemy King. Another point that may
make White want to retain the Queens is the fact that the Black
King is now free to run to the center and help hold things
together. With the Queens on, the Kings would both stay at home.

1...Qxc5
2.Rxc5 b6

> 1550: "Must move my Rook since I want to double on the c-
> file. I will play Rc3, which allows the doubling and defends
> e3 and allows for attacks like Ra3."

3.Rc3 c5

> 1550: "White wants to challenge Black's pawns. Black has
> opened up the diagonal for his Bishop so White wants to
> move his Rook on f1; at the same time he also wants to
> protect his pawn on f4."

So both amateurs (1000 and 1550) allowed Black to advance
his pawn to c5. In this case, White noticed the possibility but just
allowed it to happen. You don't have to let your opponents do
what they want. Stop them!

4.g3?

Absolutely horrible. White was worried about moving his f1-
Rook since an eventual ...d4 would undermine his pawn on f4. By
fixing his gaze on random will-o-the-wisps (I am reminded of a
deer transfixed by the headlights of a car), he forgets about more
important factors that are about to hit him on the head. 4.Rd1
would have been much better.

4...Bb5

> 1550: "That is what I was trying to avoid! Well...it's too late
> to do anything about it now. White's pressure is on the c-file
> so I'll play Rfc1 when both my Rooks are safe from the
> enemy."

It's becoming clear that the most common error that the
amateur makes (in any situation) is to ignore the opponent's
possibilities. Only when a direct threat (real or imagined) appears
on the board do they respond, though this response tends to be
filled with panic.

5.Rfc1 Rd8?

I played this poor move to see if he would panic at the prospect of the d-pawn rushing forward. However, White rises to the occasion and comes up with a wonderful reply. Black should have played the obvious 5...Bd3.

> 1550: "Black is threatening a pawn push on the d-file so White will start a counterattack on the c-file by sacrificing a pawn with b4."

6.b4!

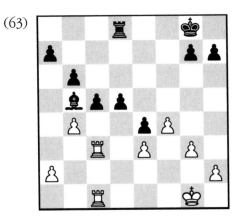

(63)

White cracks the Black position with 6.b4!.

Impressive. White is willing to give up a pawn to open a file for his Rooks. Now 6...c4 7.Rd1 leaves Black in a bad way—Black has gotten a passed pawn, but all his potential activity has been permanently stopped. White would then play his King to d4 and advance his pawns on the kingside.

It's also important to point out that 6...cxb4 fails to 7.Rc8 Rxc8 8.Rxc8+ Kf7 9.Rc7+ Kf8 10.Rxa7 Bc4 11.g4 followed by f5 and Kf2-g3-f4-e5.

6...Bc4

> 1550: "Black threatens the a-pawn. First, I'll trade."

7.bxc5 bxc5

> 1500: "Black has a bit of play but White's Rooks are also more mobile. White also wants his King in the game."

8.Kf2?

It's interesting to watch White play a very thoughtful idea on one turn and then do some lazy "pass" on the next. Instead of this useless time-waster (where is the King going? I'm sure that White has no idea), he had a couple of moves that deserved consideration. For example, 8.Ra3! a6 9.Ra5 ties Black down to the defense of his pawns, and 8.Rb1!? Bxa2 9.Ra1 Bc4 10.Rxa7 with a Rook on the seventh and the threat of Rc7 is also possible.

It's strange that White worked so hard to create an open file for his Rooks, and when he succeeds in this plan, he refuses to make use of them.

8...Rb8

> 1550: "Ouch! I missed this move. Now he's getting activity and creating some threats so I'll sacrifice the Exchange back and put pressure on his other pawns. This should put me in charge."

Here he goes again. After the bad 8th move (8.Kf2?) he comes storming back with a nice idea.

9.Rxc4!? dxc4
10.Rxc4 Rb2+
11.Kg1 Rxa2
12.Rxc5 a5?

A bad move. Black could (and should!) get an easy draw with 12....Ra3 13.Kf2 Ra2+ but I didn't want the game to end yet. Instead, I play to see what he remembers of our endgame lessons.

13.Re5

> 1550: "Might as well eat the e-pawn and get a passed pawn of my own."

13...a4
14.Rxe4 Kf7

> 1550: "I will advance my g-pawn to g4 to limit Black's King activity and at the same time expand my majority. If I can get his queenside pawn for one of my kingside pawns, I will be a clean pawn up."

I wasn't happy to hear this last comment. I had told him in the past that a Rook ending with three versus two pawns (or two vs.

one) that are all on the same side of the board is drawn. If Black can trade his a-pawn for White's pawn on e3, then a draw would result in spite of White's extra guy. At this point, White is winning and he should do everything he can to avoid any kind of drawish situations. The fact that his opponent is much higher rated is no excuse.

15.g4

Fortunately for White, he can't find any way to trade the a-pawn for the e-pawn so he instead continues to play good moves and soon builds up an overwhelming position.

15...h6

1550: "I will keep advancing and claim more space."

16.h4 Kf6

1550: "I will move my Rook along the fourth rank, which allows the e-pawn to advance."

17.Rb4 h5

1550: "I want to prevent Black's King from entering the battle so I will first drive him away with a check."

18.Rb6+ Kf7
19.g5

1550: "Now I have three versus one. If I took on h5, it would just be two versus one since the doubled h-pawn would be useless."

19...a3

1550: "White would like to get his King into action since it's doing nothing at the moment. First I'll activate my f-pawn by pushing it to f5. Then, if ...g6, I will advance to f6 and White should win."

This is the very moment that I was waiting for when I went into this endgame. I wanted to see if he remembered the extremely important rule: **Rooks belong behind passed pawns.** If he had played 20.Ra6! I would have been delighted, though 20.g6+! first and only then 21.Ra6 is probably even more accurate.

20.f5??

If White's Rook were on a6, then this pawn move would be completely winning. Unfortunately for White, Black is actually able to win the game now.

20...Rb2

> 1550: "I think I made a big error. White can't trade Rooks."

21.Ra6 a2

> 1550: "I can't believe it. I'm actually losing now."

22.g6+ Kf8
23.e4 Rb1+
24.Kf2 a1=Q
25.Rxa1 Rxa1 and the game was stopped

Tips

★ Once you learn how to break down the imbalances in a position, you have to practice coming up with a plan based on these factors.

★ Use this same understanding of the imbalances to figure out what the opponent should be doing and then make some effort to stop his plans (unless you are sure your plans will come to fruition first).

★ Don't ignore your opponent's threats or ideas. Just because you have a superior or even winning position doesn't mean there is nothing for your opponent to do!

★ You must also avoid getting into a place where all you do is worry about your opponent's intentions. Then you will spend the game reacting to his moves and will almost surely lose.

★ Avoid the quick, lazy moves that all of us are prone to on occasion. A lazy, ill-considered move often turns out to be the losing blunder.

★ A material advantage doesn't just win by itself. You have to make use of the extra wood and demonstrate its usefulness. A Bishop or a Knight can easily beat a Rook if the Rook doesn't find a useful file. Point-count chess is a useful guide but it doesn't mean anything if you don't prove why your numerical superiority gives you an advantage.

★ Basic endgame knowledge is very important. Rules like **Rooks belong behind passed pawns** are knowledge that everyone of every class must have!

In our next example, we see that owning a material advantage doesn't mean that you can ignore the positional factors that are normally so important in any given game. Often a small material edge (like an extra pawn) can be used as endgame insurance but has no enormous meaning right away. In this case, you must play to earn new advantages, i.e., space, superior minor pieces, etc.

(64)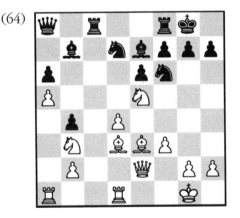

Silman-Blankenau, National Open 1989.
Black to play.

White has an isolated d-pawn but the Black pawns on a6 and b4 will also need attention. White enjoys some advantage in territory while Black can use the hole on d5 for his pieces. At the moment, White has placed his Knight on e5 and Black must figure out what he wants to do about it. Should he leave it on this strong post or should he chop it off? Black makes a very bad decision.

1...Nxe5?

Giving White's dark-squared Bishop more scope and turning the potentially weak pawn on d4 into a strong attacking e5-pawn.

2.dxe5 Nd7?

Leaving the Knight undefended on d7. The amateur must be very careful when he sees that his pieces are undefended; many bad things can befall them when this happens.

3.Bxh7+

A simple combination that nets a pawn.

3...Kxh7
4.Rxd7 Rfe8

White has won a pawn and could easily fall asleep with the thought that his game will win itself. How many promising positions are lost in this way?

Since the extra pawn is not going to make itself felt for a long time, White must work hard to insure that other positional factors will be in his favor. The most glaring thing about the position is the fact that Black has two Bishops. What are the rules for this type of situation? Going back to the chapter on minor pieces, we see that the side with the Bishop and Knight should trade off one of the enemy Bishops and create a Bishop versus Knight position. Then you must concentrate on making your Knight superior to the enemy Bishop. With this in mind, White comes up with a detailed plan designed to make his Knight as good or better than any Bishop.

5.Qf2!

Covering the important c5-square with gain of time since Black must do something about the threatened 6.Rxe7 Rxe7 7.Qh4+, picking up a piece.

5...Kg8
6.Bc5!

Trading off a set of Bishops and preparing to give the Knight a nice home on c5.

6...Bxc5
7.Nxc5 Bd5
8.Na4!

The c5-square was nice but it was not permanent since no pawn defended it. Due to this, the greedy Knight heads for greener pastures on b6.

8...Qc6
9.Nb6 Rcd8
10.Rxd8 Rxd8

11.Qd4 and White was in complete control. The final moves saw White give the material back in order to weaken the Black King: **11...Qb5 12.h4 Rb8 13.h5 Rb7 14.h6 gxh6 15.Rc1 Qxa5 16.Rc8+ Kh7 17.Qg4 Qxb6+ 18.Kh2 h5 19.Qxh5+ Kg7 20.Qh8+, 1-0**.

This game is certainly nothing special, but I was quite interested to see how a strong amateur player would handle the technical questions that arose after White won the pawn.

(65)

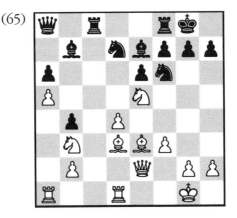

1700-Silman.
Black to play.

> 1700: "Black's pawns on a6 and b4 are weak while White's weaknesses can easily be protected. White has more queenside space than Black. White might be able to use the weak b6-square and c5 is another potential target. Black has an ideal square on d5, though White could exchange pieces there."

I reminded him that this was the wrong strategy. In a past lesson I had taught him that **the way to beat isolated d-pawns is to trade off all the minor pieces and then double on the d-pawn with a Queen and Rook.** The lack of minor pieces would take away all the isolated d-pawn's dynamic strength and turn it into a pure weakness.

Due to this rule, it is Black who would be happy to make trades on d5, not White.

> 1700: "I forgot about that stuff. Anyway, White would attack on the queenside and Black on the kingside. Does White want to allow ...Nxe5, exchanging a good Knight for a limited one? I would not allow this Knight on e5 to be exchanged. I would have played it to c4 and b6. Black should take on e5.
>
> Overall, I think that White is a bit better due to his space, control of key squares and Black's weak queenside pawns. On second thought, if ...Nxe5 then dxe5 makes the dark-squared Bishop very dangerous!

What is this talk about a kingside attack for Black? As usual, the amateur player is always thinking of attacking the enemy King, even if such a thing is unlikely in the given position.

1...Nxe5
2.dxe5 Nd7
3.Bxh7+ Kxh7
4.Rxd7

> 1700: "That was easy to see."

4...Rfe8

> 1700: "I would like to get a Knight to b6. Also the Bishop could go there."

Bishops don't necessarily need to be advanced to be effective, but Knights do! He should have given a lot of thought to his

Knight's future. Note how ideas about superior minor pieces never entered his head. I would have been so happy if he had thought of trading one pair of Bishops (**when the opponent has two Bishops, trade off one of them and leave him with only a single Bishop**), but though my students are well aware of this rule, they have trouble recognizing and implementing it during actual play.

5.Bb6 Bd5

> 1700: "Do I want to exchange my bad Knight for his good Bishop? Should I give it to him and win it back by Qd3+? Can his c-Rook penetrate along that file? No, it can't. This means that I can take the time to double."

I was happy to see him not panic over ...Bxb3, which is really not a threat at all due to the reply Qd3+. However, why does he want to double on a file that is not open due to the Bishop's presence on d5?

6.Rd1? Kg8

> 1700: "I might be able to trap his Queen with Ra7 at some point. Can I let him take on b3 and get a check on d8? No, I will just centralize my Knight. I also threaten Nf5!"

7.Nd4 Bc5

> 1700: "Trying to exchange a pair of Bishops. I thought I was the one who was supposed to do this? However, he is weakening my a5-pawn and pinning my Knight. If 8.Bxc5 Rxc5 my pawns on a5 and e5 are both weak. I think my game has gotten worse than it was at first. Critical is 8.Ra7 going after a6."

8.Ra7 Qxa7!
9.Bxa7 Bxa7
10.Kh1 Bxd4
11.Rxd4 Rc1+
12.Rd1 Rfc8 and we stopped the game since Black, for a small material price, had gotten a firm grip on the initiative.

Tips

★ When playing against an isolated d-pawn, trade off all the minor pieces and the pawn's weaknesses will come to light (no attacking chances for the player with the isolated pawn, while the remaining Queen and Rooks will be able to put strong pressure against the pawn).

★ Even if you win material, you must not forget to read the imbalances and create a plan.

DEVELOPMENT
AND
INITIATIVE

Development and initiative are almost invisible—they don't have anything to do with territory, nor do they revolve around pawn structure or any particular weakness. Instead, these terms belong in the mysterious realm of *dynamics*, compared to the *statics* that most of our other imbalances correspond to.

A static advantage is a positionally motivated imbalance. It's long-lasting, and can be used immediately or later in the game. Material is a static advantage, as are weak pawns, weak squares and, of course, extra territory.

A dynamic advantage is composed of something less tangible and permanent. Here concepts such as timing, tactical vision and playing with verve become important. The goal with a dynamic advantage is to make quick and energetic use of it, in the hopes of trading in the temporary activity for a permanent static edge or a quick knockout.

The two dynamic advantages we will discuss here are development and initiative.

Development

A lead in development is easy to spot. Simply put, you have more pieces out than your opponent. Of course, normally you would expect the other side to get the rest of his pieces into play over time. That is why a development lead is a temporary advantage; you only have a few moves until it disappears! Because of that, you must make immediate use of it or you will end up empty-handed. How is this done? What is the goal? The following rules should clarify these points:

> **RULE 1 — A lead in development usually means that you must start some sort of aggressive act. Quiet play puts no pressure on the opponent and will allow him to get the rest of his forces out.**

(66)

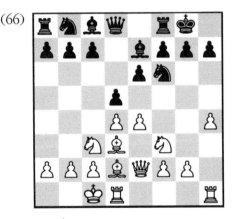

White to play.

White enjoys a clear lead in development in diagram 66. He could play in the center with 1.exd5 exd5 2.Rhe1 followed by 3.Ne5, but instead White decides to advance his pawn and chase Black's main kingside defender away.

1.e5

A strong move here, but usually the better developed side would try to open the position rather than close it.

1...Nd7

Now quiet play might allow Black time to get some counterplay in the center and on the queenside by ...c5 followed by ...Nc6. White has the use of a greater force at the moment so he decides to strike while the iron is hot.

2.Bxh7+!

Notice how White's last two moves have not allowed Black the time to get the rest of his forces out. *When you are ahead in development, take the battle to the opponent!*

2...Kxh7
3.Ng5+ Kg8
4.Qh5 and Black will be mated (4...Bxg5 5.hxg5). Poor Black was overwhelmed by the superior force of the White army.

> **RULE 2 — A lead in development means the most in open positions because the open central files should enable your army to penetrate into the hostile position with relative ease. If you have more pieces out and the position is wide open (or even semi-open), then don't hesitate to ATTACK!**

Browne-Quinteros, Wijk aan Zee 1974.
Sicilian Defense, Moscow Variation.

1.e4 c5
2.Nf3 d6
3.Bb5+

This line remains popular at all levels of competition.

3...Bd7
4.Bxd7+ Qxd7
5.c4

Black can win a pawn with the greedy (but overly risky)...

5...Qg4?

However, this move, which does give Black a static material

edge, allows White to build up an enormous advantage in development.

6.0-0 Qxe4
7.d4

White opens up as many lines as possible. These open files should be looked upon as highways into the hostile position.

7...cxd4
8.Re1 Qc6
9.Nxd4 Qxc4?

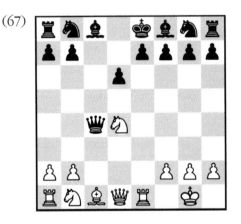

(67)

White to play and attack like mad!

Black's last move gives him a two pawn advantage. However, few things in life are free, and this suicidal capture gives White more development and more open lines. If you are the defender in such positions, remember that it is rarely a good idea to open lines if your King is still in the center.

10.Na3

From this point on, White will play with threats and never allow his opponent to bring his lazy troops out.

10...Qc8
11.Nab5

Threatening 12.Nxd6+.

11...Qd7

White answers the obvious 11...e6 with 12.Nf5!.

12.Bf4

Renewing the threat against d6.

12...e5
13.Bxe5!

It's time to crack open the Black King. White is playing for complete Armageddon and, as a result, normal material and positional considerations no longer exist.

13...dxe5
14.Rxe5+ Be7
15.Rd5!

Black is not given a moment's rest.

15...Qc8

Taking on d5 was not possible due to 16.Nc7+.

16.Nf5

Another fork is threatened on d6.

16...Kf8
17.Nxe7 Kxe7

Mate follows 17...Nxe7 18.Rd8+.

18.Re5+, 1-0. Black has taken enough punishment. 18...Kf8 19.Qd6+ does not paint a pretty picture for the second player.

> **RULE 3 — If the enemy King is still in the center and you have a lead in development, consider these factors an invitation to rip the opponent's head off! Start an immediate attack. At the very least, you will keep his King stuck in the middle and make him suffer for a long time to come.**

> **RULE 4 — A closed position often nullifies a lead in development because the blocked files stop you from effecting any real penetration. If you have a big lead in development and think you can blast the**

pawns out of the way, then by all means give it a try. However, more often than not, the side with the deficit in development will find that he has ample time to cure this problem if the central situation is locked up.

A common opening that leads to a closed center is **1.d4 Nf6 2.c4 c5 3.d5 e5 4.Nc3 d6 5.e4 Be7** (this line is known as the Czech Benoni) **6.Bd3 0-0 7.Nge2 Ne8!** Black allows himself to fall behind in development because he knows that White's pieces cannot get to him due to the traffic jam in the middle. After **8.0-0,** Black shows that he's willing to lose even more time by **8...Bg5!,** trading off his bad Bishop for White's good one. Black shows disdain for development and instead accomplishes a good strategic goal, secure in the knowledge that he can catch up in development later.

> **RULE 5 — The goal doesn't have to be mate! If you start an attack and win material (or get the two Bishops in an open position, or leave him with weak pawns, etc.) by the time he gets his forces out, then you are in possession of a fine static advantage. Don't go crazy and attempt to force an immediate decision where none exists.**

(68)

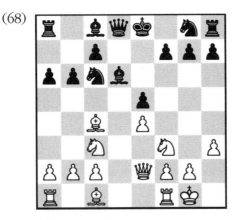

White to play.

In diagram 68, White could attempt to make use of his development lead and try to attack in some way, but why not grab material with **1.Bxf7+ Kxf7 2.Qc4+** followed by Qxc6 with a solid extra pawn? This would give White something to use for the rest of the game.

Initiative

When you have control of the game, you are said to possess the initiative. The initiative can be based on static or dynamic factors. For example, if you are attacking a weak pawn (a static plus) and your opponent is reduced to a passive defense, you have the initiative. You would still own the initiative if you have a poor pawn structure but your lead in development gives you an attack (this time you have an initiative based on dynamics).

In general, top players look upon the initiative with great favor; it is always advantageous to have the initiative. The question is, will you be able to retain it and what was the price you paid to acquire it?

For example, you may have sacrificed a pawn to take control of the game (the initiative). Will your opponent eventually be able to equalize (when his extra pawn might take on enormous importance), or will your initiative lead to gains that are greater than the sacrificed material?

(69)

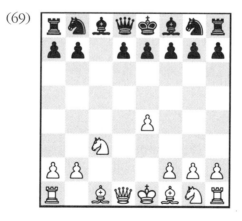

Black's pawn versus White's development.

The position in diagram 69 comes about after the moves **1.e4 c5 2.d4 cxd4 3.c3 dxc3 4.Nxc3** (the Smith-Morra Gambit in the Sicilian Defense). Why did White sacrifice a pawn? He *does* gain a lead in development, but in this case Black expects to eventually catch up. The real reason White made the offer was to create two open files and a space advantage. Of course, this particular gambit is considered somewhat unsound at the top levels, but the concept is a good one: Always fight to take control of the game.

Of course, if you can create static advantages and also retain the initiative then you have the best of both worlds. However, it's often a tradeoff, one kind of advantage for another. For example, if you are about to get pushed around, why not give up material (in trade for the initiative) and try to become master of your own fate?

The example in the diagram is somewhat extreme. White immediately goes after the initiative and feels that a pawn is a small price to pay. However, why should White give anything away? Why not fight for the initiative by positional means (grabbing tactical possibilities if they arise) and attempt to get it all at no cost whatsoever?

Though most gambits don't really work in the professional ranks (White is happy to try and make use of his extra move), amateurs can learn a lot from initiative-seeking pawn sacrifices. Ultimately, though, you have to be able to do both: mastering positional (static) ideas on one hand and making use of dynamic strategies on the other.

• • • • •

An eight year old student—rated about 1100 and visiting me for the first time—showed me a game which he lost to an opponent (another youngster) with a rating of just 800. He wasn't sure where he went wrong, but a glance was sufficient to show me that he lost due to passive play. His opponent grabbed the initiative and literally blew him off the board.

800 vs. 1100. Sicilian Defense, Rossolimo Variation.

1.e4 c5
2.Nf3 e6
3.Nc3 Nc6
4.Bb5 Nd4
5.0-0 Nxb5
6.Nxb5

So far both sides have played really well. White enjoys a lead in development while Black has a solid position and owns a pair of Bishops.

6...d6

Quite playable, but this move caused some concern in me. I would have been happier to see 6...a6, chasing the Knight back to obscurity. If Black had taken lessons from me earlier, he would have known that **you battle Knights by taking away all their advanced support points.**

7.d4

This guy is just 800 strength? White is trying to open up the position so he can make use of his lead in development. Of course, it's usually bad to open things up when your opponent has two Bishops, but the dynamic strength of a development lead must be exploited immediately or it will fade away.

7...b6?

The first poor move of the game. Correct was 7...a6 8.Nc3 cxd4 when White's Knights are being contained and Black can hope to catch up in development (nullifying White's main weapon) and eventually make his two Bishops (Black's main weapon) work for him. Remember that **you are supposed to create imbalances in the opening and then develop your pieces around those differences.**

8.Bf4?

White's heart is in the right place but he falters anyway. He should have made immediate use of his advanced Knight by playing 8.dxc5 bxc5 9.Bf4. Now Black is given another opportunity to chase the annoying horse away.

8...Ba6?

(70)

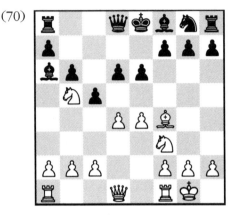

White to play.

Black's last move (8...Ba6) pins the Knight, but it allows the horse to remain on b5. It was still correct to play 8...a6.

9.c4

I would prefer 9.a4, when 9...Bxb5 10.axb5 opens a file for White's Rook.

9...Qd7

So what is Black doing? Whatever it is, it's not correct. He is not aware of the possible battle between the minor pieces—we know this because he's not doing anything to make his Bishops active—and he is letting the enemy Knight remain on its active post.

Black is also not aware of the danger of leaving one's King in the center for too long. Once you castle and get your King to safety, you can play for a long time. However, if your King is sitting in the middle, then you might get nuked at any moment.

Finally, Black is not aware of the dangers inherent in a lack of development. At the beginning of this game, he bought the two Bishops for the price of development. Now it's time to replenish his store of cash (development), but he refuses to do so. Moves like ...b6 do nothing for development at all, and ...Ba6 and ...Qd7 leave all the kingside pieces at home.

10.a4 0-0-0

White threatened dxc5 with a gang-attack on d6. Castling long defends this square but places the King in another vulnerable area.

11.e5!

White is doing everything he can to open up the position and get to the Black King. This is exactly what you want to do when you enjoy a huge lead in development.

11...d5
12.cxd5 exd5
13.e6!!

The 800 rating kept swirling around in my head. I wish my students with class A ratings could play like this! In one move, White, who is playing with a lot of energy, brings two pieces into the attack.

13...fxe6
14.Ne5 Qe7?

Note that 14...Qb7 is still met by 15.Nc6! when the Rook and the a7-pawn both hang and 15...Qxc6 fails to 16.Nxa7+.

15.Nc6 and White went on to win.

This game raised some questions. Do most amateurs see a lack of development as a major problem? Do most amateurs attack with the verve that White demonstrated in the game? To answer these questions, I had two of my students take the White side from the diagrammed position and try to blow me off the board.

(71)

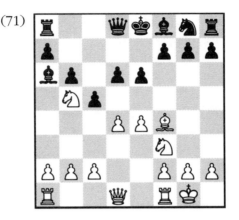

1400-Silman.
White to play.

1400: "Black has an advantage in space on the queenside and owns the two Bishops. However, Black is a long way from being castled so I'm not sure if he can make use of these things. White has a space advantage on the kingside and in the center, plus he's way ahead in development. I also see a possible weak square on c6. White should break open the center by any means possible. Even a pawn sacrifice would be justified if it meant getting to that King."

I really like what White said about breaking through the center by any means possible; that is just the type of attitude that I am trying to cultivate. However, when it came down to particulars he had surprisingly little to say. That's because he started to concentrate on his attacked Knight. Notice how he never gets too far away from this defensive thought.

9.c4 Qd7

1400: "I will bring my Queen up to d3 where it will defend c4. This move also connects my Rooks."

I prefer 10.a4 followed by 11.e5, as seen in the original game. White has become so concerned about defending b5 that he never gets his dreams for an attack started.

A large part of chess success is based on attitude. If you decide that your advantage consists of something that demands quick and vigorous play and you insist on moves from yourself that conform to those particular needs, then you will be a fearsome opponent. However, if you pay too much attention to the enemy's threats, then your mind will click into this defensive mode and you will become sensitive to every threat or non-threat that arises. You will start playing a game of reaction and your own ideas will never have a chance for expression.

10.Qd3 cxd4

> 1400: "Now the recapture dumps a piece to ...e6-e5. I'll play e5. This opens the center but blocks my Bishop."

He has already lost the game mentally. If someone's King is in the middle, then feel free to sacrifice a pawn or even a piece in order to get your army to it. In this case, White should play 11.Qxd4! e5 (the move he feared. Simply good for White is 11...Bxb5 12.cxb5 e5 13.Qd5) 12.Nxe5! (blasting his way through) 12...dxe5 13.Qxe5+ Be7 14.Nc7+ and White regains his sacrificed piece. White didn't see this because he stopped looking when he saw the fork by ...e6-e5. This is how blind spots are created; we see a move or two ahead, notice a problem, and completely stop looking. Instead, we should look one or two moves ahead, stop, and treat this future situation as our starting position. When you analyze from this new starting position you will often be amazed at what you find!

11.e5 d4

Notice how White has been reacting to Black's threats for the last several moves. In chess there are two wars being waged: one is on the physical chessboard. The other is the subtler battle of mind versus mind. In the present contest, White is doing whatever Black tells him to do. This means that Black has already won the mental part of the fight.

12.b3?

No words or thought; he just played it right away. He's still reacting to everything Black does.

12...dxc4
13.bxc4 Bc5

Now White has a permanent weakness on c4 and he has also given Black use of the c5-square.

> 1400: "I want to take on d4."

He tried 14.Nfxd4 Bxb5 15.Be3?? (15.Qe4) and didn't notice that he was a piece down. I pointed this out to him and had him do something else.

> 1400: "That's not good! I'll just keep up the pressure by moving my Rook to d1."

White is making things easy on Black. He has to get control of the game before Black develops his Knight and castles; he has to make something happen before the long-term disadvantages of the White position make themselves felt. White should play 14.Nd6+ Bxd6 15.exd6 when the pawn on d6 is quite strong and the pawn on d4 will quickly fall. **Remember: Chess is a game where you come up with an idea that supposedly improves the plusses in the position, then you do everything you can to implement that idea.** In the present case, White is just doing what his opponent wants him to do.

14.Rad1 Ne7

> 1400: "I want to trade one of my Knights for a Bishop to get rid of his Bishop pair. I'll do this by Nd2-b3xc5."

He's lost all sense of reality and reverts to rules used only in static situations. Taking the Bishop on c5 only helps Black retain his extra pawn on d4. White should have taken his pawn back by 15.Nfxd4.

15.Nd2? 0-0
16.Nb3? Bxb5
17.Nxc5 bxc5
18.cxb5 Qd5. Black threatens both ...Qxa2 and ...Ng6 followed by ...Nxe5. We stopped the game.

So White noticed what was going on in this game but he never made a real effort to realize his ideals. It was becoming clear to me that mental toughness (this *is* something that can be learned) is a major part of chess strength. You have to insist on accomplishing your goals and you can't allow anything to distract you from this path.

The next game is still from the same position, but this student's collapse comes even faster.

(72)
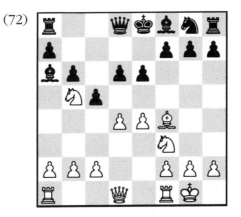

1300-Silman.
White to play.

1300: "My Bishop is undefended on f4 and my Knight is attacked and pinned. White has a space advantage in the center but this is evened out by Black's space edge on the queenside. I have a lead in development while Black has only one piece out. I'm probably just slightly better due to my development, though I'm bothered by my pinned Knight on b5. I would like to move it to safety but then he would take my Rook. I'll go to d3 with my Queen. Then if he takes my Knight I can recapture with check."

1300 didn't talk like a man who has faith in his position. Notice how he really hated the fact that his Knight was pinned, and he even was worried (unjustifiably, I assure you!) about his undefended Bishop on f4. Evidently, White doesn't realize that a huge lead in development on an open board takes precedence over most static principles.

9.Qd3

An interesting move. Now the Bishop on a6 can hang to tactics based on Nc7+ or Nxd6+.

9...cxd4

> 1300: "I might be able to play 10.Nxd6+ when he gets my
> Knight and I get his Bishop. Wait! After 10.Nxd6+ Bxd6
> 11.Qxa6 I lose a piece to 11...Bxf4. I'll just take back on d4."

Very interesting. White faces his first tough decision and he
promptly falls apart. When you are trying to make use of a
dynamic edge you should take your time and look long and hard
for a knockout. This doesn't mean that you are playing only for
mate. Far from it! A superior endgame, the win of a pawn, a huge
positional plus; all of these things are good value for your
dynamic dollar. In the present situation, White should have
played 10.Bxd6! Bxd6 11.Nxd6+ Qxd6 12.Qxa6 when threats like
13.Qa4+ or 13.Rad1 guarantee that White will pick up the d-pawn
and be a solid pawn to the good.

10.Nfxd4 e5

> 1300: "I didn't see that at all. I better attack."

White more or less just gives up. I would have been happy if
he hunkered down and tried hard to find a way out (it didn't mater
if he actually found a saving idea, I just wanted to see some effort.
If you don't make an effort, you won't get results). Instead, he
took a few seconds and makes a one-move threat.

As it turns out, White had the strong 11.Qc4, threatening both
12.Qc6+ and 12.Nc7+. Then 11...Rc8 is met by 12.Qa4!. However,
it's impossible to find a game-saving shot if you don't look for it!

11.Nc6 Qd7

> 1300: "My c6-Knight and my f4-Bishop are hanging. Things
> have gotten out of hand."

12.Nc7+

Mental and physical surrender.

12...Qxc7
13.Qxa6 Qxc6, 0-1.

In this game, White had an idea but noticed that it didn't work
at the last moment. Instead of calmly reassessing the situation, he
panicked and went berserk!

It is interesting to note that the amateurs took note of the development leads and realized that it was a favorable factor, but they were not able to make use of this advantage.

Tips

★ Figure out if the position is a dynamic one or a static one. If it's dynamic, then you must play with tremendous energy.

★ Once you decide on a goal (for example: you want to break through in the center) you must take as long as necessary to accomplish it (on the clock and on the board). A static goal might take twenty moves. A dynamic goal calls for some sort of instant result—this means that speed is extremely important. If it takes you forty minutes to figure out how to do what you want done, then take forty minutes!

★ Never let the opponent dominate you mentally! If you notice that you are meekly reacting to everything he does, you must snap yourself out of your trance and fight to establish some sort of psychic control.

★ Castle quickly! When your King is safe, you can do what you want and play without fear of a mating surprise. If you see a King in the center, do everything you can to blast things open and execute it. No subtleties here, just pure brutality!

Our next example shows what happens when one of the greatest attackers of all time gets his hands on the initiative: He never lets up until the opponent is dead.

Even more interesting is how he creates the initiative in the first place. It's almost as if he treats his opponent like a sheep—he herds him in a certain direction and the opponent obeys the commands given to him.

(73)

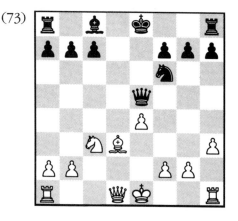

Alekhine-Marshall, Baden-Baden 1925.
White to play.

The main imbalance in this position is created by the mutual pawn majorities. White has a central majority and Black has a majority of pawns on the queenside.

Seeing that the key to his success will be whether or not he can make use of the power of his majority, Alekhine takes immediate steps to get his pawns moving.

1.Qd2

A flexible move. White prepares to make use of his kingside majority with f2-f4. He can also castle queenside.

1...Bd7

Since White's pawn majority influences the center and kingside, Black hopes to place his King on the other side of the board. Naturally, White takes immediate steps to prevent this.

2.Qe3!

A very fine idea. Black is prevented from castling queenside and the Black Queen is also kept out of the d4-square. We will see how Black made use of this square in the games that follow.

2...Bc6?!

Black decides to castle kingside, but it is rarely wise to castle into the strength of the enemy. In this case, the kingside is White's strength due to his majority of pawns.

Better was 2...Qa5, when Black could safely castle on the queenside.

3.0-0-0

With his King safely tucked away on this side of the board, White can advance his kingside pawns without being worried about weakening his King's protection.

3...0-0

When you see Kings that are castled on opposite sides, it usually denotes a wild struggle where both players strive for an attack on the enemy monarch. However, in this case Black will hardly be able to strike a blow. Why? Because the Black majority is unable to take part in the attack. White gets to land the first blow and he keeps on punching till the opponent falls to the canvas. This type of active control is known as the initiative.

4.f4

The first threat. White takes over the initiative because the advance of his pawns gains time by attacking the Black pieces.

4...Qe6
5.e5

Another threat. Once again Black is forced to react to White and not bother with his own ideas.

5...Rfe8
6.Rhe1 Rad8
7.f5

White's assault is in full swing, while Black's counterattack has not even started.

7...Qe7
8.Qg5 Nd5
9.f6 Qf8
10.Bc4!

White never gives his opponent a moment's respite.

10...Nxc3
11.Rxd8 Rxd8
12.fxg7!

Taking advantage of the fact that Black's Queen is the only defender of the Rook on d8.

12...Nxa2+

Also hopeless is 12...Qe8 13.Bxf7+ Kxf7 14.Rf1+ Ke6 15.Rf6+, etc.

13.Kb1!

The automatic 13.Bxa2 would give Black a saving check on c5.

13...Qe8
14.e6! Be4+
15.Ka1

A self-mate can be had by 15.Kxa2?? Qa4 mate. White could also win with 15.Rxe4, though this lets Black enjoy a short-lived burst of activity by 15...Rd1+ 16.Kc2 Qa4+ 17.b3, etc. Alekhine's move is simpler, safer, and more brutally effective.

15...f5

White wins more mundanely after 15...fxe6 16.Bxe6+ Qxe6 17.Qxd8+ Kxg7 18.Qd4+ followed by the capture of Black's Bishop.

16.e7+ Rd5
17.Qf6 Qf7
18.e8=Q+. Black resigned since mate follows in two moves.

This powerful performance by the legendary Alekhine was accomplished due to his insight into the opponent's possibilities. He didn't just note that his kingside majority was strong. He also took into consideration the opponent's counterplay and made a point of first preventing it. After that, the enemy never had a chance to do anything but defend.

Now let's see how mortals play the position that Alekhine handled so magnificently.

(74)

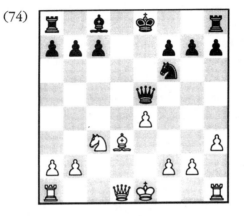

1500-Silman.
White to play.

> 1500: "White has a space advantage. Black has the more active Queen but it could also turn out to be a target. White can activate his majority with tempo by playing for f2-f4. How do I do this? I'll castle and play for a quick f4."

White, to his credit, notices the advantages that an active central majority can bring. Unfortunately, he neglects to take Black's plans into account.

1.0-0 Be6
2.f4 Qd4+

It's worth noting that Alekhine was very careful not to give his opponent access to this square.

3.Kh2 0-0-0

> 1500: "I should have prevented this. I'll play 4.Rf3. What else can I do? No! It's too passive!"

4.Bc2 Qe3

> 1500: "Can't play 5.Qe2 because of 5...Qxe2 and 6...Rd2. I need to trade Queens."

5.Qf3 Qxf3
6.Rxf3 Rd2

1500: "Ugh. Have to defend my Bishop."

Ever since Black placed his Queen on d4 and castled queenside, White has forgotten his own plans and done nothing but worry about the threats of his opponent. This all stemmed from White's refusal to look for Black's plan on the first move.

Knowing your own plan isn't enough, you also have to know what your opponent intends to do!

We decided to end the game at this point.

Next I tested this position on a slightly stronger opponent.

(75)

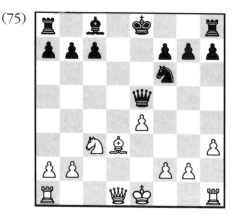

1700-Silman.
White to play.

1700: "White has a pawn majority on the kingside. Black's pieces are farther advanced and Black has a bit less development. White's pawn majority gives him a space advantage on the kingside so Black would be well-advised to castle long. White will castle short and prepare f2-f4."

1700 realized that Black should not step into the brunt of White's onrushing pawns. This is excellent. However, like the student before him, White fails to notice the potential weakness of the dark-squares in the center. This seems to be a typical failing of the amateur player: he can see tactical threats to win material or go after the King, but he has real trouble seeing that a square can also be a target.

1.0-0 Be6

> 1700: "If I play f4, he can check me with ...Qd4, but then he has to move his Queen because he can easily lose it to a Bishop discovery on b5. He could also check me on c5 when his Queen might be safer. I could just move out of the way, though, and continue my attack."

This student tends towards excessive optimism. While confidence is an important thing to have, you also need a touch of realism. Like 1500 before him, 1700 is not really giving the possibilities of the opponent a thorough examination.

The initiative in open positions will often go to the player who is first to control an open central file. In the Alekhine game, White went ahead with his pawn expansion only after stopping any counterplay on the d-file.

2.f4 Qd4+

> 1700: "Looks risky to me."

At this point White is transfixed by his threat to win Black's Queen by Bb5+.

3.Kh1 0-0-0

> 1700: "Now he's attacking my Bishop and has stopped my threat of Bb5+. I can move it to c2 or play Rf3."

4.Bc2

Did you notice that we've reached the same position as in the previous game, with the insignificant exception of the King's placement on h1 instead of h2?

Perhaps we have stumbled onto something important. Perhaps the amateur typically has some sort of idea about what he wishes to achieve but rarely takes an honest look at the opponent's plans.

4...Bc4

> 1700: "I have to defend my Rook."

Now White was in pure defensive mode. He seemed shocked that things had turned around so quickly and this depressed state of mind soon led to a blunder.

5.Re1 Qf2
6.Qc1

He moved quickly and without thought.

6...Rd2, 0-1.

Well, that was a disaster for White! Note how routine play keeps giving Black the initiative in these games. Now compare them to Alekhine's play and you will get a greater appreciation of two things: how he stopped Black's counterplay before it began and how he claimed the initiative for himself by making the most of his kingside pawn majority. The mixture of prophylaxis and aggression was quite impressive, don't you agree?

In our next example (still using the Alekhine position), we move up the food-chain a bit and test the skills of an "A" class player.

(76)

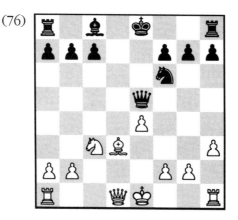

1800-Silman.
White to play.

1800: "I like White. He has his minor pieces out and he has a pawn controlling the center. He has both the d-file and the half-open c-file to work with. He has a pawn majority on the kingside while Black has a majority on the queenside. We have to kill his majority and get ours going. How do we do this? 1.Qb3 slows down his development, but he just goes 1...b6 and fianchettoes. At some point, I could play b4 stopping his pawns. I can't do this at the moment so I'll just castle and prepare to get my pawns going by f2-f4."

As a higher-rated player, 1800 looked at more than his predecessors. Nevertheless, his error is basically the same. By seeing the game as some mad race between rival majorities, he fails to take into account other possibilities for Black and falls victim to the pressure on the d-file that the others ran afoul of.

1.0-0 Be6

1800: "He has a pin coming up but there is nothing he can do with it yet. I'll get my majority rolling."

Like 1700, White sees Black's first move but discounts its usefulness.

2.f4 Qd4+
3.Kh1 0-0-0

1800: "I'm pinned and I don't see any counterplay for myself."

Here we go again! All of these players saw the punch coming but refused to give it credence until their teeth were knocked out!

How do players of C-A strength avoid this type of reversal? First, you have to work much harder at the board than these guys did! They gave the position just a cursory examination and paid the price.

As we're discovering, it's critically important to come up with an aggressive plan for yourself (based on the positive aspects of your position, of course), but you must also figure out what the opponent is going to do and strive to cross his plans. This is done by determining that your plan is faster (which means you can ignore his stuff altogether), or by simply stopping him from doing what he wants to do.

4.Bc2

1800: "I need to consolidate and this does it."

4...Qe3

1800: "He's in my position! I don't know what to do."

The once-confident commander of the White pieces succumbs to panic.

5.Qf3 Qxf3
6.Rxf3 Rd2

> 1800: "Black stands better. I need to sacrifice a pawn and get out of the bind."

White is a little too eager to give up material. Your position may be unpleasant but you must hold on tight and refuse to give up more than is necessary.

7.Bb3?

So panic leads to the loss of material. The calm 7.Rc1 was much better.

7...Rxb2 and we stopped the game.

Ready to do this one more time? Let's go to the strong expert class and see if someone of this strength can handle the position with any degree of proficiency.

(77)

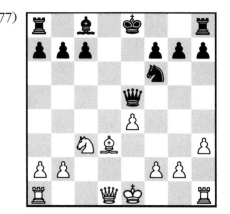

2100-Silman.
White to play.

> 2100: "The major imbalance is a kingside majority versus a queenside majority. If White can break the blockade on e5 and push his pawn to that square, his Bishop will be more active and his pawns will push the Black pieces backwards.
>
> "Of course, this sounds good but it's not so easy to accomplish. On 1.0-0 Black can play 1...Nh5 and create a

blockade on f4. My dark squares would then be conquered. I have three moves to consider: 1.0-0 with the idea of f4. I already found a good reply to this; 1.Ne2, giving up the b-pawn. I don't think I can open up the center fast enough to justify this sacrifice; 1.Qc2 with the idea of Ne2. This covers the f4 and d4 squares. Finally, 1.Qd2 is also possible but Qc2 gives extra protection to the e-pawn.

"From Black's point of view: he wants to retain his blockade and prevent f4. He doesn't want to castle queenside because there are several open files. Black could try to work on the e4-pawn but that might be slow. He should probably try to use his queenside majority and get his King to safety with ...0-0.

"For White, I like 1.Qc2 because there are potential attacks on the c-pawn."

That was nicely done! He was off on his assessment concerning the correct location for Black's King, but his efforts to take the dark-squares away from Black are highly praiseworthy (though inaccurate). Notice how he also looked for ways that Black could fight against his plans (1.0-0 being met by ...Nh5). This was something that the C-A players didn't do.

1.Qc2 Bd7

2100: "Now I'll take away those squares on f4 and d4."

Notice how the other players never even mentioned the existence of "squares." Any class player will make great strides if he realizes that the control of individual squares is as important as any other strategy in the game.

2.Ne2 Bc6

2100: "Now f3 or 3.Nc3 will make me look stupid so f4 is forced."

3.f4 Qa5+

2100: "I knew he was going there. If 4.Qd2, he can simply trade. My best option is 4.Nc3; the Knight's already done its job in allowing me to play f4. After 4.Nc3, I can also castle queenside and get my kingside majority into play."

4.Nc3 0-0-0

2100: "Now I have to decide between queenside castling and e5. It's risky to play in the center when your King is still sitting there. I'd better castle since he threatens 5...Nxe4! 6.Bxe4 Bxe4 7.Qxe4 Rhe8."

5.0-0-0

Though White's play was not the very best, he came up with a logical plan and this sufficed to give him a good position with a safe King and an active central majority.

We stopped the game at this point.

Tips

★ Don't become entranced with your own plans. You *must* also take note of the opponent's possibilities and gauge just how dangerous they really are.

★ Part of your plan can be the prevention of the opponent's goals. For example, you can be playing to win a weak pawn but can take time out to prevent his Knight from reaching a strong central outpost.

★ In an open position, the first person to dominate an open central file will usually gain the initiative.

★ The initiative will usually go to the first person who turns his plan into a reality.

During my years of teaching experience, I have noticed that nothing freaks out the amateur player more than the threat of an attack against his King. Though the amateur's play on the queenside or in the center may be highly promising, when the opponent goes "boo" to his King, all thoughts about his own plans are quickly forgotten and his pieces rush to the kingside in an effort to defend their leader. **When you lose such a game, you aren't losing because of the opponent's kingside attack (which is usually more imagined than real). You are losing because you've given up on your own plans, and this lack of direction allows the enemy to safely do anything he wishes to do.**

This leads us to the following simple but effective rule: **When players are attacking on opposite wings, it's important to follow your plans with unerring devotion.** Certain defensive moves are acceptable, but the first person to crack and go into defensive mode will most likely end up as the loser. Why? Because the attacking side can then take his time and build up his forces to his heart's content, secure in the knowledge that his opponent has ceased to make threats of his own.

The following two games both show cases where White (the amateur) is given a position with very promising queenside play. Will our amateurs panic in the face of Black's kingside counterattack? If they do panic, does this mean that such a reaction is typical of most amateurs, or is it simply a matter of style and individual temperament? Perhaps the games will provide an answer to these questions.

(78)

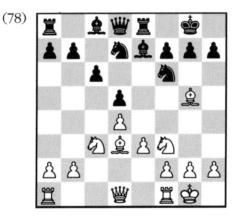

1400-Silman. Queen's Gambit Declined.
White to play.

The starting moves were: **1.d4 d5 2.c4 e6 3.Nc3 Nf6 4.cxd5 exd5 5.Bg5 Be7 6.e3 c6 7.Bd3 0-0 8.Nf3 Nbd7 9.0-0 Re8**.

This, the Exchange Variation of the Queen's Gambit Declined, features one of the most useful positional ideas in chess: the **Minority Attack**. The beauty of this plan is that White is able to implement a strategy that goes beyond the middlegame, right into the endgame. The idea is to play Rb1 followed by b2-b4-b5 and bxc6 (White is attacking a majority of pawns with a minority of pawns, hence the name) when Black will be left with a weak pawn on c6 that will bother him forever. Does this mean that Black is doomed to defend passively and hope for a draw? Of course not! It's important to note that Black's pawns are pointing towards the kingside. The pawn-pointing theory (discussed earlier in the book) states that Black should play in the direction his pawns point, so this means that Black must try to generate a kingside attack. Thus the battle lines are drawn: White will play on the queenside, making use of the pawn weaknesses that his minority attack creates there (this gives him a long-range, static advantage. As a result, endgames are favorable to White). Black's play will come on the kingside (Black hopes for a middlegame decision).

My students in these two games were given lectures about the minority attack. Would they be able to integrate that information into an actual game scenario?

> 1400: "The position looks even. White's light-squared Bishop appears to be pretty good. Looks like Ne5 followed by f4 with a kingside attack might do well here. Black has a queenside pawn majority and White has a majority on the kingside. This means that White has the possibility of using a minority attack on the queenside. The other plan with Ne5 is interesting but Black has a lot of pieces aimed at the kingside and his pawns point there also. White's pawns aim at the queenside so a minority attack must be correct. I'm considering Rb1 followed by b2-b4 starting a minority attack. I'm not sure if that is correct or if a3 followed by b4 is better."

10.a3?!

I was worried when he jumped on the Ne5 bandwagon, but it pleased me when he realized that this could be a chance to make use of the minority attack (something he'd never used before).

The best move is 10.Qc2, which gives added support to the e4-square and connects the Rooks. When the time comes for the b4-advance, though, correct is Rb1 instead of a3 since after an eventual b2-b4-b5 and bxc6 the Rook will be nicely placed on the open b-file. Another problem with 10.a3 is that after b4 Black can play ...a6 when White must move the a-pawn a second time by a3-a4 if he wishes to get in the desired b4-b5 advance. Note that Rb1 followed by b4 allows White to advance his a-pawn (if needed) to a4 in just one move.

10...Ne4

> 1400: "Looks like I have to trade Bishops by Bxe7. By doing that I'm allowing Black to back up his Knight. Due to this, 10.Bf4 is possible. Trading the Bishops probably helps me on the queenside with my minority attack so I will go ahead and snap it off.

So far White is thinking only of his minority attack. This is a good sign! He has a plan and he wants to implement it.

11.Bxe7 Qxe7

> 1400: "I'm now concerned about his Knight on e4 and an ...f7-f5 advance on the kingside. How do I get rid of his Knight? Nevertheless, my pieces are posted towards an advance on the queenside and I don't see how he can kill me right away so let's advance!"

Here we see the start of 1400's fatal weakness as a chess player: he becomes so worried about possible threats to his King that he starts to forget about his own ideas and even misses elementary tactical tricks (though, to his credit, he resisted the immediate temptation to panic and stays focused on his minority attack). At this point 1400 played 12.b4?? which hangs his face to 12...Nxc3. I had him take the move over.

> 1400: "I can play 12.Qc2 to guard c3 and put pressure on e4."

12.Qc2 Nf8

> 1400: "Black is definitely setting his sights on a fierce attack against my King. In order to counteract that I can play Nce2-g3."

White's fear of being mated has left all his previous dreams of a minority attack in the dust. From this point on, he plays a fearful defensive game and hands the initiative to Black. He didn't realize that the time White takes to "defend" himself allows Black all the tempi he needs to set a real attack in motion.

13.Ne2 Ng6

> 1400: "Now I'll bring my Knight around and get more protection for my King."

White is now so preoccupied with thoughts of defense that he no longer entertains any hopes at all of continuing his queenside play.

14.Ng3

The game was stopped here. Though the move isn't bad in itself, White's reasoning is a disaster waiting to happen! White has reduced himself to just reacting to the opponent's ideas and is getting so confused about stopping all of the enemy's possibilities (real or imagined) that he has become afraid to move anything at all.

In the next game, I played pretty much the same position but this time I brought in my ever-confident 1700 student. Would he bravely follow his own plans or would he, like 1400 before him, succumb to the whims of fear and panic?

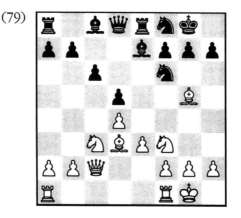

(79)

1700-Silman. Queen's Gambit Declined.
White to play.

The starting moves were **1.d4 d5 2.c4 e6 3.Nc3 Nf6 4.cxd5 exd5 5.Bg5 Be7 6.e3 c6 7.Bd3 0-0 8.Nf3 Nbd7 9.0-0 Re8 10.Qc2 Nf8**.

> 1700: "I want to prevent …Ne4 by taking the f6-Knight. This also allows me to play b4 immediately and begin my minority attack."

This is more like it! White is going after his plan with as much speed as possible. However, how long will he retain this enthusiasm?

11.Bxf6 Bxf6
12.b4 Be7

Seeing that his Bishop is doing nothing on f6, Black wants to redirect it to d6 where it will menace the White King.

> 1700: "He's attacking my pawn. I can now push my pawn up or guard it with the Rook. If I play b5 then he can try …c5. So maybe it's better to guard it first."

He didn't figure out why I played …Be7 (other than to attack his b4-pawn) and he didn't seem to care what my plan was. We also get to see a bit of laziness present itself: he notices the possibility of answering b5 with …c5 but doesn't take time out to see if that idea works for Black. After 13.b5 c5? 14.dxc5 Bxc5 15.Rad1 Black would experience real problems with his weak d-pawn (after all, White's original plan was the creation of a pawn weakness and the lame creature on d5 certainly qualifies) and the undefended Bishop on c5. Don't look at a move for your opponent and just decide that it works for him. Prove it!

13.Rab1 Bd6

> 1700: "He's going right for a kingside attack. I should ignore that and continue with my idea."

Bravo! As the old saying goes, "The best defense is a good offense."

14.b5 Re6

> 1700: "Still going for my King. I will capture on c6 and create a target there."

Black wishes to mix offense with defense. His Rook will defend c6 and join in the kingside attack. Note how both sides are following their respective plans (both sides are fighting for the initiative) and are not allowing side issues to distract them.

15.bxc6 bxc6

1700: "I can bring my Knight back to e2 where it guards the kingside and uncovers my Queen on c6."

Now that a weakness has been created on c6, White can spend a little time shoring up his kingside. However, great care must be taken to insure that his own threats on the queenside never let up (if White can get Black to react to queenside threats, then Black's attack will lose its momentum). He must also make sure that he doesn't fall into a defensive frame of mind.

16.Ne2

Instead of this somewhat passive reassignment of the Knight, better would have been 16.Bf5! (since endgames favor White, trades can only make the first player happy. In this case, the c8-Bishop was aiming at White's King so this equals one less attacking piece for Black) 16...Rh6 17.Bxc8 (17.h3!? followed by 18.Rfc1 may be better. With the light-squared Bishops gone, White suddenly has access to the f5- and b7-squares) 17...Rxc8 (and not 17...Bxh2+?? 18.Nxh2 Qh4 19.Bh3) 18.h3 (stopping the threatened 18...Bxh2+ 19.Nxh2 Qh4) 18...Ng6 (bringing up reinforcements. Neither side is losing sight of his goal.) 19.Rfc1 (threatening 20.Nxd5) 19...Nh4! (this allows the remaining Black forces to get closer to the enemy King) 20.Nxh4 Qxh4 and now 21.Rb7 or even 21.Qf5 Rd8 22.Rc2 Rf6 23.Qg4 keeps Black's kingside play under control, still leaving him to deal with the weaknesses on c6 and a7. Note that 21.Nxd5! is also possible (21...Qg5 22.Nc3 with the threat of 23.Ne4 retains the pawn). I'll leave it to the reader to decide if Black can get any compensation after the chop on d5.

I admit this is long-winded, but the point should be obvious. Even in the face of a kingside attack you must keep a clear head and not lose sight of your goals (like in this instance where trading pieces is good for White since most endgames favor him). After all, White owns a static advantage, while Black's play is based on dynamics.

16...Rh6

> 1700: "I can't take on c6 due to ...Bxh2+ winning my Queen. I should block his Bishop on d6 by 17.Ng3 or 17.Nf4."

17.Nf4??

White first played Ng3 and just before letting go placed it on f4 saying, "Here is better." Naturally, this type of last second change of plan can only lead to trouble. If you touch a piece and suddenly have a change of heart, put the piece down, take a deep breath and rethink the position. You do have to move the piece you touch but at least you can make sure that you place it on a good square.

17...g5

> 1700: "Attacking my Knight. I have to move it when he can continue to advance via ...g5-g4. Then I will play Ne5."

White's mistake on the 17th move has given Black several free moves and a firm grip on the initiative. White must now ride the storm and allow Black to dictate the play.

18.Ne2 g4
19.Ne5 Bxe5
20.dxe5 Qh4

> 1700: "I have to play h3. I don't like it but I no longer have any choice."

21.h3

White's last few moves have all been forced. Though things look hopeless, Black's lingering weaknesses on c6 and a7 give White some hope of surviving if a mate or further loss of material can be avoided.

21...gxh3
22.g3 Qg4

> 1700: "He threatens to go to f3 with mate on g2."

The game was stopped here. For those that have always wondered what the initiative is, this game provides an excellent example. White was forced to deal with all the Black threats and was not able even to think of continuing his own play on the queenside.

Tips

★ Always be aware of your opponent's plans and ideas.

★ Don't panic in the face of a kingside attack. Size up his real threats, make defensive moves when needed and continue with your own plans.

★ Follow your plans with gusto. Be devoted to your plan and it will serve you well.

★ Don't play with fear in your heart. If you play with courage, the worst thing that can happen to you is a loss. Since we will all lose many games in our lifetime, we might as well go down with honor and make every game as instructive as possible. Playing passively and getting routed is no fun at all and teaches you nothing.

★ Worry, confusion and hasty moves leads to gross blunders. If you find your mind fogging up, sit back, relax and take a fresh look at the position.

★ Chess is a game of willpower. Don't let the opponent's will dominate yours. Stick to your plans and don't allow him to distract you from them.

★ Take nothing for granted. Don't feel or hope that some line is good or bad. Make sure it is!

★ The best defense is a good offense. When you have to defend, try to make a move that also furthers your own plans.

MANY
IMBALANCES,
ONE BOARD

The vast majority of chess games contain battles between several different types of imbalances. One person may have high hopes for his advantage in space and superior pawn structure while the opponent will insist that his two Bishops and greater activity is what really counts. Often it's not clear which particular imbalance will triumph, but no one doubts that the first player who stops trying to make use of these positive attributes will allow the opponent to dominate.

Though it's important to be aware of the general rules concerning the imbalances, it's equally important to be conscious of the fact that one rule might negate or strengthen another.

When contemplating the imbalances you have and imbalances you would like to create, always make sure that they complement each other. For example: you may have two Bishops (vs. a Bishop and Knight), a passed pawn and the chance to gain extra space by advancing and locking the pawns. The desire to gain space may be great, but will this decision aid or hurt your Bishops (remember that they don't like closed positions)? Will the passed pawn be useful or will it make the enemy Knight (which might sit in front of the passer and act as a blockader) stronger?

• • • • •

Our first example of several imbalances interacting with each other is obviously in White's favor. He clearly enjoys the superior pawn structure and he also has a fine Knight versus a poor Bishop. Is this enough to win? Yes, White should win, but the process is far from easy.

(80)

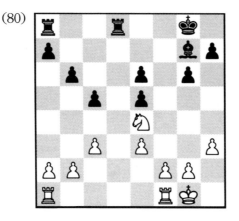

Alekhine-Euwe, London 1922.
White to play.

1.Rfd1

Staking a claim to the d-file. To win this game, White will play to keep the Black Bishop bottled up while attempting to create new weaknesses (points of attack or penetration) on the queenside.

1...Kf8
2.Kf1

More obvious stuff. Once an endgame is reached, both sides should rush their Kings towards the center.

2...Ke7
3.c4!

This does two things: It keeps a Black Rook out of d5 and it fixes the Black c-pawn on c5 where it blocks its own Bishop.

3...h6
4.Ke2 Rxd1
5.Rxd1 Rb8

Let's let Alekhine tell us what's going on:

"Black cannot exchange Rooks since after 5...Rd8 6.Rxd8 Kxd8 White wins as follows:

"1st phase: 7.h4 followed by g2-g4 and g4-g5, against which Black has nothing better than ...h5, since the exchange of pawns will give the White Knight the square h4.

"2nd phase: b2-b3 followed by Kd3, Nc3 and Ke4.

"3rd phase: the transfer of the Knight to d3, which ties the Black King to d6 in order to hold the twice-attacked e5-pawn.

"4th phase: finally f2-f4, forcing the win of the g or e-pawn, after which White wins easily.

"By avoiding the exchange of Rooks, Black makes his opponent's task more difficult."

6.Rd3 Bh8
7.a4!

White intends to play a4-a5 and create new weaknesses in the Black position. Since 7...a5 8.Rb3 wins material for White (the threat of Nxc5 is hard to stop), Black is unable to prevent this advance.

7...Rc8
8.Rb3 Kd7
9.a5! Kc6
10.axb6 axb6
11.Ra3

White will use the a-file to penetrate into the Black position. Black cannot do the same along the d-file since the White King and Knight cover all the entry points.

11...Bg7

And not 11...Kb7?? 12.Nd6+. White's Rook becomes more active than its Black counterpart mainly due to the fact that his Knight is taking part in the effort. Compare the horse to the pathetic Black Bishop and you will see the vast difference in strength between the two pieces.

12.Ra7 Rc7

Now White could trade Rooks and carry out the winning plan that Alekhine mentioned earlier; however, he decides that his Rook is better than the enemy's and keeping it should allow him to shorten the winning process.

13.Ra8! Re7
14.Rc8+ Kd7
15.Rg8! Kc6
16.h4

Now White has the superior minor piece, a structural advantage and a more active Rook. Since Black is unable to do anything active, White takes his time and plays to tie Black up. **If you have an opponent backed up against a wall, take away any and all potential counterplay before going for the final kill.**

16...Kc7
17.g4 Kc6
18.Kd3 Rd7+
19.Kc3 Rf7
20.b3

Still taking his time and doing little things that make his position more compact and safer.

20...Kc7
21.Kd3 Rd7+
22.Ke2 Rf7
23.Nc3! Re7
24.g5 hxg5
25.hxg5 Kc6
26.Kd3 Rd7+
27.Ke4

White has just added a superior King to his list of advantages. Now the win is just a matter of time. The final moves were: **27...Rc7 28.Nb5 Re7 29.f3 Kd7 30.Rb8 Kc6 31.Rc8+ Kd7 32.Rc7+ Kd8 33.Rc6 Rb7 34.Rxe6**, 1-0.

We have seen that, in top flight chess, the diagrammed position is considered to be a matter of technique, but at the amateur level virtually anything can happen. Let's see what kind of mistakes the amateur makes while trying to realize his advantage.

(81)

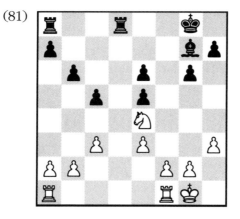

1467-Silman.
White to play.

1467: "My Knight is better than his bad Bishop and the open d-file is not a problem since White can easily challenge it. The queenside seems even. The only thing I can see is to play Rfd1."

He saw the basics (though I was surprised that he never mentioned Black's doubled pawns) but was not sure how to make use of his advantages. In this type of position, a player should look for ideas rather than concrete moves.

I certainly don't expect 1467 to come up with the plans that Alekhine laid out, but there are three things that a player of any rating can do: **1) Make each of his pieces better than, or at least equal to, their enemy counterparts; 2) If the opponent cannot do anything active, then don't rush the position; instead you should let him sit there, suffer, and beg you for**

a draw; 3) Try to make your plusses expand while making sure that his negatives don't cure themselves.

1.Rfd1

> 1467: "Now, if 1...Rxd1+ 2.Rxd1, White threatens Rd6 and Rd7."

1...Kf7

> 1467: "I can check on g5 and win a pawn!"

He decides that I just hung a pawn and rushes to cash in his ill-gotten gains. This type of decision should be made slowly; after all, White is moving his Knight from a dominant central location and placing it on the far rim of the board.

Instead of this impulsive act, White would have done well if he had simply brought his King to the center.

2.Ng5+ Ke7

> 1467: "I don't know if this is good, even though it wins a pawn."

He should have figured this out before he made the check.

3.Nxh7 Bh6

White's greedy idea, which forced the Black King to the center, has left him with a poorly placed Knight.

4.h4

The only way to free his embattled Knight. White has now taken on the role of the defender—someone who must react to his opponent's will. How did this transformation take place? White failed to make his pieces better than or equal to the Black ones and he failed to make use of his fine Knight (instead, he stuck it in a ditch).

4...Rh8
5.Ng5 Bxg5
6.hxg5

> 1467: "I probably should have exchanged Rooks first."

He's no longer thinking of positive things to do. From here on, he goes completely on the defensive.

6...Rh5
7.f4 Rf8

> 1467: "Attacking me."

8.g3 Rfh8

> 1467: "I have a bit of a problem here."

9.Rf1 e4!

> 1467: "I should have exchanged a pair of Rooks while I could."

The sickly doubled pawn now controls and contributes to an attack on the White King.

10.c4 Rh1+

> 1467: "Damn! Now he wins the b2-pawn. I should have played b3."

11.Kf2 R8h2+
12.Ke1 Rxf1+
13.Kxf1 Rh1+, 0-1.

He lost this game because he did a couple of negative things: He allowed his proud Knight to be exchanged for the horrible Bishop, and he allowed the enemy King to become centralized. This happened because he tried to cash in his advantage too quickly. Remember: **When your opponent is helpless, take your time and make sure he doesn't generate any counterplay!**

1467 was so upset about losing this nice endgame that he set the same position up and insisted on trying it again.

(82)

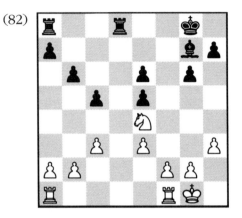

1467-Silman.
White to play.

1.Rfd1 Kf7
2.Kf1

> 1467: This time I will leave my Knight on its dominant square and bring my King up to the middle. No more adventures for me!

2...Ke7
3.Ke2 c4

> 1467: "I should have played c3-c4. This would have kept his pawns on the same color as his Bishop."

Seeing things after they happen won't be of much help during a game. If he had asked himself (before playing 3.Ke2) how he could have made sure that the bad Bishop *stays* bad, he would have found c3-c4. Always ask yourself, "How do I make the negative areas of his position even worse?"

4.Rd2 Rxd2+
5.Kxd2 Rd8+
6.Ke2 Rd5
7.Rd1 b5

> 1467: "My game has deteriorated."

White is still better but Black has made some progress: His Rook is happy on d5 and the Bishop can eventually find some life on the f8-a3 diagonal.

We stopped the game here since he wanted to try it one last time from the beginning.

(83)

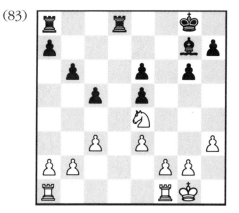

1467-Silman.
White to play.

1.Rfd1 Kf7
2.c4

> 1467: "All right! I don't know what I have to do to get this right, but I actually have the feeling that I kind of know what I'm doing."

2...Ke7

> 1467: Now I can bring my King up.

3.Kf1 h6

> 1467: "I'm not penetrating, but right now I don't see how to do it. I need to activate my King and Rooks. A good plan is 4.a4-a5 when ...bxa5 leaves him with a weakness on a7 and c5."

Quite a difference from the other two games! Here he's killing my counterplay, centralizing his pieces and probing for weaknesses.

4.a4 a5

> 1467: "His Bishop is even weaker and now I have b5 for my Knight. I could bring my King up and change all the Rooks,

but does that win? I need to get his g6-pawn to go to g5
when his Bishop is a horrible piece. To get him to play ...g5
I must threaten his pawn, but how? I guess I should play b3
first to improve my game. I have time."

He must have taken vitamins or something! Keep in mind that
1467 has not yet seen the Alekhine game but now, after a couple
of trial runs, he is actually coming very close to the World
Champion's ideas.

Why the drastic change? I think he suddenly realized that his
advantages are not going away and that a slow handling of the
position leaves Black without any play at all.

In a way, these three examples show how chess should be
studied. All great players look at thousands and thousands of
master games. By doing so, you see important patterns (positional
and tactical) that can be emulated, you see how the opening,
middlegame and endgame are all interrelated, and you get a feel
for natural but strong moves.

By playing the position three times, he learned a lot about its
needs and secrets. His play improved enormously on the third try
thanks to his newfound knowledge of this game's particular
patterns.

5.b3 Rab8
6.Ke2 Bf8

> 1467: "I'm thinking of playing Nc3 and e3-e4 to close the
> ·position. I don't like that, though. I should expand on the
> kingside via h4. Then I can consider Rh1-h3-g3."

His original idea of playing e3-e4 was horrible since it killed a
square that was a potential home for his Knight and his King.
However, his 7.h4 followed by Rh1-h3-g3 deserves quite a bit of
praise since it gains space and begins to pick on some of Black's
weak pawns.

7.h4 Kf7
8.Rxd8 Rxd8
9.Rd1

> 1467: "I know that I can at least draw this position."

I wish he had given his original idea of Rh1-h3-g3 a try.

9...Rxd1
10.Kxd1 Be7
11.g3 Ke8
12.Ke2 Kd7
13.Kd3 Bd8
14.Nc3 Ke7
15.Ke4 Bc7

> 1467: "Now 16.Nb5 Bb8, so I need to get my Knight on d3 or f3 when I attack e5 with all my pieces."

I like the way he first picks a weakness to attack and then brings all his pieces to bear on that target.

16.g4 g5
17.hxg5 hxg5

> 1467: "Now I'll get my Knight to f3 to attack both g5 and e5."

18.Nb1 Kf6
19.Nd2 Bb8

> 1467: "I can't chase him from g5 and e5. I needed to get my Knight on g4 to win. Now it's a draw."

We stopped the game.

Tips

★ If you own a long-term advantage, don't be in a hurry to make use of it.

★ If the opponent has a passive position, never allow him to get counterplay.

★ Even if you already have several advantages, always be on the lookout for ways to create new targets.

When it comes to positions with several imbalances, humans, computers and other chess playing creatures may find themselves with differing views about who has the advantage. I recall once having a little argument with a well-known chess writer in the pages of a certain American chess magazine. In one of his books, he declared that Black stood better in the following position.

(84)

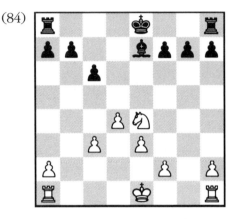

White to play.

I disagreed, saying that the ending was far from clear (I actually preferred White but decided to be kind). He disagreed with my disagreement and pointed out that his chess computer validated his opinion. I...well, we never did come to terms on this position.

Why the difference of opinion? Why would a computer be in error? This example showed me why some players and many computers run into trouble: When the heart of a position takes accepted principles and turns them inside out, many players find themselves at a loss to understand what's really going on. This means that though basic laws such as "Always capture towards the center," "Don't move the same piece twice in the opening," "Doubled pawns are bad", and "Bishops are better than Knights in open positions" are often correct, they also lead to a close-minded bigotry that can stunt the growth of just about any student of the game.

Computers, of course, are even more vulnerable to this type of thing than humans are. They are given specific rules and they stick faithfully to these dictates—often to the exclusion of everything else. We biological organisms, however, can (hopefully) go beyond this one-dimensional view.

In diagram 84, we have a situation where the basic laws of chess add up to a Black advantage. He has a Bishop versus a Knight in an open position and White has three pawn islands versus Black's two. However, placing any credence in these two laws serves only to blind a player to the truth—which is that White's mass of center pawns are far more threatening than their Black counterparts (a good plan for White is a2-a4 followed by Ke1-e2, Rhb1 and Ke2-d3).

This unwavering faith in beginning principles has harmed many players who have come to me for help. How many times have I recommended a position with doubled pawns and how many times have they cringed in horror? How often have I caught myself in this situation: During the first lesson I say, "Why did you move the same piece twice in the opening? You should know better." Then, during the next lesson I find myself pointing out how they could have gotten a strong game by breaking that rule and moving the same piece twice or even three times!

This confusing state of affairs is enough to drive anyone crazy. Indeed, I have even run into cases where masters get trapped in the world of basic rules. A good example of this is the game between Beatriz Marinello and Sharon Burtman (diagram 85).

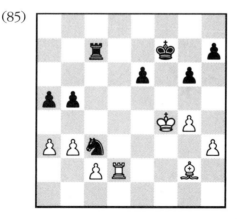

(85)

Marinello-Burtman, U.S. Woman's Championship, 1993.
White to play.

Here the players agreed to a draw since White was exhausted from a long trip and Black was disgusted that she had blown a winning position from the opening. At the time, the players and the tournament's other participants thought that White had the advantage and should have continued the battle. A glance shows that this is a reasonable assessment: White's Rook is on a completely open file, White's Bishop is very active, White has a queenside majority of pawns, Black has an isolated pawn on e6 and White enjoys a clearly superior King position.

An impressive list, but I shocked Sharon when I declared that Black's position looked quite nice to me. What was I seeing that others didn't? Nothing at all! I just preferred to look at all the so-called negatives in a positive light.

Here's what I mean:

➤ White's Bishop is indeed slicing down that h1-a8 diagonal, but what is it doing there? On the other hand the Black Knight is quite bothersome and threatens to pick up the a3-pawn by ...Nb1.

➤ White's Rook is on a completely open file but it is not attacking anything there. The Black Rook, though, is eyeing the morsel on c2.

➤ White does have a queenside majority, but the purpose of such a majority is to create a passed pawn. Black's so-called weakness on e6 is in reality a tower of strength since it is already passed. Thus, I will not look at it as isolated—instead, I look at is as an active attacking unit!

➤ The White King is better placed than the Black one. You got me on that point!

Naturally, I immediately gave this position to a class C student and had him play me one of my patented "talk out loud games."

(86)

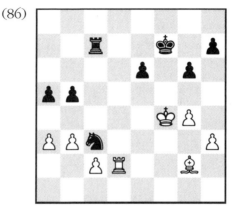

1470-Silman
White to play.

> 1470: "Black has an isolated pawn and a passive King. My Bishop is also dominating his Knight, though the pawn on g4 makes my Bishop bad. I think that I should be able to do something really good here; Black must be busted. I will use my superior King to march into h6 and win the h7-pawn."

1.Kg5?

By looking at the e6-pawn as a weakness, White was unable to see its dynamic potential. Something is only weak if you can attack it. Names such as "doubled" or "isolated" don't make things weak!

White's best try is probably 1.Rd6. This activates the Rook and prepares to attack the Black queenside from behind by Ra6.

1...e5!

> 1470: "Oh-oh. This pawn is threatening to go to e4, e3 and e2! Have I done something really stupid or can I stop the silly thing? I can't believe that this pawn can really go too far! I will continue with my plan and make him defend. That way he will never have the time to push the pawn."

2.Kh6

Winning the h-pawn will not worry Black. He is after a new Queen and certainly won't blink an eye at such a tiny threat. White is making the mistake of assuming that Black will go into a panic at this first nibble. Instead, he will ignore White's King-walk and continue with his own ideas.

2...e4

> 1470: "Giving me material. There is no turning back now; I have to take it and dare him to do his worst!"

Black could have dispelled White's illusions with 2...Ke6, but I felt it was more instructive to give up the h-pawn and demonstrate the strength of the runner on e4.

3.Kxh7 e3
4.Rd3 Re7

We ended the game. That "weakness" on e6 took White right out of the game!

The next time I gave the position to a student, I made a couple of small changes to make things look (cosmetically) even more attractive for White. Incredibly, my student insisted that Black stood better, so I found myself on the White side!

(87)

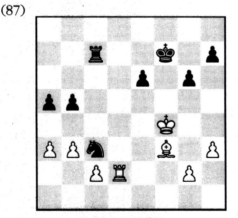

Silman-1650.
White to play.

> 1650: "So we have an endgame with Rook and Knight versus Rook and Bishop. The question is: which is better, the Knight or Bishop? White has a queenside pawn majority. White's Bishop controls a nice long diagonal. White has a

hidden weakness on c2, so his Rook is forced to stay on the second rank to defend it. Black's Knight is kind of trapped on c3 so that covers the weakness at the moment. However, the threat to move it to b1 and win the a3-pawn is very annoying for White. So overall, I will give the edge to Black.

"I think that way because, aside from the threat of ...Na3, Black also has three pawns to two on the kingside."

Not bad at all! 1650 is not a prisoner of memorized preconceptions and instead tries to figure out the present position in a fresh way. I decided to try to freak him out with a central King rush.

1.Ke5

> 1650: "White is aiming for d6 with an invasion on the queenside. I want to prevent this!"

1...Ke7
2.Bg4

> 1650: "He is going after my pawn but this is an easy threat to stop."

2...Rc5+
3.Kd4 Rc7?

> 1650: "Time to bring my Rook back to safety."

Missing two important possibilities. The first (but weaker) one is 3...Kd6 when 4.Ke3+ Ke5 leaves Black with the superior King. However, 3...Kd6? turns out to be an error due to 4.Bxe6! Kxe6? 5.Kxc5 Ne4+ 6.Kxb5 Nxd2 7.Kxa5 when White's pawns are stronger than Black's Knight. Nevertheless, if Black had played 3...Kd6 I would have been very happy, since it would have shown an awareness of the need to activate one's King in an endgame (the tactical flaw doesn't take away from the move's good intentions).

The second possibility is 3...Rd5+!, a move that he looked at but rejected due to 4.Kxc3 (note that 4.Ke3 Rxd2 5.Kxd2 Nb1+ wins a pawn for Black). Now Black can take advantage of the loosely guarded White Rook by 4...b4+ 5.axb4 axb4+ 6.Kxb4 Rxd2 with an extra Exchange and a sure win. **If a piece is not well defended, you should always look for ways to win it.**

4.Ke5

1650: "He wants a draw but I hate draws and I won't allow him to get one! I will just go after his pawn."

I like his attitude but he makes the mistake of placing the Knight on the rim. Of course, it ends up being out of play there.

4...Nb1?
5.Rf2 Nxa3

1650: "I hope my Knight can get back in the game!"

Whether he can get it back into play or not is beside the point—he should have asked this question before putting it on a3.

6.Bxe6 Rc5+?
7.Bd5

1650: "This doesn't scare me. He wants to check me on f7 and win the h-pawn. He has no mating possibilities so it all comes down to a race."

He was not aware (though we had discussed this point several months before) that a Knight is much worse than a Bishop in a mutual pawn race situation. The speed of a Bishop puts a Knight to shame in those cases.

7...Nxc2
8.Rf7+ Ke8
9.Rxh7 Ne3

1650: "I think I have him!"

10.Ke6

1650: "He had a way out. He wants to mate me but that is easily stopped. I'm still doing well."

He also missed 10.Kd4 (attacking Black's two undefended pieces at once), which would have led to a draw.

10...Kd8
11.Be4

1650: "A trap! He's hoping for 11...Rc7 12.Rh8 mate! I will play 11...Nf5 which defends my g-pawn and threatens ...Nd4+. Then I will follow up with ...a5-a4 and try to promote my pawn."

Note how the Bishop is dominating the Black Knight. This Bishop is so much better than the Knight that White is now winning.

11...Nf5?

Leading to a quick finish.

12.g4

> 1650: "I expected that, but I don't mind giving up my g-pawn for his b-pawn."

12...Nd4+

White also wins after 12...Ng3 13.Bb7!. I invite the reader to work out the variations himself.

13.Kd6

> 1650: "Oh no! He threatens both Kxc5 and Rh8 mate."

We stopped the game here. It should be apparent that leaving one's pieces in vulnerable, undefended positions is asking for trouble.

Tips

★ The basic rules we learned when we started out are good guidelines but must be broken often. Don't fall in love with these concepts and become blind to the reality of any given situation.

★ Every imbalance is capable of doing something positive. Don't look at a thing as negative just because it's supposed to be weak or bad. You have to ask: "Is it bad in this particular position?"

★ Undefended pieces can easily lead to trouble.

★ When pawns are racing to promote on both sides of the board, a Bishop will usually beat out a Knight due to its ability to jump from one side of the board to another in one move.

The next game shows a battle based on very different imbalances. Both sides nurse what they have and try to make it grow but, of course, only one side's vision will be proven correct.

2120-Silman. English Opening.

Our game only started after I played the first eight moves for both sides: **1.c4 Nf6 2.Nf3 e6 3.Nc3 Bb4 4.Qc2 0-0 5.g3 b6 6.Bg2 Bb7 7.a3 Bxc3 8.Qxc3 d6**.

> 2120: "Lots of moves: 0-0, b4, d3. What's my plan? Black's plan is to play ...c5 and ...d5 and break open the center. How am I going to activate the dark-squared Bishop? I could play Bg5 with a pin or place it on the long diagonal. 9.d3 controls e4 and keeps options open."

While it's all right to play an obviously useful move (like 9.d3), there is also a bit of laziness in the equation. White should really have at least a partial plan mapped out for himself. For example: White has the two Bishops and would like to make them better than the Knights. Since the dark-squared Bishop is the one piece that Black does not have, White should try his best to make it as active as possible. Thus d3 (limiting the enemy Knights), followed by b2-b4 and Bb2, placing the Bishop on the fine long diagonal, would be a simple but effective strategy.

9.d3 Nbd7

> 2120: "Where is his Knight heading to? If I develop my Bishop on the long diagonal, he could play ...e5 and block it. 10.Bg5 is also silly due to ...h6."

He is still not quite sure what to do, so he holds off on any clear decisions and simply castles. This is fine here, but in many situations such trepidation might lead to problems.

10.0-0 c5

> 2120: "Takes away this square from the Knight. Now he can't play ...e5 since d5 would be weak. I could play b3 or b4. On 11.b4 cxb4 he opens up the a-file for me. I could also play d4 and open up the d-file so as to get play on d6. He wants to play for d5. My Knight on f3 is not doing anything so where do my pieces go? I'll get play by b2-b4."

In closed or semi-closed positions, you should lead with your pawns. For this reason, Black had no intention of playing ...Nc5 since it would just get chased back by b2-b4. Instead, Black gains space with ...c7-c5 and keeps his pieces flexibly posted behind his pawns. A d3-d4 advance would give Black use of the e4-square and activate his Knights. It should also be mentioned that Black won't hesitate to play an ...e6-e5 advance if White posts his Bishop on the b2-h8 diagonal. True, it leaves a hole on d5. But can White actually use that hole? No, he can't. So, since this weakness is more illusion than reality, Black will be happy with ...e6-e5 since it blocks the a1-h8 diagonal and gains central territory.

11.b4 Qe7

2120: "Playing for d5. How can I mix things up? A good slow plan is b5 and a4-a5."

Black has no intention of playing ...d6-d5 (unless it achieves some very positive goal) since that would open up the position for the enemy Bishops. Instead, he will place his Rooks on squares that will inhibit White from playing in the middle. Once that is done, Black will seek counterchances on the kingside.

12.Bb2 Rac8

2120: "Threatens to take on b4 and then follow up with ...d6-d5 so I will prevent this and grab queenside space with b5."

13.b5 Rfe8

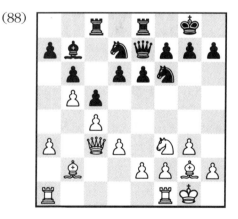

(88)

White to play.

> 2120: "A wealth of riches. What do I want to play? I'm ignoring the center, which is bad. However, 14.d4 gives him the e4-square. What does he do here? Play for …d6-d5? My g2-Bishop is doing relatively nothing. How do I get my pieces into play? I'd like to play for a4-a5 but that has nothing to do with my b2-Bishop."

It's strange to see a guy with such a "wealth of riches" be so confused about how he's going to get play! His 13.b5 took the tension out of the center so he might as well continue on the queenside with a3-a4-a5.

Funnily enough, it's Black who has most of the options here. He can play …e6-e5 or he can play …d6-d5 with the idea of …d5-d4.

14.Nd2

> 2120: "To transfer it to b3 in anticipation of a4-a5."

Leaving White with only one Bishop instead of two. Black is also happy to make this exchange since it leaves White's King a bit less secure.

14…Bxg2
15.Kxg2 e5

> 2120: "He has no threat. I could play e4 when my Bishop cold get into play via c1 since d5 still scares me. Pushing to e4 leaves me with play on the queenside."

So White has stopped …d6-d5 once and for all. However, his dark-squared Bishop is now all but useless (the locked position will be friendlier to the Knights) and the whole game will now come down to a race between White's queenside play (he will open lines with a3-a4-a5) and Black's kingside play (he will play for …f7-f5).

This game has seen a few imbalances parade by: First we had a Bishop vs. Knight battle (which still exists) and now the emphasis is on mutual wing attacks (made possible by the closed center).

16.e4 Nf8

> 2120: "Transferring to e6 and d4. I will go ahead with my plan."

17.a4

2120: "I'm only worried about a kingside attack, so I would like a Queen trade."

I like this comment very much. He is quite aware that his chances lie on the queenside and he knows that the presence of the Queens only helps Black, who will do his utmost to break through on the kingside.

17...Ne6

2120: "I see no threat."

18.a5 Nd4
19.axb6 axb6
20.Ra6 Nd7

2120: "Does he want to transfer his Queen to that side? Since my Bishop is doing nothing I will try to trade it off."

21.Qa3 Ne6
22.Ra1 Rf8

2120: "Trying to get some activity."

Black wasted time with his Knight maneuver to d4; once it got there it moved away since it didn't want the pathetic Bishop to snap it off.

23.Nf1 f5

2120: "I could take and gain a tempo with Ne3 or I could play Ne3 and sink at f5 or d5. Does he have anything? He has no threat right away."

24.Ne3 f4

2120: "Now I have two squares. Nd5 wins b6. I'd like to get my Queen into the defense. 24.Nf5 attacks d6 and closes the file. I am winning a pawn."

Yes, White will win a pawn, but his King is far from safe.

25.Nf5 f3+

2120: "Is he really going to mate me? I refuse to believe it!

A good attitude, but the reality of the situation is quite different. White's King is in grave danger.

26.Kh1 Qg5
27.Qb3

> 2120: "My Queen will come back and defend the g2 mating square."

27...Rxf5
28.exf5 Qxf5

By giving up a very tiny bit of material, Black has made his pawns safe and is free to pursue his kingside desires. White's whole strategy has failed.

29.Qd1 Rf8

> 2120: "I will trade Rooks."

30.Ra8 Nf6
31.Rxf8+ Nxf8
32.Bc1 Ng4
33.Kg1 Ne6

> 2120: "More pieces into the attack."

The Black Knights are suddenly looking quite good. In the meantime, the White Rook and Bishop are unable to help out on the kingside.

34.Ra8+

> 2120: "Can't be bad."

34...Kf7
35.Ra7+ Kg6
36.h3 Nf6

> 2120: "Now 37.g4 Nxg4 38.hxg4 Qg4+ is complicated and gives him several pawns and an attack for the Rook. Since he has no threat, I will be safe."

He must be kidding. No threats? If I was White, I'd be terrified!

37.Kh2 Nd4

> 2120: "If g4, he will retreat since 38.g4 Nxg4+ 39.hxg4 Qxg4 40.Qg1 Qxg1+ 41.Kxg1 Ne2+ picks up the Bishop but leads to a favorable endgame for White."

38.g4 Qe6

2120: "What do I do about ...Ne2 when ...Nxg4+ is really strong? It's time I went for his King!"

A panic reaction. I would have been happier to see 39.Ra2 intending 40.Be3 and 41.Bxd4. Then 39...Ne2 would be met by 40.Rxe2, sacrificing the Exchange back.

39.Bg5??

Going berserk. The final moves were: **39...Kxg5 40.h4+ Kxh4 41.Rxg7 Nxg4+ 42.Kg1 Qh6 43.Rg8 Qf4**, 0-1.

White lost this battle because he didn't work hard enough to make his Bishop active and then, once he closed the center (and as a result lost the minor piece duel), he did not take proper precautions on the kingside.

Tips

★ Always try and make your pawn structure conform to whatever minor piece you happen to own.

★ Creating a hole (a weak square) is only a problem if your opponent can make use of it.

★ When you own two Bishops, you usually want to retain both of them.

★ When the center is dead (closed), you must find play on one of the wings. Even if your opponent breaks through on his side of the board first, your plan must still move ahead.

★ It's not too hard to deduce that if you're playing on one wing, your opponent must have some play on the other. Never discount this! Get your attack going as fast as possible, but don't allow yourself to lose sight of the enemy's correct plan.

HOW TO PLAY THE OPENING

When we first learn how to play chess, we are force-fed certain rules. Basic endgames, middlegame ideas, basic tactics, and how to play the opening correctly. In the opening, we're told to develop all our pieces ("Don't move the same piece twice!" gets repeated over and over like a never-ending mantra). Then we're told to castle quickly so that our King finds a safe haven and our Rooks can connect, like long lost lovers, and work together. Fighting for control of the center with our pieces and pawns comes next. At this point, we get a little cocky, thinking that we know everything there is to know (discounting the memorization of variations) about this phase of the game.

All this advice is useful when we are starting out; however, as we progress up the rating ladder we lose more and more games in the opening (or due to the opening) and we begin to suspect that there is something that we are not quite understanding. Sadly, we invariably discover that we can't find this mysterious missing knowledge in any books. We memorize more and more lines in an attempt to shore up our opening I.Q., still lose countless games and, in a fit of despair, run off to Tibet to seek the mystical light that will eventually lead us to the discovery of the inner game of chess (at least, this is how I started out. I can only guess that it's the same for everyone).

What is the real purpose of the opening? Is it really correct to mindlessly develop our pieces, only to discover that we often stand badly when everything is out? The answer is repeated again and again in the earlier parts of this book: we are trying to create favorable imbalances (or imbalances that have the potential to eventually become favorable) and develop our pieces and pawns around the differences that we have created at the beginning stages of the game. **Once an imbalance is created, every developing move we make, every pawn that we push, must address this imbalance in some way.**

For example, after **1.d4 Nf6 2.c4 e6 3.Nc3 Bb4** (the Nimzo-Indian Defense) **4.a3 Bxc3+ 5.bxc3**, White accepts doubled pawns for the two Bishops and a space advantage in the center. White will play to increase this edge in territory via f2-f3 and e2-e4, while Black will strive to show that White's weakness on c4 is of greater consequence (via ...b6, ...Ba6 and ...Nb8-c6-a5). Once again: it's this battle of ideas that determines where we develop our pieces, where we place each and every pawn, and delineates the fight that will be waged throughout the middlegame.

Another common opening battle that is created in the first few moves comes about from the popular French Defense:

1.e4 e6
2.d4 d5
3.Nd2

So that White can meet the ...Bb4 pin with c2-c3.

3...Nf6
4.e5 Nfd7

White has an obvious space advantage in the center while Black will attempt to place pressure on the d4- and e5-pawns.

5.f4

Greedily claiming even more space. This makes a lot of sense. White gained a certain advantage and he wants to place his pawns on squares that enable him to increase it.

5...c5

Black claims some space of his own on the queenside and simultaneously attacks the White pawn on d4. Mindless developing moves like 5...Nc6 would leave Black without territory or threats after 6.c3.

6.c3

Following an important rule: Try to make your center as strong as possible so that the opponent will eventually be engulfed in its space-gaining coils.

6...Nc6

And Black devotes a lot of energy to attacking d4. This forces White to make concessions and defend his pawn.

7.Ndf3!

Why would White move an already developed piece a second time? Wouldn't 7.Ngf3, bringing a new piece out, be more logical? No, after 7.Ngf3?! Qb6 (stepping up the pressure on d4) White would have trouble guarding d4; he would be forced to place his Knight (it would have to move again after all!) on the unpleasant b3-square. The correct 7.Ndf3 allows White to support his center with all his pieces.

7...Qb6
8.Ne2 and d4 is well-defended.

These two examples have shown us that both sides use the opening to create some difference and then try hard to demonstrate that their difference is more important than the enemy's. This means that the opening is not really about development at all, it's about ideas and their implementation.

● ● ● ● ●

Our first game shows both sides sparring to gain anything that might be of use later in the game. Targets, space, good and bad minor pieces; all these things come into consideration when we start out a serious game of chess.

2100-Silman. Reti Opening.

1.Nf3 d5
2.b4 Nf6
3.Bb2 e6
4.a3 Be7

I made him play these first few moves, curious to see how he would handle this unorthodox type of position. White has gained some queenside space and has a powerful Bishop on b2 that eyes the central dark-squares. Black has a solid position and some central space but, at the moment, he doesn't have any clear plan or targets to aim at.

> 2100: "I can fianchetto my other Bishop if I want to. I have space on the queenside. I could play for e2-e4 via d3. I must make use of my dark-squared Bishop. Since I like the e2-e4 push, I should fianchetto, castle and play to advance with that move."

The kingside fianchetto does not make much sense to me since the h1-a8 diagonal will be firmly blocked by the pawn on d5. I would prefer e3 (gaining more control over d4) followed by Be2, 0-0 and c2-c4. This increases White's advantage on the queenside by adding to the territory that he already possesses.

5.g3 0-0
6.Bg2

> 2100: "I don't understand the point of b4 since he can play ...a5 or ...c5. If 6...a5, then both 7.b5 and bxa5 are possible."

Moves like ...a7-a5 and ...c7-c5 could be answered by b4-b5 (gaining more space) if White's light-squared Bishop stood on e2 (where it would defend b5). The light-squared Bishop does not participate in queenside operations on g2.

Remember: White gained queenside space on move two, so he should continue to add to the gains that he has already made. All his pieces should work together in this (or any other) effort.

6...c5

> 2100: "There's no life to this game. If 7.b5, the pawn might be weak since nothing is defending it. I could take. Any pawn sacrifice fails and 7.c3 is extremely ugly. My plan is to utilize the dark-squared Bishop and play on the kingside. Since he is playing on the queenside, I could try to hold with b5 but I don't like it due to ...a6 when the a-file might open and a3 could become weak."

He said that there's no life to the game, yet the position is full of interest. Subtle decisions must be made, plans found, imbalances created. Who could want more?

As for his comment about getting a kingside attack, this is pure bluster. There's much too much play in the center for thoughts of a kingside attack to enter anyone's head.

7.bxc5 Bxc5

> 2100: "I could either castle or play d3. Oh, oh! I just noticed that 8.d3 loses to 8...Qb6 with a double-attack on f2 and b2. I have to castle."

I mentioned earlier that Black wanted a clear plan and targets. His last two moves have left him with play against White's isolated a3-pawn and possibilities of creating pressure down the half-open c-file (the c2-pawn might become weak). This isn't much, but it's a beginning.

White's plans also need to be clarified. After castling, White must, at some point, play c2-c4. This advance strives to open up the g2-a8 diagonal and to make the c-pawn an active participant in the coming battle (before it gets stuck on c2 and turns into a permanent target).

8.0-0 Nc6

> 2100: "I have to come up with a plan. My b2-Bishop is undefended and bothers me in many lines. Change of plan! He has too much control of open center squares for me to do a kingside attack. I'll just play for e4 as originally intended."

With 8...Nc6, Black developed and tried to regain some control of his central dark-squares on e5 and d4. White's whole plan of e2-e4 is incorrect since that would leave him with a weak c-pawn on a half-open file. Better, as mentioned in my note to Black's seventh move, is a plan involving c2-c4.

9.d3 Qe7

> 2100: "I will continue to develop my pieces and play for e2-e4."

10.Nbd2 Rd8

> 2100: "Does he really want to play ...d5-d4 himself? I'm probably choosing incorrect plans. I can't tell if I want an open or closed position. I want to play e4 but that doesn't work at the moment due to 11...dxe4 with a nasty pin on the d-file. So I'll play e3 and if 11...d4, then 12.e4."

Usually a player with two fianchettoes wants the position to be as open as possible since that will benefit his heat-seeking Bishops. A closed position blocks them and makes them both useless.

As stated earlier, White should play 11.c4 when 11...d4 12.Nb3 opens the h1-a8 diagonal and gives White play on the queenside because of the extra space there and the open b-file. If Black answered 11.c4 with 11...dxc4?, then 12.Nxc4 would lead to a beautiful position for White. Both his Bishops enjoy wide-open diagonals, his Knights both aim at e5, all his pawns are safe, and he can generate play down the open b-file and c-file.

11.e3?

Now a c2-c4 advance would leave the pawn on d3 weak.

11...b6

> 2100: "Playing to fianchetto on b7."

12.Qe2

> 2100: "Still preparing for my central advance."

12...Ba6

(89)

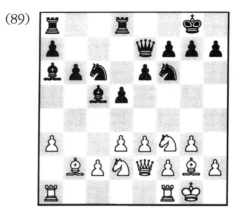

White doesn't know what to do.

> 2100: "He hampering my intended e2-e4 so I'll switch to a different plan. His c6-Knight gives him good control of the dark-squares so I will trade it off."

Notice how Black has placed his pieces on squares that fight for central control and restrain any central pawn advances by White. At the same time, Black has opened a key file (the c-file) and left White with weaknesses on c2 and a3.

White, on the other hand, hasn't done much of anything. He has allowed weaknesses to appear in his position and, aside from randomly developing his pieces, has not made any effort to create points of attack in the enemy camp or to gain space for himself.

13.Ne5 Nxe5
14.Bxe5 Rac8

I didn't fall for 14...Bxa3?? 15.Nb1 when White would win material due to the two loose Bishops on the a-file.

> 2100: "He is trying to hit c2. I'm not active enough. My kingside stuff is not happening since f2-f4 is slow. I also have to worry about the a3-pawn. It may be time to push it out of harm's way."

15.a4 Bb4

> 2100: "What's the point?"

Black understands that pawns are not the only things that can become weak. The new target is the c3-square, and Black rushes to claim it.

16.Nb3 Bc3

> 2100: "He is getting rid of my strong Bishop."

17.Bxc3 Rxc3
18.a5

> 2100: "I need to try to get rid of everything."

Exchanging off a weak pawn is a good idea, but unfortunately he forgets that his Knight on b3 is not as safe as it appears to be.

18...Bxd3!
19.cxd3 Rxb3

I stopped the game because White is a pawn down for nothing.

Tips

★ If you gain space early, you should continue to add to the gains that you have already made. All your pieces should work together in this (or any other) effort. The same can be said for an early minor piece advantage (make all your pieces and pawns help to improve your piece and restrict his), a structural edge (show that his pawns are weaker than yours), or virtually any other imbalance.

★ Don't just develop pieces. You must make gains with every move.

★ Bishops on long diagonals want those diagonals to stay open. Only allow them to close up if you feel that you are getting something good in other areas.

Admittedly, this was a rather one-sided contest. Our next game shows a more balanced battle.

The moves that I forced him to play were: **1.c4 c5 2.Nc3 Nc6 3.g3 g6 4.Bg2 Bg7 5.e4 d6 6.Nge2 Nf6 7.0-0 0-0 8.d3 Ne8.**

(90)

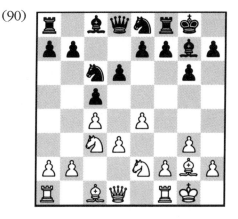

2100-Silman. English Opening
White to play.

> 2100: "His Knight wants to go to c7 to guard d5, prepare ...b5 and make way for a defensive ...f7-f5. Black's fianchettoed Bishop is annoying. I want to play f4 but the position doesn't call for the move. The hell with it!"

Why doesn't the position call for f2-f4? The move gains more kingside space and prepares for f4-f5 with a dangerous kingside attack.

The Black Knight on e8 *is* heading for c7, but it may continue on to e6 and d4 if given the chance. White's opening with pawns on c4 and e4 gives the first player plenty of space but it also leaves a hole on d4 which Black would like to make use of.

9.f4 f5

> 2100: "I wanted to provoke that. I knew he would not let me play f4-f5. Now I have many possibilities. If I go Nd5, he will kick it out with ...Nc7. I will just develop and defend the d4-square and perhaps push to d4."

The developing 10.Be3 is a good all-purpose move that eyes his weakened d4-square and connects the Rooks.

10.Be3 Nd4

> 2100: "He doesn't want me to play d3-d4. I have an idea to sacrifice a pawn to get some sort of activity with 11.Nb5 when the b2-pawn goes but I get lots of open lines. I want to get a quick d4 in to take advantage of his lack of development."

I don't like the idea of him bringing his c-pawn to the vulnerable b5-square but I do like the fact that he's trying to open the position and take advantage of his lead in development. He is forcing the play and making Black dance to his tune. The move may be a bit dubious, but his heart's in the right place.

11.Nb5 Nxb5
12.cxb5 Nc7

> 2100: "Didn't fall for 12...Bxb2 13.Qb3+. The b5-pawn isn't threatened at the moment so I can do anything I please. My original plan was to play d4."

13.d4 cxd4
14.Bxd4

> 2100: "Weakening his King by swapping Bishops."

14...Ne6

> 2100: "Now there's a lot of pins coming up. If 15.exf5 Nxd4 and ...Qb6 kills me. I have two moves: either 15.Bxg7 or 15.Qb3. Since I'll probably take on g7 anyway, I should try to win a tempo."

15.Qb3 Kh8

> 2100: "No choice."

16.Bxg7+ Nxg7

> 2100:" I want to play Kh1 but it's so slow. I'll let him do it for me."

17.Rad1 Qb6+
18.Kh1 Be6

> 2100: "I have no idea what's going on here. Should I sacrifice the b-pawn? No...I'll make him work for it!"

The opening stage is over. Black has caught up in development and is now trying to take over the initiative. This won't be so simple, though. True, Black does have the long-range advantage of superior pawn structure, but White has potential pressure down the e-file (against the e7-pawn) and his pieces are more active than the Black guys. Note that both sides came out of the opening with certain plusses and are now trying to milk these advantages for all they are worth.

19.Qd3 Rac8

> 2100: "Hitting c4. I could play Rc1 but I will go for b2-b3 which controls some squares but gives him the c-file."

White was hoping I'd play 19...Bxa2?? when 20.b3 traps the Bishop and threatens to pick it off in a number of ways (21.Rd2, 21.Ra1, 21.Qc2, and 21.Nc1).

20.b3 Rc5

> 2100: "I'm starting to regret b2-b3. I'm giving you time to double-up. Too late now; I have to continue with my plan."

21.Nd4 Bd7

> 2100: "It may be time for my a4 advance. It gives him a free move but may be the only way to defend b5."

22.a4 Rfc8

> 2100: "I still can't assess this. I have to get some counterplay to challenge his domination of the c-file. I have to get something going on the e-file."

He finally notices his potential down the e-file.

23.Rfe1 e6

> 2100: "Saying no to my counterplay. But now I have a new target."

24.exf5 gxf5

> 2100: "Whose King is weaker? What are my ideas here? His Knight looks silly but it guards lots of squares. I could sacrifice an Exchange or a Rook but maybe I don't need to go for any wild stuff. I'll force him to create holes."

25.Qf3 d5

> 2100: "Cool! It feels great to push him around for a change. Now I can run to e5."

26.Qe3 Qd6

> 2100: "I hate that! He wants an endgame. I want to play Nf3-e5 but that weakens b3!"

27.Nf3

> 2100: "Now I'm going to get mated—my King is so weak!"

I don't know why he felt that his King was weak; it looks perfectly safe to me. The advantages acquired from the opening are still influencing the moves for both sides. White still has to defend his queenside pawns while Black, due to the doubled White pawns, is virtually a pawn up in the center. White's biggest plus is his control of the juicy dark-squares on d4 and e5.

27...b6

> 2100: "Still have no idea. I'll play Ne5 cause it looks nice. Is that a bad reason?"

Making a move because it "looks nice" is not a good reason at all! I prefer putting the Knight on d4 where it guards b3, blocks the d-pawn, keeps the enemy Rooks out of c2 and eyes e6.

28.Ne5 Kg8

> 2100: "Now I can challenge the file."

29.Rc1 Be8

> 2100: "I will re-maneuver the Knight."

30.Nd3 d4
31.Qd2 Rc3

We stopped the game due to lack of time. The battle is still raging around the imbalances created in the opening.

Tip

★ The advantages you create in the opening often still have influence deep into the middlegame or endgame.

This type of cut and thrust battle becomes more and more common as your rating and the rating of your opponents grows. However, a beginner never looks at these things. Instead, he simply wants to get his stuff out and have some basic idea of what to do once his development is completed.

The game that follows shows some of the typical mistakes that players in the 1100 range and below often make.

900-Silman. Ruy Lopez, Exchange Variation.

1.e4

> 900: "Attacks the middle and the f5- and d5-squares. Also helps develop the Queen and Bishop."

1...e5
2.Nf3

> 900: "Attacks e5, develops and prepares to move the Bishop and castle."

2...Nc6

> 900: "Protects and develops."

3.Bb5

> 900: "Attacks the Knight and will someday threaten to win the pawn on e5. I remember you telling me that an immediate 4.Bxc6 dxc6 5.Nxe5 fails to 5...Qd4 with a double attack on my Knight and pawn."

3...a6

> 900: "Attacks my Bishop."

You must always ask why your opponent played his move. That way you won't experience any horrible surprises.

4.Bxc6

> 900: "Chops off a piece with no loss of time."

4...dxc6

(91)

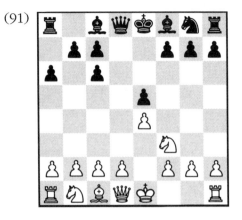

White to play.

900: "I want to castle but I am a bit worried about him getting a Bishop to h3 and a Queen to f3. Then I may be mated on g2. I will just develop and see what happens."

While I was happy that he thought about mating patterns of that type, I was quick to point out that you can't live in fear of every shadow that comes your way. Getting the Black Queen to f3 and the Bishop to h3 would only be possible if White lost or advanced his g-pawn and made other blunders as well. The usefulness of seeing such patterns in advance is that, once you are aware of them, you can make a point of not allowing them to happen.

A more advanced player would know that Black has gotten the two Bishops in exchange for a slightly compromised pawn structure. White's best plan is to play for d2-d4, exchanging the d-pawn for Black's e-pawn. Then White would own a healthy 4 vs. 3 majority of pawns on the kingside.

I didn't go into this stuff too heavily with 900 since I just wanted to concentrate on some easier concepts first. For example, one of the biggest problems a beginner has is making use of his Rooks. He just doesn't know how to get these pieces into play. If he had tried d2-d4 with the idea of opening the d-file for his Rooks, I would have been delighted. Instead, I constantly see players of this class play d2-d3 and suffer through chronic Rook-clog for the rest of the game.

5.Nc3 Bc5

Putting the Bishop on an active square and playing to stop White from opening a file with d2-d4.

6.0-0

> 900: "Since you told me that I don't have to worry about his Queen and Rook coming down on me, I suppose that castling will be okay."

He never even noticed Nxe5 which, however, can be answered by 6...Qg5 or 6...Bxf2+ 7.Kxf2 Qd4+ when Black has taken advantage of the undefended piece on e5.

6...f6
7.d3 Ne7

> 900: "I remember that you once told me that 8.Be3 Bxe3 9.fxe3 would be a good idea. However, I really am attracted to 8.Na4 with an attack on his Bishop."

8.Na4

White finds another typical error. One-move attacks are useless if they don't torment the attacked piece or if they don't accomplish other goals. Here White is sticking his Knight on the rim and, after Black moves his Bishop to safety, the first player will have to deal with the stupid placement of the poor horse on a4.

Much better was his first thought of 8.Be3 Bxe3 9.fxe3 which brings a pawn to the center (where it controls the useful d4- and f4-squares) and opens the f-file for his Rooks. The exchange of Bishops also gets rid of Black's Bishop-pair (when your opponent has two Bishops, trade one of them off!). Compare this with 8.Na4 Ba7 which does nothing at all to improve White's position.

8...Ba7

> 900: "I would like to play d2-d4 but I can't. I will play 9.Qe2, which connects my Rooks and prepares Be3."

A really good idea. White would love to trade off Bishops with Be3 since that develops, gives White more control of d4 and gets rid of Black's Bishop pair (as discussed above).

9.Qe2, and we stopped the game.

Tips

★ Don't play mindless one-move attacks which, after the opponent moves his attacked unit to safety (and you must believe that he will see your threat), leave your attacking piece on a useless square.

★ If you advance your pawns in the center, you will be able to open central files for your Rooks. Be attentive to the needs of your Rooks and they will serve you well.

★ If the opponent has two Bishops, trade one of them off. It's much easier to deal with one Bishop than two, since a pair of them is able to control both white and black squares.

USING THE ROOKS

M ost chess players are aware that Rooks need open files to be effective. However, these files don't just appear out of thin air (well, sometimes they appear to, but don't count on this type of lucky manifestation), you must go out of your way to create them.

The amateur player often has trouble using his Rooks; they just seem to sit there, trapped behind their own pawns, and often don't play a part in the game at all. The following thoughts should prove worthwhile to those who have trouble with Rooks:

RULE 1 — Use your pawns to blast open files. This holds true in open and closed positions.

(92)

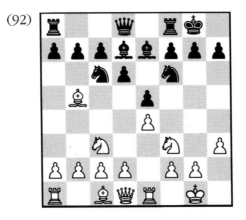

White to play.

In diagram 92, many amateurs might play 1.d3, which gives another defender to the e-pawn and frees the dark-squared Bishop. However, what does this do to help your Rooks? Nothing at all! Much better would be 1.d4 followed by Be3, Qd2 and Rad1. Now the White Rooks are showing a hint of activity on the d-file.

(93)

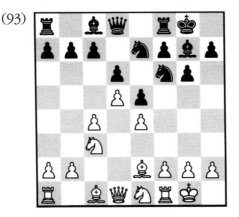

Black to play.

The position in diagram 93 also seems to offer a bleak prospect for the Rooks. Because of this, both sides play to open files and get these towers of uselessness into the game.

1...Nd7!

This frees the f-pawn in anticipation of …f7-f5, gaining kingside space and giving the f8-Rook more room to breathe.

2.Nd3!

White plays for c4-c5, gaining queenside space and preparing to blast open the c-file for his Rooks.

This type of systematic preparation for the opening of a file is a necessary skill if you want to progress in chess.

> **RULE 2 — Don't open a file if you think that the opponent will take it away from you.**

> **RULE 3 — If the creation of an open file has nothing to do with your other positive imbalances, then don't waste your time creating it.**

In diagram 93, Black's pawns pointed to the kingside so he not only played to open files, he also played to gain extra territory in that area. White's dreams of c4-c5 also attempt to open files on the side of the board where he enjoys more space.

> **RULE 4 — At times you can allow the opponent to dominate an open file, as long as you make sure that no penetration points exist along it.**

(94)

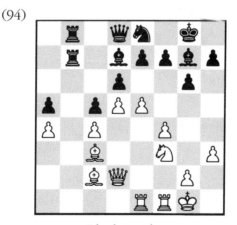

Black to play.

Black appears to have pressure along the open b-file in diagram 94, but this is really an illusion because these Rooks can't penetrate into the enemy position. The squares b5, b4, b3, b2, and b1 are all covered and are taboo to the Black Rooks.

• • • • •

The following position shows that a file without penetration points is more or less useless.

(95)

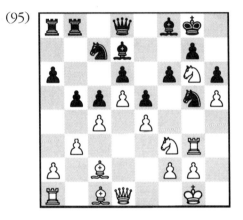

Karpov-Andersson, Stockholm 1969.
Black to play.

The center is closed and Black's superiority on the queenside is just as obvious as White's on the kingside. Hoping to add to the flames of his queenside assault, Andersson played to open as many files there as possible.

1...a5

Intending to blast everything open with ...a4.

2.a4!

An excellent move that stops the enemy a-pawn dead in its tracks. True, Black does gain the open b-file. True, White has weakened the b4-square. However, White feels that he can successfully deal with one open file. He certainly did not want to allow Black two of them!

2...bxc4

3.bxc4 Na6
4.Qe2

Karpov knows that his chances on the kingside are not going away, so he carefully deprives his opponent of the entry points along the b-file. Once this is done, and the enemy Rooks are neutralized, White will be free to play for his own attack in relative safety.

4...Ra7
5.Bd2 Rab7
6.Bc3 Nb4
7.Bd1 Na6
8.Nd2

White's pieces keep Black out of b5, b4, b3, b2 and b1.

8...Nb4
9.Re3 Be8
10.Nf1 Qc8
11.Ng3 Bd7
12.Qd2 Nh7
13.Be2

White goes about another positional plan before he starts an attack. He wants to trade off his light-squared Bishop for its counterpart on d7. Then the f5- and g6-squares will be permanent homes for the White Knights.

13...Kf7
14.Qd1 Be7
15.Nf1 Bd8
16.Nh2 Kg8
17.Bg4 Ng5
18.Bxd7 Qxd7
19.Nf1

Now that the Bishops are gone, White heads for the nice home on f5.

19...f5

Getting rid of the hole before White can use it. This doesn't work out very well, but to allow White Ng3-f5 followed by g2-g3 and f2-f4 would also be hopeless.

20.exf5 Qxf5
21.Ng3 Qf7

Black sees that 21...Qc2 22.f4! would give up material, since 22...exf4 23.Re8+ leads to mate.

22.Qe2

With all his basic positional goals taken care of (the nullification of the b-file and the trade of his bad Bishop), Karpov plays to open files of his own. He knows that if his Rooks get in the game, the Black position will fall apart.

22...Bf6
23.Rf1

White will play f2-f4, when both his Rook charge into play.

23...Qd7
24.f4 exf4
25.Rxf4 Bxc3
26.Rxc3 Re8
27.Re3 R7b8
28.Qf2

Threatening 29.Re7! Rxe7 30.Rf8+.

28...Nh7
29.Nf5 Rxe3
30.Qxe3 Nf6
31.Nge7+ Kh8
32.Nxh6 Re8
33.Nf7+ Kh7
34.Re4! Rxe7

Giving up, since he saw that 34...Nxe4 35.Qxe4+ leads to a quick mate.

35.Rxe7, 1-0.

A beautiful game in which Karpov nullified the enemy files and used his own to create a decisive penetration into the hostile position.

I thought that this idea of taking away penetration points along a file might be unfamiliar to most amateurs. To test out this theory, I tried the same position on several of my students. Sure enough, none of them knew how to keep Rooks from penetrating along an open file. Here is the most instructive of these contests.

(96)

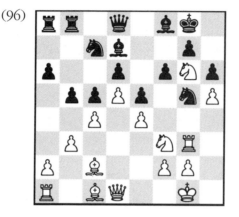

1400-Silman.
Black to play.

1400: "Black's dark-squared Bishop stinks. White has more space in the center and a great Knight on g6. Black has more territory on the queenside and would like to open the b-file. Though it's Black to move, I still like White. Black would like to trade pieces, particularly the g6-Knight."

1...a5

1400: "Continues with his queenside space edge. I like 2.a4 because it will kill his pawns, though it does open up the b-file and weaken b4."

2.a4! bxc4
3.bxc4 Na6

1400: "Heading for b4. Since the center is closed, I will start to get things going on the kingside."

4.Nxg5

Before this, White played just like Karpov! However, now he shows that he feels it is a race on opposite wings (which means that you must proceed with speed). While this demonstrates a good understanding of wing situations, it's simply not true here. White could, and should, keep the enemy pieces out (via Bd2-c3 which, by the way, also eyes the Black a-pawn) and then take all the time he wants on the opposite side.

4...fxg5

> 1400: "I'm trying to figure out the best way to get in. Since the center is locked, I would like to use my kingside pawns. An immediate f2-f4 fails but I do want to push f2-f4 at some point. The only way to do it is a Rook move followed by g3 and f4. Seems like it's too slow, though. Well, I have to get my Rook out of the way but I don't know where to put it."

Notice how he played 4.Nxg5 without detailed thought. He didn't bother looking at the ramifications of his decision. This move was an act of aggression on the kingside that made him feel better but did nothing to open lines on that side of the board. On the contrary, it made it *harder* for White to play the file-opening f2-f4.

5.Rc3 Be7

> 1400: "He wants to play ...g5-g4 followed by ...Bg5, trading off his bad Bishop. I will stop this with g2-g4, when his dark-squared Bishop remains very bad."

6.g4?

He thought that he saw a threat and became so distracted by it that he forgot all about opening lines on the kingside. Instead, he stopped the "threat" of ...g5-g4 (which in actuality places the pawn in grave danger after Bd3-e2) and closed up the very side he was hoping to open.

Don't become so entranced by the enemy's ideas that you forget all about your own.

6...Bf6

> 1400: "That makes it hard to push f2-f4. I still want to play for f4 and if he takes ...exf4 then e4-e5 is possible. So 7.Qe2 is an idea."

Black is making sure that any tactically based e4-e5 advance fails. Once he does that, he will have a free hand on the queenside. In a way, this is the reverse of what happened in the Karpov-Andersson game.

7.Qe2 Be8

> 1400: "That was inevitable. I want my Queen to go to h2 so
> f3 clears the 2nd rank."

8.f3 Bxg6
9.hxg6 Qe8

I wanted to see how he would react to the loss of material. I
was hoping he'd notice that, after Black takes on g6 (via 10…Qxg6),
White can make use of tactics (created by the c2-Bishop's
potential X-ray to the Black Queen on g6) by 11.f4 gxf4 (11…exf4
12.e5) 12.Bxf4. Of course, this still fails due to 12…exf4 13.e5 Qe8,
taking advantage of the unprotected White Queen (14.Qd3 Qxe5
is nothing for White), but such tactics can often turn a game
around and must be noticed if you want to have any real chance
of saving a poor position.

10.Qh2?

> 1400: "Eyeing h6 and if he takes on g6 I go to h5 and trade."

What is this madness about trading? Why would he want to go
into an endgame after he has lost a pawn? The threat to the g6-
pawn seems to have blown one of his fuses!

10…Qxg6
11.Qh5 Qxh5
12.gxh5 g6
13.hxg6 Kg7

> 1400: "Black has an extra passed pawn but I don't know if
> that pawn makes such a big difference. My two Bishops
> help and his Knight is useless since b4 is a nowhere square.
> I will trade Rooks since all his pawns are on dark squares
> which makes his Bishop bad. Ideally I would like to trade
> my bad Bishop for his Knight."

I was very pleased at how he continually thought about
getting rid of bad Bishops. However, his desire to trade when
down material concerned me. Usually it is the person who is *up*
material that wants to trade!

14.Rb1 Rxb1
15.Bxb1 Rb8

16.Bc2 Kxg6
17.Rb3 Rb4

> 1400: "He is threatening two pawns. I will trade and if he retakes with either one, I can block on b3 with my Bishop."

Still trading away to his doom.

18.Rxb4 cxb4

Now Black has a new passed pawn and a nice square for his Knight on c5.

19.Be3 Bd8

> 1400: "He has two passed pawns. I have to improve the position of my King."

20.Kg2 Nb8!

> 1400: "I think the push works now."

Black intended to trade his bad Bishop (or get it outside the pawn chain) by ...Nd7 followed by ...Bb6.

21.c5 dxc5
22.Bxc5 Nd7
23.Be3 Bb6

> 1400: "Trading his bad Bishop for my good one. I don't want his Bishop to go to d4 but what can I do about it?"

24.Bd2 Bd4
25.Kg3 Nc5. The game was stopped at this point.

Tips

★ Trading bad Bishops is fine, but don't think about that to the exclusion of everything else.

★ Open files are only valuable if you can effect some sort of penetration on them.

★ If you can stop the opponent's play, you don't have to be in a hurry with your own.

In the diagram that follows, we see a position that is far from enticing for Black. Aside from having the inferior pawn structure, he is also about to lose a pawn. Masters know that in Rook endgames it is of the utmost importance to keep one's Rook active. This rule should be followed even if you have to sacrifice a pawn. However, I suspected that in the amateur ranks this well-known principle was unknown.

(97)

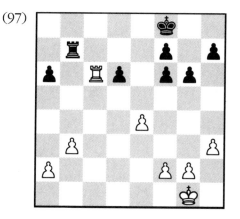

Silman-1480
Black to play.

How would an amateur defend such a position? I tried it against several students to see if their reactions were uniform or varied from individual to individual.

> 1480: "The position is miserable for Black. I need to give up a pawn and penetrate with my Rook so it gets active. However, 1...Ke7 2.Rxa6 leaves him with two connected passed pawns on the queenside. My Rook could penetrate then and his Rook would be in front of his pawns but that probably doesn't make any difference. The other problem is that if I let him chop on d6, then the f6-pawn would also hang. I would consider the game lost here and I would not have a positive attitude. I would play 1...Ke7 2.Rxa6 Rc7 and penetrate with my Rook. Maybe I could get some play."

1...Ke7?

Poor 1480 didn't enjoy this position at all! Apparently he was not aware of the old saying, "All Rook endings are drawn."

This is actually an old joke saying, but there is more truth to it than one would imagine. Why? Because all Rook endings take patience and skill to win. Such qualities are not always present, and a dogged resistance can easily bring rewards.

He gave up the a-pawn because he had already given up the game. When you adopt a loser's attitude you will play loser moves. You must believe that you have a chance. If you don't, then your moves will echo this sentiment. His 1...Ke7 gave White two connected passed pawns after 2.Rxa6, and these two pawns will easily win the game for the first player.

We stopped the game since 1480 was too disgusted with the position to continue!

Silman-1500 (also from diagram 97)

> 1500: "I can't save both pawns so I have two choices. One is to save the d6-pawn and advance the f-pawn and create a passed d-pawn. Second, is to try to keep the a-pawn by advancing it and give up the d6-pawn. I can get my Rook behind his pawns and try to prevent him from queening. The first plan gives him two passers on the queenside so the second is the way to go.
>
> "I have 1...a5 or 1...Ra7. The former allows 2.Ra6. I'm not crazy about 1...Ra7 because it dooms my Rook to passivity, so 1...a5 is better."

I was very happy about what he had to say. He wanted to avoid a passive Rook and did not want to give White two connected passed pawns.

1...a5

> 1500: "If 2.Ra6 Rb5."

2.Rxd6 Ke7

> 1500: "Protects the f-pawn, centralizes my King and attacks the Rook."

So far he's done quite well. This natural move, though, just forces the White Rook to a better square. For the superior 2...a4, see the next game.

3.Ra6 Rb5 and here we stopped the game since Black is a pawn down with a passive position.

(98)

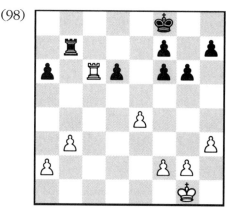

Silman-2100
Black to play.

2100: "Losing the a6-pawn is bad because connected passed pawns on the queenside are fatal for me. However, my Rook is not active and ...Ra7 does nothing to help. I have to activate my Rook *and* stop his queenside pawns. I must hold the a-pawn and ...a5 followed by ...Ra7 is the only way to do it. I don't care about my d-pawn but my a-pawn is everything. Unfortunately, my King can't be activated either. So 1...a5 is forced since ...Ra7 is death. After 1...a5 2.Ra6 Rb5 or 2.Rxd6 a4!, and if he takes on f6 I liquidate and the four vs. three should draw."

Excellent! He intends to play this as actively as possible in order to avoid a passive pawn-down Rook endgame. I was especially pleased that he noted the drawn four vs. three endgame—whenever you have pawns on only one side of the board you create excellent drawing chances.

1...a5
2.Rxd6 a4!

2100: "2...Ke7 does not really activate my King so I have to liquidate. White has to get his King into play. Now (after 2...a4) if 3.bxa4, I get counterplay with 3...Rb4."

He is doing a superb job. White's best chance for victory is
3.bxa4 Rb4 4.f3 Rxa4 5.Rd2 when White is the one with the
passive Rook. Nevertheless, White could still torture Black by
bringing his King over to the queenside and relieving his Rook
from guard duty. Whatever the result, Black has done his utmost
to make the win hard for White to achieve.

3.Rxf6 axb3
4.axb3 Rxb3 and Black got his four versus three endgame.
The game was agreed drawn after **5.h4 h5 6.Kh2 Kg7 7.e5 Rb5
8.f4 Rb4 9.Kh3 Rb3+ 10.g3 Rb2**.

Tips

★ A game is always easier to draw if there are pawns
on only one side of the board.

★ A bad, defeatist attitude will get you only defeat.

★ Two connected passed pawns almost always win in
a Rook endgame.

THE CURSE
OF THE
MINDLESS
KING HUNTER

Everyone likes to attack the opponent's King. If it works, you get a quick win with a lot of flash. However, it drives me to distraction when a player tries to do this without any regard for the particulars of the position. The amateur *must* learn that you have to do what the *position* calls for, not what you want to do! This means that you may be the finest attacker of all time, however, if the position calls for a queenside attack against a weak pawn, then that is what you should do.

Attacks against the enemy King only make sense in the following situations:

> ➤ If the center is locked, you should play in the direction that your pawns point. You play where your pawns point because that is where your territory lies.

(99)

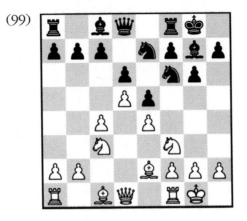

White to play.

Black's pawns point towards the kingside (from c7 to d6 to e5...getting closer and closer to White's King) in diagram 99, so he should be playing for a kingside pawn storm by ...Nd7 and ...f7-f5. This also fits in nicely with rule number two.

➤ If the center is locked, you should try to attack with pawns. This gives you extra space and allows your Rooks to come into play.

➤ It is very important to understand that you play on the wings when the center is closed, but if the center is open, the middle is the most important area to concentrate on. Central play almost always beats wing play!

(100)

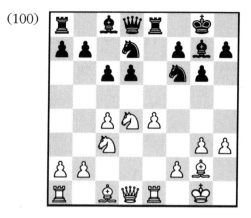

Black to play.

In diagram 100, Black should not even think of a kingside attack since there is too much play in the center. Instead, he should concentrate on strengthening his position in the middle by ....a5, ...Nc5, ...a4 and ...Qa5 with piece pressure on the White position.

➤ You only play where you have a favorable imbalance or the possibility of creating a favorable imbalance. In other words, if you have nothing positive on the kingside you cannot expect to be successful on that side of the board.

(101)

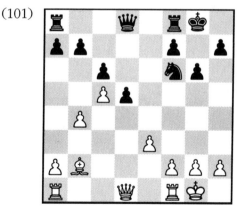

White to play.

In diagram 101, White is justified to look at the kingside since his main imbalance (the Bishop versus the Knight) is aiming in that direction.

1.Qd4 Kg7

The only move. Any Knight move would have allowed mate on h8.

2.g4!

Threatening to advance to g5.

2...h6

No better is 2...g5 3.f4 when the Rook on f1 joins in the fight.

3.f4 and Black is overwhelmed.

➤ You may also start a King-hunt if you have a large lead in development and think you can land a knockout blow before he can recover his balance.

After **1.e4 e5 2.Nf3 f6?** we get the position in diagram 102.

(102)

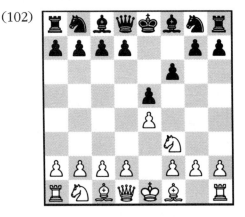

White to play.

White has a lead in development and Black has weakened his King position by playing the horrible ...f7-f6. It is this weakening of the a2-g8 and h5-e8 diagonals that makes White seek out a hard-hitting solution.

3.Nxe5! fxe5
4.Qh5+ Ke7

Or 4...g6 5.Qxe5+ when White picks up the Rook on h8.

5.Qxe5+ Kf7
6.Bc4+

White's army comes out with gain of time.

6...Kg6
7.Qf5+ Kh6
8.d4+ g5
9.h4 and Black cannot stave off White's threats.

• • • • •

In the game that follows (between two amateurs, rated 1061 and 1466 respectively) we see White build up an excellent position on the queenside only to be tempted by the siren call of a non-existent kingside attack.

Minders-Gonzalez, U.S. Amateur West 1993.
Queen's Gambit Declined.

1.d4 d5
2.c4 Nf6?!

A common error at the amateur level. Black is allowing White to trade his inferior c-pawn for the strong central d-pawn. Better is the immediate 2...e6 or 2...c6 when Black can retain a space-gaining pawn on d5.

3.Nc3?!

Transposing back into the main lines of the Queen's Gambit Declined. White should have punished Black by 3.cxd5 Nxd5, after which White can always gain a full pawn center by e2-e4.

3...e6
4.a3?!

Fearing the pin by ...Bb4, White throws away a tempo without just cause. You can't let every little possibility by the enemy cause you to panic. If you see something that worries you, look at it closely and make sure that it's worth stopping—you may find that you are often preventing a bad move that the opponent never intended to play!

Note that after the calm 4.Bg5 (also fine is 4.Nf3) 4...Bb4 5.e3, White need not fear the doubled pawns that arise after 5...Bxc3+ 6.bxc3 since he could always get rid of them by cxd5 followed by c3-c4 (in other words, the doubled pawns were illusory). In this case, Black has actually helped White; his capture on c3 brought the passive b2-pawn to a more dynamic central post.

4...Be7
5.Bg5

Having chased away the ghosts with a2-a3, White gets back to his own plans.

5...c6
6.Nf3 h6
7.Bh4 Nbd7
8.c5

Giving up some time (tempos) for lots of queenside space. More natural is 8.e3, but I will never criticize a move that aggressively fights for something (be it two Bishops, material, development, superior pawn structure, or in this case, space)—it shows that one's heart is in the right place. An insistence that every move you make creates some sort of gain will get you far in chess.

8...b6
9.b4 b5?

Wasting a move and destroying the tension that 8...b6 created. White's pawn moves (a3 and c5) allowed Black to take a lead in development, and he should try to take advantage of this by ripping open the position. He could castle first before initiating a fight, but the immediate 9...bxc5 10.bxc5 (better is 10.dxc5, creating an interesting fight between White's queenside majority and Black's central majority) 10...e5! (destroying one of the defenders of c5) should turn out pretty well for Black: 11.dxe5 (the solid 11.e3 allows Black to make his own spatial gains in the center after 10....e4) 11...Ne4 12.Bxe7 Qxe7 with threats to win the White pawns on e5 and c5.

By ignoring the one advantage he had (lead in development), Black quickly finds himself in an inferior position.

10.e3 a5
11.Bd3 0-0
12.0-0 Re8

(103)

White to play.

White has come out of the opening with a nice game: he has more space on the queenside and has possibilities to expand in the center with e3-e4, thereby stopping Black from doing the same thing with a later ...e6-e5.

In the actual game, White was blind to the fact that his fortunes were tied to his extra queenside space and central possibilities. Instead, he decided that a kingside attack was in order. Why? My guess is that he likes to go after Kings and thought that this was as good a time to do it as any. Needless to say, this is not the way to play good chess!

13.Ne2?

White thinks that a Knight on g3 will help him create a kingside attack simply because he has an extra piece on that side of the board. However, you should lead your pieces to squares where they have a future. Once the poor horse reaches g3 it will be badly posted since it can't go to e4, f5 or h5!

13...Bb7
14.Ng3??

Trapping his own Bishop on h4.

14...axb4

15.axb4 Rxa1

16.Qxa1 and now Black can win the Bishop with 16...g5. In the end, White did indeed hang his Bishop and he eventually lost the game.

Noting White's reluctance to play in the center or on the queenside, I began to wonder if my students would make the same mistakes, even though I had warned them of this type of error in the past. The next two games begin from the position after move twelve.

(104)

1600-Silman.
White to play.

1600: "The first thing I have to do is find the candidate moves for White. They are 13.Ne5, 13.Bxf6, 13.Qc2 and 13.Re1. Those are a few of them. Now I will see if we have even material. Yes, it's all even. Next, I will look at King safety—both Kings appear to be safe. What are my weaknesses? White is solid, my dark-squared Bishop controls a good diagonal. On the queenside, any trade opens the a-file and no weaknesses are created so I don't have to worry about that . Do I have any combination on the board? I don't see any for White. Any for Black? Nothing. His c6-pawn is weak but I don't see any way to get at it.

"So my plan is to kick Black's Knights and make them retreat. Best is to move the Queen from the first rank so 13...axb4 14.axb4 Rxa1 15.Rxa1 gives me files."

13.Qc2

He played a good move, but his reasoning was confused—to say the least! *Never* start by looking at the candidate moves—that's the *last* thing you should do! My student, though, immediately began to list them (I had not seen him for two years, so it seems that he had forgotten what we had discussed in our old sessions). Next he jumped from one thing to another, never noticing that he possessed extra queenside space. Finally, he makes the cryptic statement that he is going to kick Black's Knights (how?) and then he plays 13.Qc2.

At the risk of repeating myself, you start by listing all the imbalances. Then you ask which side of the board you (and your opponent!) are going to play on (you will only play where you have a favorable imbalance). You only look at candidate moves when you have assessed these other factors.

13...Nh5
14.Bxe7 Qxe7

> 1600: "I want to mate Black on the kingside. How do I get there? His h5-Knight is awkward so I don't want to chase it back into play. I have a Knight on c3 that's doing nothing so I should re-position it and make it more active. My pawn on e3 keeps his Knight on h5 out. I want to break in the center, though, and occupy d6. To do this I must get counterplay in the center. By playing e3-e4, I get play in the middle but give his Knight access to f4."

My heart sank when he said that he wanted to mate on the kingside! What justification does he have for this, other than desire? Are there targets there? Is my King denuded? Is his whole army posted in that sector?

Interestingly, he then forgot about this idea and found more logical ideas. His comment about my Knight being offside and his not wanting to drive it back into play is excellent—attacking a piece is useless unless you improve your position by doing so or force his piece to an inferior square. I also loved his newfound idea to break in the center by e3-e4 and, hope of hopes, make use of the d6-square. Unfortunately, this is where his good intentions ran into that oh-so-common fear of ghosts—he didn't want to allow Black to answer e4 with ....Nf4. By concentrating on this unimportant Black possibility (who cares if Black takes two moves to trade Knight for Bishop; wouldn't White be able to make significant gains by then?), he got lured into the same error that we saw in the original example!

15.Ne2?

> 1600: "This keeps him out of f4. My long-range plan is to play a Knight to d6."

Horrible. One idea of playing e3-e4 is that he can answer ...dxe4 with Nxe4 when the dream of using d6 becomes a reality. With the Knight on e2, however, this is no longer possible. Another idea associated with e3-e4 is that he can follow up with a Rook to the e-file when White would have considerable pressure in the center.

The immediate 15.e4 was called for, when Black could not counterattack with ....e6-e5 since d5 would fall. The Knight's absence from the center gives Black the time to free himself.

15...e5

> 1600: "I will counterattack."

16.e4

With Black suddenly showing signs of activity, White feels compelled to strike back. However, instead of being the one to dictate the tempo of the game, now White is reacting to Black.

16...Nhf6

The Knight rushes back to the center where it defends d5 and attacks e4.

> 1600:" I must watch out for 17.exd5 e4 with a fork. How do I exchange without allowing this fork?"

Decentralizing and time-wasting moves like 15.Ne2 usually lead to the opponent taking the initiative. Remember: you want to be the one who tells the other guy what to do. Passive moves have the opposite effect.

17.Ng3 axb4

Black sees that an undefended White Rook on a1 might lead to problems for his opponent.

18.axb4 Rxa1
19.Rxa1 exd4

> 1600: "Now I'm getting closer to his weakness on c6. Since my e4-pawn is attacked three times and guarded three times I have time to follow my plans. I can play Nf5, Nxd4 or exd5. I must watch out for back-rank mates on e1 after Nxd4 but everything seems safe."

White's three to three count is a bit off (Black is attacking e4 four times), though another oversight is the straw that will break his back.

20.Nxd4??

You should always be aware of all your weak points and undefended pieces. In this case, White must carefully watch his Rook on a1, his pawn on b4 (when a Black Knight comes to d5) and his pawn on e4. By not taking the opponent's possibilities seriously, he allowed himself to be knocked out. Much better was 20.Nf5.

20...Qe5

> 1600: "Pinning me and threatening my d4-Knight. The c6-pawn is poison now and I can't easily chase his Queen from its good square. On 21.Nf5, he has 21...dxe4 so I must defend my Knight."

21.Nge2?? dxe4 and the game was stopped.

Tips

★ Moving a piece away from the center (called a decentralizing move) should always be viewed with suspicion.

★ Only go after the enemy King if the position justifies it. A King-hunt is not something you decide to do because you "feel like it."

★ Undefended pieces often lead to nasty tactical surprises. Make sure your pieces are well-guarded.

One of the amateur's greatest weaknesses is his inability to grab the initiative. He wants to attack but he does not realize that the concept of attack must encompass the whole board. Real attacking means putting pressure against a particular target; this can be an enemy King or a weak pawn. You should strive to create a target and then force your opponent to react to your threats against it.

In our next game, White astutely notices the creation of a weakness and jumps all over it.

(105)

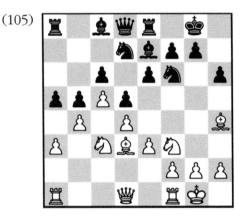

1400-Silman.
White to play.

1400: "Central space is even. There is some action on the queenside and I have more space there due to my pawn on c5. The squares and pawns on c6, d6 and b6 are weak but not easy for White to get to. White is safe on the kingside. White's pawns are pointing to the queenside. I would like to put my Bishop on the h2-b8 diagonal where it hits e5 and d6—it's not doing much where it stands.

"Now for a plan. I want to play either in the center or on the queenside. I like Bg3, which aims at both sectors, followed by Ne5."

I'm extremely happy with his appraisal. He didn't even look at the kingside since there were no favorable imbalances in that area. The only thing he didn't notice was Black's ultimate intention of advancing his pawn to e5. Don't forget to look for your opponent's best plans! By doing that, you won't run into any unpleasant surprises.

13.Bg3

1400: "I'm a bit better because Black is cramped due to my space-gaining c5-pawn."

13...Bf8

Trying to snag his Bishop with 13...Nh5 runs into 14.Ne5! Nxg3? (14...Nxe5 15.Bxe5) 15.Nxc6.

1400: "Black is thinking of fianchettoing his King Bishop since it has no future on e7."

14.Ne5

Played without thought. Why he chose this aggressive-looking move (which incorrectly permits the side with less space to trade pieces) over the logical 14.e4, remains a mystery.

14...Nxe5
15.Bxe5 Nd7

1400: "Now it's looking bad for me. He will get the two Bishops if I stay on e5. However, if he takes me on e5 I get the d4-square."

When he played 14.Ne5 he lost momentary control of the game. The mild panic that resulted from this is why he immediately began to think that something had gone wrong. Fortunately, he makes a nice recovery.

16.Ne2

It's odd, but all three of our test subjects have resorted to this ugly move!

16...Nxe5

This and Black's following moves are very weak since they give the White Knight a beautiful central post and force him to improve his position. However, this student always had trouble attacking the enemy King (preferring quiet positional play) and I wanted to give him the opportunity to test his skills in that area.

17.dxe5 Qc7

1400: "I must defend my pawn."

18.f4 Be7
19.Nd4

White has built up a significant advantage in territory and also enjoys a great Knight on d4 versus a pathetic Bishop on c8.

19...f6

So far, I had made simple one-move threats or done nothing at all. Now I lash out and try to get counterplay in the center. Will he fold at the first sign of pressure or will he rise to the occasion?

> 1400: "Black is trying to open lines for his two Bishops. He is weak on the light-squares so I'm going to take advantage of that with Qh5."

20.Qh5!

Bingo! All of a sudden my position takes a turn for the worse. He wants to blow me off the board and it's not clear if I can do anything about it. This switch from more space to an attack on the wing is quite natural—the side with more territory can move his pieces from one side to the other with great speed. Note, however, that White has only decided to go for a kingside attack after Black weakened the light-squares around his King. In other words, this decision was not made lightly—he had a clear reason to attack my King.

20...Rf8

> 1400: "I'm looking at how much damage Qg6 does. He can play ...f5 and shut off my Bishop. Since ...f5 makes Qg6 useless, I will bring up more pieces."

21.Rf3

I like the idea of bringing more pieces into the attack. However, 21.Qg6 f5 22.g4! should be winning for White because 23.gxf5 will pick up some wood. Remember that mate is not the only goal of a kingside attack. A safe material advantage would be more than adequate.

21...Qd7

Black's ugly contortions deserve a grim death.

22.Rg3

> 1400: "Threatening Qxh6. I think I've got him!"

22...f5

> 1400: "He didn't like the mating possibilities that my Bishop gave me."

23.Qxh6

See what the initiative does? By playing forcefully to take advantage of a weakness on the kingside (note the word "weakness"), a player with a 1400 rating has pushed someone around who is over a thousand points higher!

23...Rf7

He is treating me like a dog! I waited expectantly for him to put me away.

> 1400: "Now I want a way to finish him off. Rg6 aims at e6. I must be careful about breaking this pin, though."

24.Rg6?

With an extra pawn and an attack, he begins to get greedy for small gains. Instead of this move, which restricts the mobility of his pieces, he should do two things (if no immediate crush exists): 1) take away all possible counterplay—he is a pawn up and winning, so if he takes all my cheapo chances away he should easily score the point. 2) Reorganize and then break through with the remainder of his forces.

Aside from 24.Bxf5! exf5 25.e6 which wins at once, White could play quietly and lock in the victory with 24.Rb1 (defending the b-pawn and stopping any nonsense down the a-file) followed by Qg6 and Rh3. The beauty of this line (if something like 24.Bxf5 did not exist) is that Black would be completely helpless and would likely resign.

Once again: If you have a long-range win (in this case, White has a material advantage and an enduring attack) but don't have an immediate knockout, *stop all enemy counterplay!*

24...axb4

1400: "Black is struggling for counterplay on the other side. Should I defend or ignore him and go for the kill? I'm still focusing on the e6 point. I just noticed that my intended 25.Nxe6 runs into 25...Qxe6! 26.Rxe6 gxh6. I will back off and get out of the pin."

25.Qh5

Just giving up. Black has broken through on the queenside and now White must find a way to kill his opponent on the opposite wing. The move he played is simply too slow. 25.Bxf5! was still possible.

25...Bxc5 and we stopped the game since lines like 26.Nxe6 Bxe3+ 27.Kf1Qxe6 28.Rxe6 Bxe6 are good for Black.

Tips

★ Only play where you have some sort of favorable imbalance. Simply wanting to attack on the kingside is not justification for doing so. However, if weaknesses appear there then by all means go after him with gusto!

★ Always try and force your ideas onto your opponent—get him to react to what you are doing. Of course, you must also make sure that what you are doing conforms to the needs to the position.

★ Never allow counterplay when you have a lock on the game.

Our final example in this chapter starts with a quiet positional opening. White is supposed to play on the queenside and in the center but somehow his amateur eyes still stare longingly at the Black King.

The first moves were: **1.d4 Nf6 2.c4 e6 3.Nc3 Bb4 4.e3 0-0 5.Bd3 d5 6.Nf3 b6 7.0-0 Bb7 8.a3 Bd6 9.cxd5 exd5 10.b4 a6** and now 1500 had to annotate the book moves for both sides:

(106)
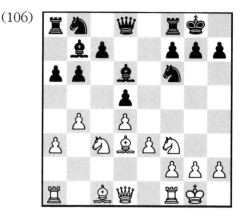

White to play.

> 1500: "White wants to push his pawn on f2 to f4. To do this he must move his Knight to e1."

I asked where White should be trying to play.

> 1500: "Black's Bishops are aimed at White's kingside. So Black is attacking the King. I still like Ne1 followed by f4, though, with a kingside attack for White."

Amazing! Look how the amateur player always wants to go after the King, no matter what the position calls for! He tells me that Black is attacking the King but he ignores this and says that he wants to do the same via Ne1 and f4 (which weakens e4 and e3 along an open file). Why so stubborn? Black's semi-open e-file is closer to the kingside than White's semi-open c-file. Where is White's space advantage? On the queenside, or course. Since you are supposed to play where your advantages are, this means that White should be setting his sights on the queenside.

11.Qb3

> 1500: "Not the kind of move I would play. This pressures d5 but I don't like it since d5 is well defended. What's the point if something is already guarded?"

11.Qb3 has several points. By attacking d5, White ties down two Black pieces (Knight on f6 and Bishop on b7) to its defense. The real purpose, though, is based on the semi-open c-file. White wants to place his Rooks on that file and bring pressure to bear on the Black c7-pawn. However, White sees that the Black Bishop on d6 not only eyes his kingside, but also defends c7. White's plan is to trade off this fine Black piece for the bad Bishop on c1 via a3-a4, Ba3 and b4-b5. This would exchange a poor piece for a good one, hurt Black's chances for a successful kingside attack and leave the c-pawn more vulnerable to an assault by the White Rooks.

11...Qe7

> 1500: "This pressures the center and centralizes a piece."

It does those things but it also eyes b4 and makes a2-a4 and Ba3 more difficult to achieve.

12.Rb1

> 1500: "Protects b4 so he can push a4 and a5."

He does not see the real point of White's play but I did not expect him to. White is using an advanced idea that would probably be overlooked by most players under 2100. The main point of this exercise was to see if 1500 could concentrate on a queenside attack. Unfortunately, his wistful glances towards my King made it clear where his heart was.

The game was stopped at this point.

Tips

★ You must be able to play in all three areas of the board (queenside, center, and kingside), depending on where your favorable imbalances are.

★ A person that does nothing but attacks the enemy King will end up a loser most of the time. Balance, and a willingness to do whatever is called for, is the key to success in chess.

The center of the chess board is the area you would like to control the most. Play there with as much energy as you can because the rewards are great for those that succeed in this quest. Why is the center important? Because your pieces can quickly reach any area of the board from the center. Pieces huddled on one wing are more or less committed to play in that area, leaving the other two parts of the board defenseless.

Of course, if the center is blocked by pawns, both armies are forced to seek employment elsewhere. This decision is *not* a matter of taste—closed centers call for wing action, and the proper wing to play on can be ascertained by using the "pawn-pointing technique."

So, how does this tie in with a correct approach to understanding a position? That should be obvious! You can't find a good move if you don't know which side of the board you are supposed play on. To do this, you first take note of all the imbalances for both sides. Once this is done, try to find a plan based on those imbalances—try to use those favorable aspects of your game as guidelines that will tell you where to seek extra space, where to attack weak enemy pawns and where to create effective homes for your pieces.

For example, the center is locked up. Your opponent has a weak, isolated pawn on the queenside and you also have a space advantage in that area. Your opponent is the one with the advantage in space on the kingside and most of his pieces are massed in that area. Where should you play? You may dream of running over to the kingside and trying to clobber his King, but that is just an emotional reaction that has little to do with the reality of the board. You must conquer this illogical desire and quietly go after his weak pawn on the queenside. That's your side of the board, that's where you should play.

●　●　●　●　●

During my private lessons, I constantly harp on certain key themes: Always pay attention to Bishop versus Knight; never play without a plan; before playing a move, always ask yourself, "What wonderful thing does this move do for my position?" And, of course, I remind my students to follow one of the finest general rules in chess: **The best reaction to an attack on the wing is a counterattack in the center.**

When a person first comes to me, they either don't know this rule or, if they have heard of it, they've never bothered to follow it. However, after a few sessions of me nagging them, they usually begin to develop an awareness of such possibilities.

Of course, if "C", "B" and "A" players are able to use this rule, then one would think that Grandmasters would never be victims of it. The following game, though, shows that this is simply not the case—players of all strengths leave themselves open to its effects. If you want to punish them, all you have to do is pull your arm back and punch them in the center!

Alekhine-Maroczy, Carlsbad 1923.
Queen's Gambit Declined, Lasker's Variation.

1.d4 Nf6
2.c4 e6
3.Nf3 d5
4.Nc3 Be7
5.Bg5 0-0
6.e3 Ne4

In modern times Black throws in 6...h6 before deciding on
7...Ne4 or the more popular 7...b6.

7.Bxe7 Qxe7
8.Qb3 Nxc3
9.Qxc3 c6
10.Bd3 Nd7
11.0-0 f5?!

Creating a big hole on e5. If Black ever brings his Knight to e4,
White will get a superior minor piece by trading it for his Bishop
and planting his Knight on the permanent e5-square.

12.Rac1 g5?

(107

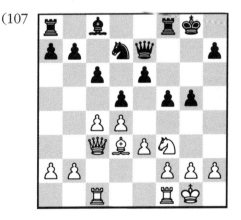

White to play.

Alekhine calls this "inexplicable," though the amateur has no
problem understanding it at all! Many players would think that

Black is starting a strong kingside attack. However, the experienced master knows that this type of wing attack will always fail if he can initiate a counterattack in the middle; in this case, White can blow open the center with Nd2 and f2-f3 followed by e3-e4. So why did an experienced Grandmaster like Maroczy make such a mistake? To answer that, we would have to know what he drank before the game—demonic possession is another theory.

13.Nd2! Rf7?

Pointless.

14.f3

White continues his preparations to rip open the center.

14...e5
15.cxd5 cxd5
16.e4!

The center gets nuked and Black's open King and lack of development begin to become serious liabilities.

16...fxe4
17.fxe4 Rxf1+
18.Rxf1 exd4
19.Qc7!

Pinning the Knight and tying up all of Black's pieces. Black is completely lost.

19...Kg7
20.Rf5! dxe4
21.Nxe4 Qb4

Giving up. The obvious 21...h6 would have held out longer.

22.Rxg5+, 1-0.

A pathetic performance from Maroczy.

Let's go back to the position after 12...g5.

(108)

1000-Silman.
White to play.

In the next few examples, I tested my students' ability to recognize when a central counterattack was called for by giving them the White side of the diagrammed position. If they showed a mastery of the necessary concepts, they would be rewarded in the usual way: a new car, a date with some super-model, a microscopic rendition of Elliott Winslow's signature, etc. However, if they failed to understand what was going on, they would have to pay ten times the normal lesson fee (the idea of fines during a lesson has been espoused by IM John Grefe).

> 1000: "Black has a weak square on e5 which White could use for his Knight. If I could trade off my Bishop for his Knight, I could use it but I don't know if that is possible. Black is starting a kingside attack which is justified since the center is locked; there are no open files. He will play ...g4 and chase my Knight to a poor square. I can trade Queens with Qa3 but I'm not sure if that does any good. I can take on d5 when ...cxd5 allows Qc7 with a pin on his Knight. If ...exd5 my Bishop gets more scope. I will play cxd5 and try to get play in the middle."

This guy's rating is only 1000 yet he pointed out some profound things! He noted the possibility of gaining a superior minor piece if his Knight could stay on e5. He also remembered me telling him that a wing attack is only justified if the center is under your control or is closed. He was well aware that he should try to open the center up and so he tried 1.cxd5. I suppose the idea of Nd2 followed by f3 and e4 was too difficult since the Knight move to d2 looks like a retreat and it also goes away form the desired e5-post. Don't be afraid of retreating moves it they help achieve an important goal (in this case, blasting open the center with e3-e4).

13.cxd5 exd5

> 1000: "I would love to get his Knight or play e3-e4. Maybe that push would be possible after Rfe1."

This earned a hefty fine. Words like "maybe" should not play a part in one's choice of move—you should *know* what your moves will lead to! For example, if he had tried 14.b2-b4 with the idea of opening the c-file with b4-b5, I would have been proud of him (it doesn't matter if it's the best plan or not, at least he is following a clear course of action and trying to do something positive by opening a file for his Queen and Rook) since that would have continued his reasoning behind 13.cxd5. Unfortunately, when I refused to open the c-file for him (via 13...cxd5) he simply gave up on the idea.

14.Rfe1 g4

> 1000: "At this point, I have to jump into e5."

Now he's just reacting to my moves and is no longer trying to follow any kind of plan. **Try to notice when the transition between thinking of your own ideas and reacting to the opponent takes place.** In this game, 1000 got lazy on move two and never woke up.

15.Ne5 Nxe5
16.dxe5

> 1000: "This is not working out well because I'm blocking my Queen."

A typical post-laziness mental process. The first stage is to get depressed and tell himself that he is doing badly.

16...Re8

> 1000: "I'm losing a pawn! I should have played h2-h3 earlier and stopped his ...g4 push."

The next stage is to panic and live in the past (I know because I've done it several hundred times in my career). Now he is thinking about all the things he could/should have done earlier in the game. Notice how even these dreams (h2-h3 to stop my ...g4 push) are defensive in nature.

We stopped the game and brought him back to reality with smelling salts.

Our next game starts from the same position.

(109)

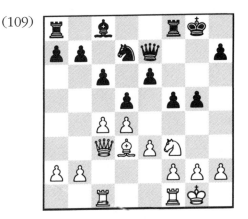

1700-Silman.
White to play.

1700: "All of Black's weaknesses are covered. His King is safe since his Queen and Rook defend. Black has a kingside attack. Material is even. White must defend the e4-square; Black would love to stuff a piece there. Black has more space. Where would both sides like to place their pieces? Well, e4 and e5 are the squares. Black also has an unguarded Queen on e7. If White can push his pawn to e4, followed by Re1, then the Queen on e7 would be bothered. So what is White's best move? I think White is in trouble. Black has space and kingside pressure. Black threatens ...g4 followed by ...Rf8-f6-h6. What can White do to prevent mate on h2?"

Very interesting! He noted that the e4- and e5-squares were important but he failed to note that e5 is a permanent weakness while anything on e4 can be chased away by f2-f3 or even taken by the Bishop. All the positive things that he said about Black's position would be true if the center stays closed. He mentioned the possibility of playing for e3-e4 (opening the center) but he gave up on it immediately. After the game, he told me that it would be too difficult to get e3-e4 in. Listen! If serious chess means you need thirty minutes to find an answer to the position, then that is time well-spent. If you can't solve the position, at least you will have the satisfaction of knowing that you tried as hard as you could. If you are White here and see that White's only hope is to play for e3-e4, don't just give up on the idea. That's like giving up on yourself! Insist on finding a way to make positive things happen.

13.Ne5 Nxe5
14.dxe5

1700: "Now his Rook can't go to f6."

I suppose this is kind of clever in a way. I decided not to fine him yet.

14...Bd7
15.f4

1700: "Trying to restrict his Bishop and equalize space on the kingside."

15...g4

1700: "I will block his Queen's path to h4 via g2-g3."

16.g3?

He is now in a completely defensive mentality. Who cares if my Queen goes to h4? A Queen by herself can't do much damage. He should have played on the queenside by b2-b4 or even c4-c5 (gaining more space). It's important to note that with the g-pawn on g2, Black's ...h7-h5-h4 advance has no sting since ...h4-h3 can be met by g2-g3 while ...g4-g3 is met by h2-h3. Now Black can advance his pawn to h4 and force open the h-file. White's fear led to the worsening of his own position.

16...h5

1700: "I still like Black but White stands better now than he did before. White has a much better minor piece but Black still has chances on the kingside. Black wants to pile up on the h-file."

17.Rf2 h4

1700: "I will bring my defenders around."

He has been reacting to my possibilities from the very beginning and he is still doing it. No wonder that his position gets worse with every move.

18.Rg2 Rf7

1700: "Expected. Now I run my King to safety."

19.Kf2 Rh7
20.Rh1 Kf7

1700: "Black is still piling up on the h-file by ...Rah8. Black will exchange on g3 and White must be ready for that but I can't stop him from killing me on the h-file."

The game was stopped here.

Our next example is from the same position, but now we have two children (a six-year-old girl and an eight-year-old boy) playing as a team against me.

(110)

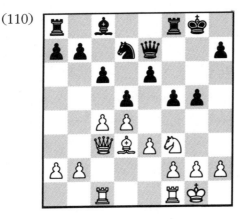

800 and 1100-Silman.
White to play.

800: "Black wants to attack us. It's scary."

1100: "I want to open files by cxd5, then I might move my Knight to e5."

13.cxd5 exd5

1100: "That's the best recapture. I want to get his King by Ne5 which might open the center and allow my pieces to get to him."

800: "That's a good idea."

I liked that 1100 saw that the Black King was getting a little open. Neither player is reacting to me yet; they are both still trying to create their own ideas.

14.Ne5 Nxe5
15.dxe5 Re8

1100 and 800: "We have to guard our pawn."

16.f4 g4

1100: "I will go Rce1 to attack in the center and bring my pieces over to the kingside."

800: "I want to play g3."

They argued for a while. So far, 1100's heart is in the right place—he wants to take control of the game but he does not know how to do it. His dreams of a central advance come too late, and queenside play via b2-b4-b5 was indicated. Unfortunately, 800 wants to react to imaginary threats and begins their demise by playing a defensive game.

1100: "17.g3 just moves a pawn and does nothing. My move is better."

800: "I want to block his pawn and stop ...Qh4."

1100: "You have to concentrate on our plan and not worry about his."

800 won the argument (showing an advanced knowledge of marriage but little of chess) and got her way because they had agreed on 1100's ideas earlier. 1100's last comment was very wise and he deserves praise for it.

Ultimately, 800 got punished for her defensive strategy: I took all the change in her pockets.

17.g3 Be6

> 1100 and 800: "We are not impressed with this move since your Bishop is blocked and bad."

They are both aware of good and bad Bishops.

18.Rce1

1100 made this useless move since it was his turn to get his way. Is this getting his Rook into the game? No. Is this creating open files for his Rooks? No. You must create open files for your Rooks, so b2-b4 followed by Rcb1, Rfc1 and b4-b5 was called for (this plan is known as a minority attack).

18...h5

> 800: "I hate it when people do scary moves. He's threatening ...h4."

> 1100: "I want to move Qc2 to defend on the second rank and attack f5."

> 800: "I'm really worried about ...h4 and want to play h4 myself."

Having talked themselves into a state of panic, they both agreed.

19.h4

> 1100 and 800: "Oh no! He can take enpassant!"

We stopped the game at this point.

Tips

★ Find a chess teacher who won't fine you for your errors.

★ Don't fear retreating moves if they accomplish some sort of important goal. It is not unmanly to move a piece backwards!

★ Take note of the transition between positive thoughts involving active plans and negative thoughts revolving around reactions and defense.

★ Insist on making good things happen for your position. If it takes you a lot of time to find these ideas, then consider this time well-spent.

★ Before you take time out to stop a threat, make sure that his move is something you should really be afraid of. If it isn't, then go ahead with your own ideas!

★ If someone tries to attack you on the wing, break open the center as quickly as possible.

In our next game, we see how an amateur handles a quiet position. Will he demand kingside action or will he calmly look to the center or queenside for answers?

1.d4 Nf6 2.c4 g6 3.Nc3 Bg7 4.e4 d6 5.Be2 0-0 6.Bg5 (the Averbach Variation of the King's Indian Defense) **6...c5 7.d5 e6 8.Qd2 exd5 9.exd5 Re8 10.Nf3 Bg4 11.0-0 Nbd7** are the moves that led to the position in diagram 111.

(111)

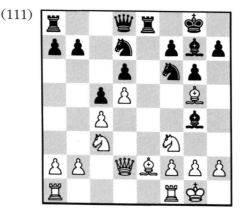

2100-Silman.
White to play.

2100: "There is no way to direct an effective attack on d6. What is a good strategic plan? Black's light-squared Bishop is not in a good position. It is not doing anything on g4.

Black's dark-squared Bishop is strong, though. The Bishop on g5 is not doing anything other than pinning the Knight. One plan is to trade the g4- and e2-Bishops; my e2-Bishop is horrendous. My first plan of action is to create some sort of imbalance. 12.h3 Bxf3 leaves me with two Bishops. He gets the e5-square but it's something to work with."

He did not mention that White had more central space. I did like his thought that, though the two Bishops are nothing to crow about in this position, at least it gave him something to work with. His willingness to create an imbalance and then try to make use of it in the future shows that 2100 has improved his understanding of the game.

12.h3 Bxf3
13.Bxf3 a6
14.a4

> 2100: "Stops any sacrifices with ...b5 and threatens a4-a5 with potential queenside play based on the extra territory there."

I love it! He is killing counterplay and gaining space. This sounds simple—in fact, it *is* simple. However, most amateurs aren't able to employ this kind of positive (since it gains space) prophylactic maneuver.

14...Qe7

> 2100: "What does that do? I want to play Rfe1 when ...Ne5 is met by Be2 and Bf1 with a solid game and a pin along the e-file."

15.Rfe1 Qf8

> 2100: "Yech! One of his ideas is to defend d6 and chase off the g5-Bishop. However, the Queen is entombed on f8 so I don't like the maneuver much. I will continue to play for a queenside space-advantage with a4-a5."

Nothing much is going on in the center (except a bunch of trades along the e-file) and Black's King is far too safe to attack. Due to this, White plays to gain the upper hand on the queenside and also hopes to make use of his two Bishops in a later endgame.

16.a5 Rxe1+
17.Rxe1 Re8

> 2100: "Getting rid of the Rooks. What's that do? My imbalance consists of two Bishops so I must open things up. If I trade Rooks, his minor pieces will probably kill me due to the various weak squares. I'll try to get some play with Rb1 and b2-b4."

I don't know what he is talking about when he alludes to the weak squares in White's camp. However, his decision to play Rb1 and b2-b4 is excellent. He has a space edge on the queenside and now intends to increase it with the line-opening b2-b4.

18.Rb1!

> 2100: "Black has the center under control. I have two Bishops but they are not doing much at the moment."

18...h6

> 2100: "Since my plan is b2-b4, I want to hit c5 with everything I have. 19.Bf4 does nothing due to ...Ne5."

Another excellent piece of reasoning. By playing Be3, he begins to eye a common target (c5) with several units. Don't just attack a point with one piece. Use everything you own!

19.Be3 Ne5
20.Be2 Nfd7

> 2100: "Now I should continue my plan by b2-b4. Winning a piece with 21.f4 is tempting, but it fails to 21...Nxc4! 22.Bxc4 Rxe3 23.Qxe3 Bd4. I will continue on the queenside and at a later time push him back with f2-f4. It is important for me to realize that his Knight on e5 is not permanent—I can chase it away some day."

21.b4 and we stopped the game since our lesson time was over. White has the advantage because he recognized that his play would come on the queenside and he went for it with great energy.

Tips

★ Some imbalances, like the two Bishops, may not be too useful right away. However, they could easily become a force later in the game.

★ In closed or semi-closed positions, you usually play in the sector where you own the most space.

White's queenside strategy was very effective in the last game, but most amateurs have a tendency to reject queenside or central play; their eyes are only aimed at the King. This tunnel vision is not acceptable! You can't become good at chess unless you can make use of all three areas of the board.

Our next position (from the Tartakower Variation of the Queen's Gambit Declined) was reached after **1.d4 d5 2.c4 e6 3.Nc3 Nf6 4.Bg5 Be7 5.e3 0-0 6.Nf3 h6 7.Bh4 b6 8.cxd5 exd5 9.Be2 Bb7 10.Bxf6 Bxf6 11.Rc1 Nd7 12.b4 Re8**.

(112)

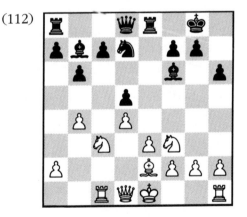

1550-Silman.
White to play.

1550: "Black's light-squared Bishop is blocked in and his c-pawn is backward. I have good central control of the light-squares. I could attack his d-pawn with Qb3 when ...c6 defends it though it blocks in his Bishop. I'm not castled yet but my King is in no immediate danger, though it would be useful to get my other Rook into the game. The points of attack are d5 and c7. As much as I'm tempted to attack the d-pawn, I think I'll castle and complete my development."

So far, so good. He notices that c7 and d5 are the targets, though he did not mention that b2-b4 gained queenside space and prevented Black's liberating ...c7-c5 (nor did he notice the powerful 13.Nb5!, a move I stop on my next turn).

13.0-0 a6

1550: "This seems silly because it blocks his Bishop. It prepares ...b6-b5, I guess, but I don't really know what that would accomplish. It doesn't really seem to do much of anything for him. Maybe he is trying to play ...c5 and it stops me from answering with b5. This must be what he has in mind. This is not such a terrible threat, so I should get back to my own plans. If 14.Qb3 c5, 15.Nxd5 is possible. What are my other points of attack? Let's look at the kingside. There's nothing there; his Bishop on f6 is a little suspicious— without a Knight there I have some possibilities. His h7-square looks weak to me. 14.Qd3 eyes both h7 and a6.

"Let's go back to basics. What are the imbalances? He has two Bishops so I would like to trade a pair of Bishops, but how do I go about it? That's one thing that a6 does, it keeps me off of b5. How about Qc2 and Bd3 and e3-e4? That would liberate his Bishop. How about Bd3 followed by Ne2 and Nf4? Does this do anything? Back to Qb3. How does he defend his pawn? He has ...Nf8 or ...c6. He won't want to stick his Knight back in the corner so 14...c6 15.Bd3. Maybe even Bd1 with the idea of Bc2 and Qd3. Yes! That would threaten a mate. Then Ne2-f4 follows his ...g6 defense with an attack."

He had quite a think! Several important points were mentioned and he even asked about the imbalances. However, he is so caught up in creating immediate threats that he didn't seriously entertain a slower plan based on a gradual buildup of queenside pressure by Qb3, Rc2 and Rac1 (eyeing c7). He could also pressure the d-pawn by Ne1-d3-f4 and Bf3.

What is most interesting is that he knew that the queenside is where he is supposed to play, but he is desperately looking for any excuse to initiate play on the kingside. Once he noticed the

Bd1-c2 followed by Qd3 idea (which is quite wrong), he was helpless to resist!

14.Qb3 c6

> 1550: "He did what I thought he would do. Is there any drawback to my Bd1 idea? Seems all right."

He was tempted by the prospect of a kingside attack and he can't say no to the siren call. White should continue on the queenside or switch to a central break with Bd3, Rfe1 and e3-e4. This is now effective since Black's light-squared Bishop no longer influences the e4-square.

15.Bd1 Be7

> 1550: "What is this? Oh, he is attacking b4. Is this a threat? No, I can ignore his threat for now and play either Bc2 or Ne2. My point of attack is c6 but only my Rook can attack it unless I can somehow get in Ne5. I could also double Rooks so I can afford to take some time. I think I'll go ahead with Ne2 and my attack. This also gives me options of Qd3 followed by Bb3."

All of a sudden, he decides that he has plenty of time (which he does) but he still goes ahead with his kingside hopes. One of the things he's done well during the last several moves is to always try to understand the point behind his opponent's move. This is a good habit that will save him in lots of games. If you know what the enemy is up to, you will not have to suffer through unpleasant surprises. This doesn't mean that he actually understood what Black was really doing, but he gave it his best shot.

Another highlight of 1550's thinking is his ability to ignore the opponent's threats. Once he sees what Black is up to, he refuses to react to it, always preferring to follow his own plans.

16.Ne2 Bd6

> 1550: "I didn't anticipate that. It stops both Nf4 and Ne5. My Knight can go to g3 but where can it go from there? His Bishops are starting to look menacing. His pawns are potentially weak but at the moment they are all well defended. I'm losing track of my points of attack while I screw around with this mating attack. 17.Qd3 pressures his

a-pawn and also threatens Ba4 with an attack on c6. Oops…if I play Qd3, my pawn hangs. Perhaps a2-a3 is in order to free my Queen."

Since Black's pawns point to the kingside, Black turns his Bishop's attentions to that side of the board. Black has stopped White's plans, so 1550 starts to panic. To his credit, he defends his pawn and tries to keep everything safe.

17.a3 Qe7

1550: "He is trying to play for ...a6-a5 to free his Rook. He's slowly taking the initiative by finding my points of attack. How do I stop this threat? My Rooks are not linked. What if I go back to my original plan with Qd3? What does that open up for me? After Bc2 and Qd3, he will be forced to play ...g6. Then I can follow with Ng3 and Nh5. Can I just ignore his stuff?"

This whole kingside idea is bogus since Black can safely defend h7 with ...g6 or with ...Nf6 or ...Nf8. The student should take note of the White pieces. Are they all working for a central break with e3-e4? No. Are they working together to pressure the queenside? Two of them are, the rest are just sitting around doing nothing.

White went wrong by playing a bit on one side and a bit on the other. You must figure out where you want to play right away and make your whole army devote itself to that plan. We stopped the game.

Tips

★ Pick a side of the board and stake a claim! Go after it with gusto and don't allow the opponent or your secret desires to distract you.

★ The kingside is not the end-all and be-all of chess. Seeking play in the center or on the queenside is just as effective (often more so) as a kingside attack.

A direct kingside attacking set-up in an open position can be very dangerous, and the defender should start a central and/or queenside counterattack right away. When facing a kingside attack in an open position, speed is of the essence and you must play with a lot of energy or fall victim to the enemy's attack.

The moves that led to diagram 113 were: **1.e4 c5 2.Nf3 e6 3.c3** (the Alapin Variation of the Sicilian Defense) **3...Nf6 4.e5 Nd5 5.d4 cxd4 6.cxd4 d6 7.a3 Nc6 8.Bd3 Be7 9.0-0 0-0 10.Re1 dxe5 11.dxe5 Bd7**.

(113)

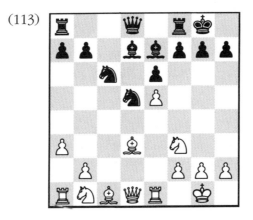

2100-Silman.
White to play.

2100: "A plan involving Qe2-e4 looks very strong."

This is a dangerous idea for Black and it fits very well into the placement of the other White forces: both his Bishops aim at the Black kingside and the e5-pawn stakes a claim to kingside space.

12.Qe2 Na5

> 2100: "Heading for the b3-square. I probably don't mind giving him my dark-squared Bishop for his Knight. Since Nd2 fails to ...Nf4, I can look at letting him into b3 via ...Nb3 when Bxh7+ can be met by ...Kh8 and several of my pieces hang. So I can't rely on cheap tactics. I have to somehow get my queenside pieces out. I'll stop his threat by a calm Bc2."

13.Bc2?

This poor move shows that White is beginning to react to the Black counterattack; just what the second player had hoped for. White should have made a play for the initiative with 13.Qe4 when 13...g6 14.Bh6 Re8 15.Nbd2 takes care of everything in an economical way.

13...Rc8

2100: "Now on b2-b4 he has ...Nc4 but I don't know if this really does anything."

14.b4?

White is still playing on the wrong side of the board. 14.b2-b4 creates new weaknesses on the c-file and forces the Black Knight to a nice square.

14...Nc4

2100: "I want to play Nbd2 but that would leave my Bishop on c2 undefended. First, I will defend it with tempo."

15.Qd3 g6
16.Bh6

2100: "Taking advantage of the newly-created dark-square holes."

16...Re8

2100: "Black has two nice Knights but his kingside is badly weakened. If I don't play actively, I can get mauled on the queenside. I would like to transfer my Queen to the kingside but I'm not sure how to do this. His Knights are strong and I would like to trade one of them. His d5-Knight is really bothersome so I will get rid of it with 17.Nc3 (I showed him 17...Nb2 which wins a piece so he took it back and placed the Knight on d2)."

17.Nbd2 b5

2100: "If I take his Knight, his passer is dangerous. However, his c5-square is also weakened but I think I will ignore this and play for mate."

He should have followed this "mate or die" philosophy much earlier in the game. If your game is geared for a kingside attack, you must attack like a maniac or risk drowning in the opponent's counterplay.

18.Ne4 Qc7

> 2100: "How to stop his threats? Both 19...Nxe5 and 19...Nb2! are in the air."

We stopped the game, though White could have gotten right back in the game by 19.Qd4! when the threat of Nd6 (since a capture on d6 opens up thye d4-g7 diagonal) is annoying (play would be about equal after 19...Qb6).

It's clear that you can't appreciate your possibilities if you give up on your own position!

Tips

★ If the board calls for a kingside attack, then you *must* attack.

★ In an open position, you must get your attack up and running as quickly as possible. If you do things too slowly, the opponent's counterplay will lead to his taking the initiative.

I t's time to develop an attitude! Since chess is largely a game of psychology, you must believe in yourself if you are going to have any hope of achieving good results. As soon as doubts enter into the equation, the moves come more slowly, a tendency towards passivity raises its ugly head and you find yourself entertaining destructive thoughts concerning the horrible things (often imaginary) your opponent is going to do to you.

To illustrate how strong a part attitude plays, let's compare two of my students. Student number-one is ten years old and knows very little about the game. He has no positional understanding at all, plays the opening very poorly and thinks the endgame is an entirely different sport. With a style geared only for mating attacks one would think he would do poorly, but it turns out that he owns a 1900 rating and often beats players hundreds of points higher than himself! His success is made possible by an overwhelming desire to win every game. When he plays a move, you know it has some mean intention behind it.

Student number-two is fifty years old and possesses the positional understanding of an expert, a solid opening repertoire and a fair knowledge of the endgame. Superior in almost every respect to student number-one, he only has a rating of 1500. The reason? He lacks confidence and is too quick to give up on his plans in the face of imaginary threats.

The following suggestions should prove helpful to anyone who regularly makes mental errors during a chess game:

1) **Always expect the opponent to see your threat and make the best reply. This forces you to look for moves that improve your position even if he is aware of your plans.**

2) **Play to win against anyone and everyone. Even if a draw suffices to give you a high placing in the final round of a tournament, playing to split the point is one of the best ways to lose a game. Play to win and make *him* beg *you* for the draw!**

3) **If you find a plan that conforms to the demands of the position, follow through with it. Don't allow the opponent to say "boo" and scare you from your proper path.**

4) **Play with confidence. Never allow yourself to believe that you are playing some sort of perfect chess machine (they don't exist). All human opponents make errors and have lapses. This means that everyone can be beaten. Play without fear (after all, we are all going to lose lots of games, so there is nothing to be afraid of, is there?) and you will instill fear into your opponents.**

5) **If you find yourself in a lost position, tighten everything up and hang on like grim death—don't play one last cheap shot and resign. Play the move that you would hate to see if you were in his situation. Extending the game in this manner will make**

him work hard for the point and, if he gets tired or frustrated, may even lead to a mistake on his part and a success for you.

6) If your opponent is in time pressure, never try to move quickly and push him over on the clock. Take your time and concentrate on making the best moves. Moving fast places you in the same situation that he is in and gives you an excellent chance to make a major error.

• • • • •

The most common mental error in chess is that of supplication: you begin to get worried about your opponent's plans, you stop implementing your own ideas and just react to his and, finally, you end up completely on the defensive. We have seen examples of this condition throughout this book. Here is another look at a disease that must be tamed before you can expect good results.

Our diagrammed position came about after **1.c4 e5 2.Nc3 Nc6 3.g3 g6 4.Bg2 Bg7 5.d3 d6 6.Nf3 Nf6 7.0-0 0-0**.

(114)

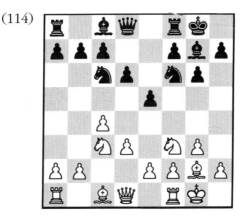

1378-Silman. English Opening.
White to play.

1378: "White's pawns are pointing towards the queenside, so according to the Silman pawn-pointing theory I should be playing on that side of the board. What about Black? His pawns are aiming at my kingside—I don't like that at all! Black will probably play ...Ne8 followed by ...f7-f5 and try to mate me. I can't allow him to do that so I'll stop his plans with Bg5, pinning and immobilizing his Knight."

White's correct plan is 8.Rb1 followed by the space-gaining b4-b5. Unfortunately, after only seven moves White demonstrates a losing attitude by concentrating on Black's ideas to the exclusion of his own plans. It is very important to realize that White has already planted the seeds of his own defeat by refusing to take a more aggressive stance. This doesn't mean that you always have to attack. It means that every move you play should do something positive for your position. Keep this idea in mind: After deciding what move you want to play, write it down, look at all possible checks and captures and ask, "What wonderful thing does this move do for my position?" If your move doesn't stand up to this simple question, then don't play it!

Actually, White's 8.Bg5 is not bad. By getting rid of the Knight on f6, White fights for control of d5. Unfortunately, this is not why White played it. He was thinking about nothing more than stopping the enemy from attacking him—pure defense and nothing else. The best way to get an opponent to stop his aggressive intentions is to worry him with your own plans.

8.Bg5 h6

> 1378: "Taking his Knight would be bad because he would just recapture, move the piece away, and advance his pawn to f5. I need to retain this Bishop with a retreat."

Still mesmerized by Black's kingside potential, White accepts a further loss of time. He still has not made one move towards his queenside attack. Best was 8.Bxf6 when the d5-square has been weakened and White is free to proceed with his own plans on the opposite wing. Don't just wish you had play somewhere. The great players insist on getting play—they *make* it happen!

9.Be3? Be6

> 1378: "He might be getting ready to push his pawn to d5. I can move my f3-Knight and put more pressure on the d5-square."

White is still in defensive mode; he's twitching to Black's tune. 10.Rb1 followed by 11.b4 is indicated. Actually, White would be happy if Black played for ...d6-d5 since that would lead to an open queenside file (the c-file) after cxd5.

10.Nd2? Ng4

> 1378: "He's attacking my Bishop and I can't move it to safety. I suppose I should get things started on the queenside with 11.Rc1, when a later ...d5 allows me to create a semi-open file."

More incorrect thinking. Rather than take matters into his own hands, White plays a move that may be good "someday." I'm sorry, but this is not good enough. There is no room in chess for words such as "maybe," "someday" and "somehow." Either a move does something, or it doesn't. Don't rely on your opponent to make your moves useful.

11.Rc1? f5

> 1378: "I have to chase his Knight away."

White has given up all hope of finding an active plan or even of thinking ahead. He is now simply reacting from move to move and has completed his slide into mental paralysis.

12.h3?

This horrible move wastes more time and weakens the kingside. An aggressive move like 12.Nd5 (preventing ...f5-f4) would at least force Black to think a little bit.

12...Nxe3
13.fxe3 h5

> 1378: "He threatens ...h5-h4 so I have to stop him."

Poor White is so freaked out that he sees danger in every Black move. Why did Black play his 13th move? Chess is largely a game of targets (weak pawns are the most common type of target, but weakened squares and a vulnerable King may also fall into our category) and I often talk of "target consciousness" in my lessons.

Two skills must be honed: 1) the ability to recognize and create targets; 2) the ability to attack them with as much energy as possible. Black's last move, ...h6-h5, was designed to allow the g7-Bishop to start an attack against White's newly weakened e3-pawn.

14.h4

Attacking on different wings is a common part of chess and such a situation often creates a very violent struggle. The first player to give up on his own play and pay attention to the opponent's will most likely end up losing. In fact, it's your job to sell him on your plan. I liken this to grabbing the opponent's head and physically turning it in the direction you want him to face. Once you get him reacting to your threats (playing your game), he will no longer be thinking in terms of progressing with his own ideas. Then your victory will only be a matter of time.

14...Bh6

> 1378: "Now he's attacking e3. I can only defend with the King and the Rook. If 15.Rf3, e4 16.dxe4 Ne5 is possible so the King move is forced."

Though 1378 was being trained in my system of thinking (as explained in the third edition of *How To Reassess Your Chess*), he didn't make use of it at all in this game. As you can see from 1378's experience, living from move-to-move without ever looking at the imbalances or trying to assert mental mastery over the opponent will give you nothing but a miserable defensive chore and a likely loss.

15.Kf2?

Strange, White got so worried about the weakness on e3 that he completely forgot about the danger to his own King. 15.Nd5 would have held out a little longer, but White's game was already an unhappy mess.

15...f4

Destroying the King's protection. Why have White's worst fears come true? Picture a car race. You have two ways to avoid defeat. You can either beat your opponent to the finish line or you can stand in front of his car and try to stop it.

In this game, White could not really stop Black from carrying out his plan of kingside pressure. His only hope was to go for the finish line and try to prove that his queenside play was more valuable than Black's play on the opposite wing. Failing to do this, White played into Black's plans, created weaknesses in his own camp and got run down by an opponent who was bigger and stronger on the kingside due to Black's space advantage in that area. This is where reading the imbalances comes into play: if you can't list the imbalances, you won't know which side of the board to play on. In other words, you'll be playing blind.

At this point we decided to stop the game.

How is it that 1378, an aggressive player who works hard at the board, played so passively? The answer is that when you get involved in a particular frame of mind, it's hard to extricate yourself from it (ever hear a song and have it play in your head for the rest of the day?); any person who starts thinking in a passive, fearful manner will find his/her attitude getting progressively worse. This disease can only be prevented by recognizing the problem and making a concerted effort to eradicate it.

I recommend the following simple study technique for those players who are affected by this defensive/reactive malady: Go through your losses and make a note at the point where you think you gave control to your opponent **(note the distinction between the opponent taking control and you giving it away)**. When you have done this, look at the imbalances and try to find what the correct moves and ideas should have been (of course, the moves and ideas must be based on those imbalances!). If you want to win, you must demand a constructive continuation from yourself, so don't give up until you find something that fits the above criteria. What we are trying to do is create an attitude where you will not accept anything but a complete effort from yourself. The creation of proper mental habits will lead to a more satisfying tournament experience.

Another common mental error is the tendency to see threats where none exist. When you react to imaginary threats, you are often wasting time trying to prevent the opponent from making a bad move! Don't go out of your way to prevent something unless you are sure that it would *really* be a problem.

In the following example, we see an amateur who is afraid of what Black does and also of what Black *might* do!

(115)

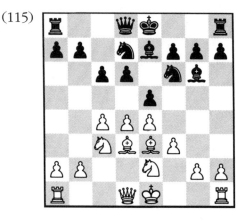

1413-Silman.
White to play.

The position in the diagram was reached after **1.d4 Nf6 2.c4 d6 3.Nc3 Bf5 4.f3 Nbd7 5.e4 Bg6 6.Be3 c6 7.Bd3 e5 8.Nge2 Be7**.

> 1413: "White has a space edge over the whole board—even in development. I think it's time to get my King out of the center."

1413 noted that he owned a space advantage but he did not even try to come up with an active plan. Of course, it's quite possible to devote all your attention to the extra space; if you can gain enough territory, your opponent might end up getting squeezed to death. Unfortunately, White made no real effort to dissect this position and his moves will eventually reflect this.

9.0-0 0-0

> 1413: "Black would like to trade pieces and relieve his cramp. I will play d4-d5 to gain space in the center and, if he takes, I get an open c-file."

Not bad, but he is basing his play on Black opening the c-file for him. You can't expect your opponent to do what you want him to do.

10.d5 a5

> 1413: "I will play a2-a4 to control b5 and shut his queenside play down."

What queenside play? Just because Black pushed his pawn to a5 doesn't necessarily mean that he has play on the queenside. Actually, White could dictate matters on that side of the board with 11.a3 followed by 12.b4 with lots of territory. Instead of this logical, positive continuation, he begins to react to the opponent.

11.a4?

Handing over the b4- and c5-squares for no reason whatsoever. The recommended 11.a3 followed by 12.b4 leaves White in control of both these points.

11...h6

> 1413: "Black wants to play ...Bh7 and ...g7-g5 and get more space on the kingside. I'm also looking at the kingside and Ng3, which eyes f5."

As usual, 1413 falls victim to the amateur malady of "King fear." Amateurs always think that the opponent wants to start a mating attack (which Black had no intention of doing), while White dreams of doing the same thing to Black's King!

12.Ng3 Nc5

> 1413: "He wants to take the d3-Bishop and maybe play ...Na6-b4. I'll shut that down with Bxc5 and leave him with two inactive Bishops."

Why would Black want to capture the bad piece on d3 with his fine c5-Knight? White's idea of playing for a superior minor piece deserves praise, but his reason for doing so was based on fear; fear of a threat (...Nxd3) that Black would never have done!

13.Bxc5 dxc5

> 1413: "I'll continue with my queenside play and go for pressure on b7."

14.Qb3

You only get real pressure on the enemy position if you can attack a point with several of your pieces. Remember that chess is a team effort, all your army should participate. 14.Qb3 is an obvious one-move threat that forces Black to move his Queen to a good square.

14...Qc7

> 1413: "He connected his Rooks and protected b7 and e5. I will prepare for f4 by Nce2."

Now he loses focus and forgets about his reasons for the capture on c5. Originally he wanted to leave Black with two inactive Bishops (actually, the Bishop on e7 is bad. The guy on g6 is good by definition but is obviously doing very little) but now he goes for f3-f4, a move that opens the position and frees the e7-Bishop.

15.Nce2 Nd7

> 1413: "Right now, Black has the Bishop pair. His dark-squared Bishop is bad but my Bishop stinks. My g3-Knight is more active than his and I have more central space. It's pretty even over all. I will go ahead with the pawn push."

He said some good things but what did all those factors have to do with him pushing his f-pawn? Nothing at all! Only play moves that highlight your positive imbalances.

16.f4?

> 1413: "Trying to open up my Rooks."

His 16.f4 did open the f-file for his Rooks but it also activated Black's dark-squared Bishop, gave Black play on the e-file and allowed the Black Knight to take up residence on e5. You tell me who got the better deal.

16...exf4
17.Nxf4 Bd6
18.Nxg6 fxg6
19.Be2

1413: "This allows my Queen access to the kingside and defends my Knight."

White now has two connected passed pawns in the center, but both of these pawns will be firmly blocked. Black has made serious gains in the form of nice posts for his pieces while White, after a brief but suicidal bit of activity, is still reacting to his opponent.

19...Bxg3

1413: "It's ugly, but I'll retake with the pawn."

20.hxg3 Ne5

1413: "I don't want to trade Rooks because my Bishop is horrible. His Knight would be far superior to my Bishop."

He noticed the minor piece situation but it's now far too late to do anything about it!

21.Bf3 Rf6

1413: "He will double up. I'll try the same thing, simply because I don't know what else to do."

Still reacting.

22.Rf2 Raf8
23.Raf1 g5 and the game was stopped.

Tips

★ If you find yourself reacting to the opponent's ideas, you're walking the road to doom and destruction.

★ Figure out which side of the board you're supposed to play on and then claim that area of the board as quickly as possible. Don't let anything distract you from this holy goal!

★ When you are about to make a move, always ask, "What wonderful things is this move doing for my position?" If you can't answer this question, don't play the move!

★ Don't just wish you had play somewhere. It's your job to make it happen!

★ Don't hand over key squares to your opponent. The idea of holding squares is alien to many amateurs. Work hard to make this concept a major part of your strategic repertoire!

★ Always be aware of the battle to make your minor piece superior to your opponent's.

___

To avoid the unfortunate spiral into the abyss (be it on the board or in one's mind) that these amateur's experienced, I give these additional recommendations:

➤ Don't look at your opponent's rating before the game. This prevents you from freezing up and getting into a defensive "I want to draw" type of mindset. Once you convince yourself that the opponent is a chess god, you might as well resign and take up knitting. Treat everyone you play with a touch of contempt! There is nothing a higher rated player hates to see more than an opponent who refuses to be respectful to a superior. A positive "win at all costs" attitude will add at least 150 rating points to your stats!

➤ Always have a plan and never forget that the only plan that matters is yours. The opponent's ideas should be treated as nothing more than minor annoyances; swat them away if they start to sting, and then go back to what you were doing.

Now let's explore two other subjects: giving up and depression. Sometimes things don't go the way we wanted and we find that defeat appears to be looming. Depressed over this state of affairs, we make a few hopeless moves and accept our fate.

Don't let this happen to you! Fight back! Often we have more play than we supposed but we are trapped in a negative mindset and become blind to these promising possibilities. I remember one game in which I had been suffering for a long time. Finally I couldn't stand the abuse anymore and so I resigned. Looking at me as if I were a vegetable, my opponent (a well-known Grandmaster) said:

"What are you doing?"

"I'm giving up. It's lost."

"Lost? I was about to offer a draw. You have an immediate perpetual check!"

When I heard this, I felt like a blindfold had been torn from my eyes. I immediately saw the draw, ripe and tempting, but now out of my reach, since I had irrationally laid down my arms.

(116)

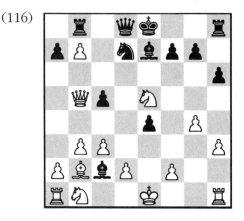

1857-1685.
Black to play.

This position shows despair in action. My student (1685) felt a deep sense of hopelessness when he looked at this situation, and a glance might tell us that this negative attitude was justified. Black is two pawns down, he is not castled, his Knight is pinned to his King and Nc6 looms as a powerful threat. In the game, Black saw the Queens were going to be traded (not something you normally want when you are down material), but since there was no apparent way out he opted for 1...Qc7?? which at least attacked the Knight and stopped Nc6. However, after 2.Qxd7+ Qxd7 3.Nxd7 Kxd7 4.Na3 followed by 5.0-0-0 White enjoyed good winning chances.

All his thoughts smacked of defeatism because Black only concentrated on the negative qualities of his position. He never bothered to ask what was *right* about his game. Though material down, he is ahead in development and has chances of an attack based on the weakened light-squares on f3 and d3. If the Queens and Knights go off, these attacking chances evaporate, so you *must* find a way to retain your army and make use of the advantages you have.

1...Rxb7!!

This stops Nc6 and breaks the pin along the a4-e8 diagonal. It's true that Black loses some more material (not that much, though—just a Rook for a Knight and pawn), but he is able to train his sights upon the weakened light-squares in White's camp.

2.Qxb7 Nxe5 and all of a sudden White is facing threats of ...Nf3+ and ...Nd3+. This turns the game around and leaves Black with a very powerful attack. Material doesn't matter; Black had already sacrificed a couple of pawns for the advantages just listed and throwing out some more ballast should not make him blink. The moral? Don't go along with the opponent's agenda! Don't allow yourself to be herded around like a sacrificial lamb! Look hard for the plusses in your position and *insist* on making use of them.

So far, we have only discussed a negative, defeatist attitude. What about overconfidence? Can that be a problem? Most definitely! When you fall into the trap of overconfidence, you cease to concentrate properly. You "know" you are going to win and, as a result, stop looking at the board in an honest manner. This lack of attention makes you miss ways to finish up the game quickly and leaves you open to tricks, traps and time-pressure blunders.

(117)

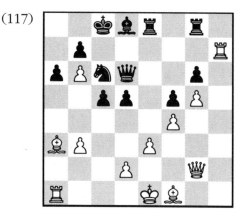

Caluag-Burtman, Los Angeles 1993.
White to play.

Black, an expert, was the higher-rated player and had been in control of the game the whole way. Burtman's advantage in space and the lack of coordination of the enemy pieces had convinced her that the win of material (the b6-pawn) and a quick victory were within reach. A few moves earlier she had been right, but she had fallen asleep during her last few turns and lost all sense of danger. After all, what could the opponent (a 1900 player) possibly do to her here? The answer proved to be a rude shock.

1.Bxa6!

All of a sudden, the White army is working together rather well! A safe advantage for Black has turned into an unpleasant tactical mess.

1...bxa6
2.Qe2

There's no good way to defend a6. For example, 2...Nb8 fails to 3.b7 mate!

2...Be7
3.Qxa6+ Kd7
4.Qb5 Ke6
5.d4 Nb4?

After the initial shock, Black once again became confident of her win and once again tunes out the tactical possibilities in the position. Here White, who was playing in a desperate frame of mind, gave in to the will of his opponent and somehow eventually lost after 6.Bxb4 cxb4 7.Rc1?? (missing an instant win by 7.b7 when there is no answer to the threat of 8.Ra6) 7...Rc8. However, White could have stolen a memorable point in another way: **6.dxc5 Qxc5 7.Rxe7+! Qxe7 8.Bxb4 Qd7 9.Qc5** (threatening 10.Qd4) with material equality and a winning attack.

It's funny, but both players were so stuck in their roles (Expert defeats Class "A" player) that neither was aware of the fact that Black was on the brink of extinction. I am quite sure that if the roles had been reversed, Sharon would have seen the danger. As Black, however, these lines were completely invisible to her simply because she had lulled herself to sleep—her overconfidence (which translates to a lack of vigilance) chopped hundreds of points off her strength.

Tips

★ A bad attitude will always lead to bad results.

★ Don't concentrate on what is wrong with your game. Concentrate on what is right with it and insist on making use of those positive imbalances.

★ It's great to be confident, but overconfidence can easily lead to a fatal loss of vigilance.

★ The game is not over until the opponent has resigned. Take pride in finishing the enemy off with gusto and never allow counterplay that might turn the battle around.

"**W**e don't have to go over this game, I already know where I went wrong."

I've heard this line from students for many years now, and in virtually every case, I find that their view of the game's errors was based on an opening mistake or a major tactical blunder. When I point out subtle errors (which are far more common and more important than mere blunders), they are often amazed to find that I'm criticizing moves and ideas that they were proud of in the actual game.

Ideally, one of the best ways to improve is to play a tournament game, deeply annotate it while trying to unearth the inaccuracies by both sides, and then show those annotations to a skilled chess teacher. The information this teacher will (hopefully!) bring to your attention will prove to be invaluable.

The following tests allow you to practice this technique. Though I'm not really there, by comparing your written comments with my answers, you should get a very personal and deep insight into the possibilities that this type of instruction offers.

What is Black's correct plan?

(118)

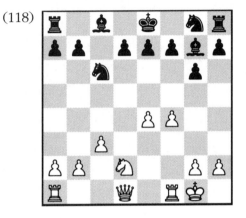

Black to play.

Find the correct move *and* the plan that goes along with it!

(119)

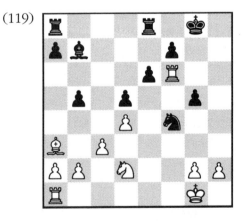

White to play.

#3

White's correct plan is far from obvious. Find his next two moves and beyond!

(120)

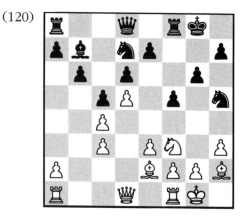

White to play.

#4

Who stands better and what is White's best move?

(121)

White to play.

#5

What is White's proper move and what's his proper plan?

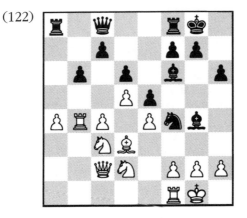

(122)

White to play.

#6

How can Black squeeze the most out of this position?

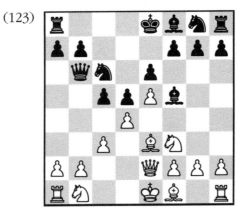

(123)

Black to play.

#7

Where should Black park his dark-squared Bishop?

(124)

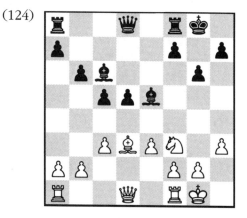

Black to play.

#8

The book move is 7...Be7. Does 7...g6 make any sense here?

(125)

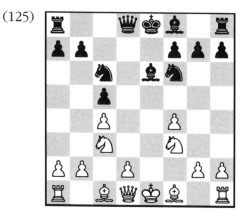

Black to play.

#9

Annotate this game and then go over my notes and see how your ideas and comments measured up.

1.e4 e6 2.d3 d5 3.Nd2 Nc6 4.Nf3 Bd6 5.g3 Ne7 6.Bg2 d4 7.0-0 Ng6 8.Nc4 e5 9.Nxd6 cxd6 10.b3 Bg4 11.Ba3 Qf6 12.h3 Bd7 13.Nd2 b5 14.Rc1 b4 15.Bb2 0-0 16.Nc4 Bc8 17.Qe2 Nce7 18.f4 exf4 19.e5 dxe5 20.Bxa8.

#10

Annotate this game and then go over my notes and see how your ideas and comments measured up.

1.d4 Nf6 2.Nf3 c5 3.e3 e6 4.Bd3 Nc6 5.c3 cxd4 6.exd4 d5 7.Nbd2 Bd6 8.0-0 0-0 9.Re1 Qc7 10.Nf1 h6 11.Qe2 Nd7 12.Bc2 Re8 13.Qd3 Nf8 14.h3 Bd7 15.N1h2 a6 16.a4 Rac8 17.Re2 Bxh2+ 18.Nxh2 Na5 19.Nf3 b5 20.Ne5 Nc4 21.Nxd7 Qxd7 22.Qg3 Kh8.

#11

What are all the imbalances? What side of the board should both you and your opponent play on? What is the best move or plan based, naturally, on the answers to the first two questions?

(126)

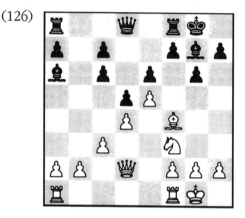

White to play.

#12

Is White doing all right in this position? What would you recommend?

(127)

White to play.

#13

List the imbalances and find a move that conforms to those differences.

(128)

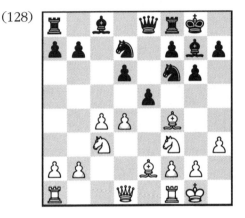

White to play.

#14

Scan the imbalances and then decide if 1.h4 followed by 2.Rh1 and h5 is justified.

(129)

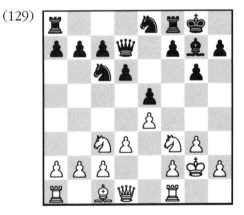

White to play.

#15

Is White justified in playing 1.h4 in this position?

(130)

White to play.

#16

Would 1.Bf4 be foolish here?

(131)

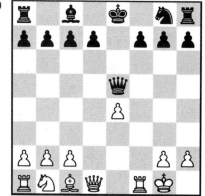

White to play.

#17

Don't bother looking for individual moves. Instead, figure out what White's correct plan is. Also, be aware of why you made this decision.

(132)

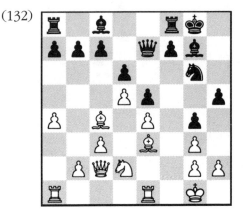

White to play.

#18

Black has just pushed his h-pawn from h7 to h5. Is this a good move, and how should White react to it?

(133)

White to play.

#19

How should White handle this position?

(134)

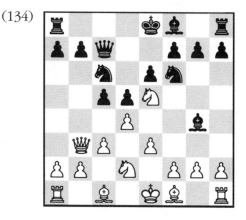

White to play.

#20

Black's center pawns look very threatening. How should White deal with this situation?

(135)

White to play.

#21

White has several tempting choices here. What would you do and why would you do it?

(136)

White to play.

#22

List the imbalances and then find a plan that helps White make use of his main plusses. What is White's best move?

(137)

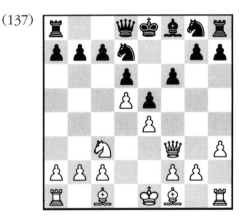

White to play.

#23

A big question comes to mind: should White capture on h6 and open up the g-file for Black's Rooks?

(138)

White to play.

#24

Black appears to have an excellent position. Is this true, and what should White do?

(139)

White to play.

#25

In the game White played 15.Bg6. Is this a good move? If you don't like it, what do you think he should have played?

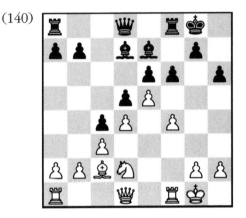

(140)

White to play.

#26

In the game, White played 1.Be4. What do you think of this move? Is it a logical choice?

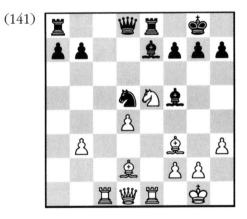

(141)

White to play.

TEST
SOLUTIONS

Each test solution starts with the problem's specifications. To offer the student the maximum instruction, I often give the moves leading to the actual problems/solutions (with copious notes) and the moves that follow. In many cases, I also add the occasional lecture and lesson summary.

Everyone has seen the term "losing the thread" in Grandmaster notes. It usually refers to a player who loses concentration and fails to understand what's really going on in the midst of a heavy battle. One useless move after another gets banged out and suddenly a good position, or even a winning one, quickly unravels into a ball of chaotic twine.

This dreaded "thread" affliction tends to be psychological in nature. You get a nice position, you relax (evidently thinking that it will play itself), one bad move leads to another (panic may set in at this point!) and suddenly you "wake up," only to discover that it's far too late.

Though everyone falls victim to this syndrome from time to time, steps can be taken to avoid it. The first thing you must do is to always INSIST on understanding the position to the best of your abilities. No position will play itself and, no matter how huge your advantage may be, almost any position can be lost if you set your mind to it.

Never tell yourself that you're winning. Doing this trivializes the technical process and can easily lead to "thread disease." Instead, learn to take great pride in pushing your opponent off the board in the safest and most economical fashion. In other words, when your position gets good, work twice as hard as you did earlier!

Class "A" player-Class "B" player. Los Angeles, 1998.
Sicilian Accelerated Dragon.

1.e4 c5
2.Nf3 Nc6
3.d4 cxd4
4.Nxd4 g6

This opening, known as the Accelerated Dragon, has long been a favorite of mine and many of my students.

5.Bc4

A rare move. White deprives himself of the "Maroczy Bind" (c2-c4) and, in addition, gives Black some original and highly tempting options.

5...Qa5+

I'm quite fond of this strange-looking move. Black tries to take immediate advantage of White's loose pieces on c4 and d4.

6.Bd2?

This is supposed to be an error (both 6.c3 and 6.Nc3 are better), but White flicked it out so fast that Black suddenly became convinced that his opponent had prepared the whole line. I suspect that part of this paranoia was forged by White's higher rating. If the first player had been rated 1200, Black would have accepted that his opponent didn't know what he was doing. However, since White was a mighty "A" player, Black has trouble believing that "big A" could make this kind of mistake so quickly!

Now, thanks to this self-imposed psychological burden, Black finds it difficult to take his mind off his opponent and onto the board.

6...Qc5

Black knew this move was supposed to be good. What had White cooked up?

7.Bc3

A good try in a bad situation. Both 7.Nxc6 Qxc4 (winning the e4-pawn) and 7.Nb5 Qxc4 8.Nc7+ Kd8 9.Nxa8 Qxe4+ (when the a8-Knight will never make it out alive), are worse.

7...Qxc4
8.Nd2

White's facade cracks, but the opening has been a disaster for the first player. Black might have been more scared by 8.Na3.

8...Qxd4

Grabbing three minor pieces for the Queen. Black now has an enormous advantage. Many players have trouble giving up their

Queen, so I was pleased to see Black (who is a student of mine) do this.

9.Bxd4 Nxd4
10.c3 Nc6
11.0-0 Bg7
12.f4

Problem Position

(142)

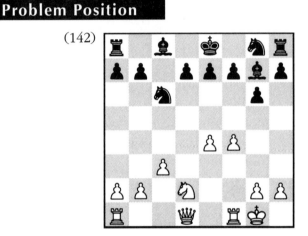

Black to play

What is Black's correct plan?

Solution

12...Nf6?

Black knew he was doing well, but his trepidation about the opening still left some residual doubt bouncing around in his head. This led to a state of confusion, and Black plays the rest of the game poorly.

Having won material, Black should have calmed down and focused himself to the task at hand. If you have the time, clearing your head with a small walk works wonders. Instead, he stayed seated, decided that he had to develop (hardly a deep assessment of the position!), and tossed his Knight out into the storm.

Better was the obvious 12...d6 when 13...Nf6 would have worked rather well. White's problem is that he doesn't have anything to attack in the Black position. Of course, Black should also be looking for ways to create targets in White's camp (this kind of basic thinking should not stop just because you've won material!). By moving his pawn to d6, he tells White that an e4-e5 advance will either lose a pawn or leave the first player with a weak e-pawn after ...dxe5. Having nullified e4-e5, Black could then have developed in peace. Plans like ...b7-b5-b4 would have eventually blasted open some lines and highlighted the superiority of Black's minor pieces over the White Queen.

13.e5 Nd5
14.Nc4

Suddenly Black's Knight is hanging out to dry, his g7-Bishop is blocked, and the c8-Bishop still can't get out of its cage. Black's still doing well, but these unexpected problems begin to drive home his earlier doubts.

14...Nb6

The c7-square was a more flexible home for this Knight. Now White will be able to gain more time battering the poor thing around.

15.Ne3 0-0
16.a4

Threatening to trap the b6-Knight with 17.a5. It's very important for White to keep Black busy; if the second player manages to get all his stuff out then his larger army will eventually overpower the lone White Queen.

16...a5?

Black has been reduced to reactionary chess: White makes a threat and Black reacts to it. The text leaves holes on b5 and b6. Less fatalistic was 16...Rb8 17.a5 Na8 18.Nd5 d6 19.exd6 exd6 when Black's pieces will finally be able to escape from their tomb.

17.Qb3

Still pointing a finger at that tortured horse.

17...Ra6

Ugly but forced.

18.Rad1

White has a limited army, so it's still very difficult to create any lasting threats.

18...Rd8
19.Qa3 d6

Black has lost faith in his position and now panic enters the picture. A serious reassessment of this situation would have told him that his dark-square Bishop isn't really doing much on g7. Thus, the calm 19...Bf8 (threatening 20...e6 followed by 21...Bc5) suggests itself.

20.exd6 Rxd6?

A serious error. Even after all his mistakes, Black could still have grabbed the initiative with 20...exd6 21.Rxd6 Bf8 22.Rxd8 Nxd8 23.Qb3 Bc5.

21.Rxd6 exd6
22.Qxd6 Nxa4?

Black's forces are not working together in any cohesive manner, and curing that problem (not grasping for material gains) should have been his main priority. This is an important thing to think about! **The creation of a unified plan should always take precedence over a random gain of material.**

23.Qc7 Ra8
24.Nc4

Black's uncoordinated forces are spread all over the place in a seemingly random fashion. The immediate threat is 25.Nd6, hitting both c8 and f7.

24...Bf8
25.f5!

An astute move, showing that White is paying close attention to detail. The immediate 25.Ra1? falls victim to 25...Nc5 26.Nb6 Ne6 when White's Queen is unexpectedly trapped! With f4-f5 thrown in, this line won't work for Black because the White Queen now has access to the newly-opened c7-g3 diagonal.

25...gxf5

Also depressing was 25...Bxf5 26.Qxb7.

26.Ra1 Bc5+

As mentioned earlier, 26...Nc5 27.Nb6 Ne6 now fails to 28.Qg3+.

27.Kh1 Nxc3

This horse, tormented throughout this game, is driven to suicide

28.bxc3, 1-0.

Tips

★ Always INSIST on understanding the position to the best of your abilities.

★ No position will play itself.

★ No matter how huge your advantage may be, almost any position can be lost if you set your mind to it.

★ Never tell yourself that you're winning. Just work as hard as possible and keep your mind centered (the victory celebration only starts after the game!).

★ Everyone blunders. If your opponent goes crazy, don't give him supernatural powers and decide that he can see mystical strands of energy that are invisible to you. Take the offered "gifts," look him straight in the eye, and dare him to do his worst!

★ A confident, defiant opponent makes the bravest (and highest-rated) player entertain a nagging doubt about his skills and yours.

★ The creation of a unified plan should always take precedence over a random gain of material.

#2

It has often been said that it takes more than one mistake to lose a chess game. Though this may not be true at the highest levels of the game, in general, we can agree that a typical amateur contest is filled with errors. Having embraced this truth, most players should be happy to realize that they will get several chances to win almost every game. Yes, you may have been the first to blunder, but somewhere, at some time, your opponent is going to slip up and give you an opportunity to claw your way back into the game.

The trick is, you must believe this with all your heart or you won't be on the lookout for those hard-to-see moves that WILL arise. A despondent, mentally-beaten player will actually find a way to lose, even if one win after another magically appears and screams to be noticed! This brings us to an interesting statement:

THE WINNER IS THE PLAYER WHO MAKES THE NEXT TO LAST MISTAKE!

Our next key point centers around psychology. If you feel that you are winning, don't refuse to pull the trigger just because your opponent is higher rated than you. Get angry, become stubborn; INSIST on coming up with a proper method of execution. Whatever you do, don't get cold feet when your instincts tell you that the game should be won. This line of reasoning takes us to our second point:

RESPECT NO OPPONENT!

So far I've painted a picture of a player (in a worst-case scenario) who goes into a game thinking that he really doesn't stand much chance of winning (fear of the higher-rated opponent) and also thinks that the guy sitting across the table is perfect and won't make any real mistakes (showing a complete lack of realism). This becomes a self-fulfilling prophecy since such a player really *won't* stand any chance!

The following game illustrates all of these points: The "mighty" higher-rated player (Black) indulges in a planless opening. Then

White (a "B" player) tosses his advantage out the window. Not to be shown up, the 2100-player once again falls into the gutter and soon has a resignable position. Not quite believing his luck (in other words, not believing that his opponent could really play so badly), White refuses to win the game, making one error after another until he becomes a mentally-beaten husk. This psychological collapse leads to yet another victory for the rating system.

Makarewicz-Darias (1780-2140), Los Angeles 1998.
Torre Attack.

1.d4 Nf6
2.Nf3 e6
3.Bg5 d5
4.e3 Be7
5.Bd3

The ever-popular Torre Attack: dynamic, easy to learn and fun to play. Who could ask for more in an opening system?

5...0-0
6.0-0

Natural but inaccurate. Better is 6.Nbd2 when 6...c5 7.c3 Nc6 could be met by 8.Ne5 with a nice game for White. The trick to this opening (from White's point of view) resides in control over e5. When Black moves his b8-Knight to d7 or c6 he threatens to "win" e5 with ...Qc7. White can't allow this! In general, White must be ready to meet ...Nc6 or ...Nbd7 with Ne5 when the threat of f2-f4 clamps down on e5 and gives him good chances on the kingside.

6...c5
7.c3 Nc6
8.Nbd2 b6?!

Missing his chance. White's opponent has just demonstrated that he doesn't understand the position at all. Correct was 8...Qc7 when the threat of 9...e5 guarantees Black good chances (note that 8...Qc7 9.Bf4 Bd6 won't help White).

It's important to point out that Black has fallen into a very dangerous mental trap: he's developing his pieces without any clear plan in mind. Such a "strategy" will usually lead to real trouble. Naturally, you should train yourself to avoid this kind of lazy thinking.

9.Qe2

White isn't aware of the Ne5 idea. Naturally, 9.Ne5 would still have been good. White was familiar with the Colle and thought he was playing that opening (and its plan of preparing for e3-e4) with the Bishop on g5.

9...cxd4?

A poor move that opens the e-file for White and cuts down on Black's options. In effect, Black is trading his good c5-pawn for White's passive e3-pawn!

10.exd4

An excellent response that happily breaks the "always capture towards the center" rule. By leaving his pawn on c3, White keeps the enemy Knight off of b4 and opens up the e-file for future operations.

10...h6
11.Bh4 Bb7

Still getting his pieces out with no plan in mind. In this kind of position, Black should be playing for a minority attack via an eventual ...b6-b5-b4 (creating open lines and weaknesses in White's queenside structure).

12.Ne5?

Much too early. What's the rush? Black can't really do much of anything so White would have been well advised to continue building up in the center and on the kingside. One plan (of many) was 12.Rfe1 followed by 13.Rad1, Bb1 and Qd3 with storm clouds brewing on the kingside.

12...Nxe5
13.Qxe5

More tempting is 13.dxe5 but Black would suddenly spring to life with 13...Nd7 14.Bg3 Nc5 when 15.Bc2 is met by 15...Ba6.

What has White accomplished by his early 12.Ne5? The first thing that catches my eyes is White's willingness to exchange Black's passive c6-Knight for White's more useful beast on f3 (the side with more space should not exchange pieces). I am also disturbed by White's joy in placing his Queen on an exposed square.

Never initiate an exchange unless you can clearly list the thing(s) you are gaining!

13...Nd7

Suddenly White is being herded in a direction that he may not have wished to take.

14.Bxe7 Nxe5
15.Bxd8 Nxd3
16.Be7 Rfe8
17.Ba3

Black has managed to trade off several pieces and now, thanks to the opposite-colored Bishops, enjoys an even game. However, now we can see the differences between the two players: while White was happy to trade off from a superior game to a even one, Black wants to push the envelope as far as possible. Seeing his d3-Knight as a strong piece, and also recognizing that the make-up of the game has suddenly changed, Black tries to extract the maximum from the position. This noble goal (in chess, any greedy goal is noble!) falls flat when White suddenly wakes up and begins to play brilliantly!

17...b5?

Planning 18...a5 and 19...b4. Unfortunately for Black, this move blocks the a6-d3 diagonal (which stops Black from defending his Knight with ...Ba6) and leaves the Knight in sudden danger!

18.f4

Forcing Black to address the threat of 19.Rf3.

18...g5

Taken aback, Black weakens his kingside, not believing that White will find a way to take advantage of this flaw. The more natural 18...a5 19.Rf3 b4 fails to 20.Rxd3 bxa3 21.b3 when White will eventually scoop up the a3-pawn with Nd2-b1xa3.

19.fxg5 hxg5
20.Rf6

White sees a very interesting idea and, in his excitement, misses Black's best response. Better was 20.g3, taking the f4-square away from the Knight.

20...Nf4??

This lands Black in serious trouble. Correct was 20...Kg7 when 21.Raf1? (White should play 21.Rf3) loses material to 21...Nf4. Notice how each side makes one mistake after another, always letting the opponent escape from fate.

Problem Position

(143)

White to play.

Find the correct move *and* the plan that goes along with it!

Solution

21.Bd6

The main imbalance in the position is the opposite colored Bishops. Once White's Bishop reaches e5, it will dominate the game by laying claim to all the weak dark squares in Black's camp. Compare this piece with Black's pathetic alter ego on b7.

21...Nh5
22.Rh6!

Excellent! White suddenly creates a mating attack.

22...Ng7

No better was 22...Nf4 23.Be5 Ng6 24.Bf6 when Black can't make a move.

After 22...Ng7, White has a completely won game. He realized that he was in charge but he suddenly became worried about the horrible 23...f5 (as he put it: "And Black gains space."). Strange, don't you agree? With a strong attack blazing, and threats mounting with every move, White stops in his tracks and becomes paranoid that the opponent must have something good (would White think like this if Black was rated 1200?).

23.Rf6??

In White's mind, he was stopping two Black threats: 23...Nf5 (forking Bishop and Rook) and 23...f5 ("gaining space"). Correct, of course, was 23.Be5 (meeting 23...Nf5 with the reasonably strong 24.Rh8 mate) when Black is busted. For example, the feared 23...f5 (threatening nothing and weakening e6 and e5) gives White various strong replies like 24.Nf3 g4 25.Ng5 or 24.Rg6 Re7 when White has a couple ways to win material.

23...Nf5
24.Be5

The difference in Bishops still leaves White with a huge advantage.

24...g4
25.Raf1 b4

Desperate, Black tries to confuse the issue. He's hoping for 26.cxb4 (this has nothing to do with White's kingside attack and he did well to ignore it) 26...Rac8 when Black's Rook penetrates to c2. Why let Black get counterplay for a silly pawn?

26.Nb3

A solid move that prepares to bring the Knight to c5. Also tempting was 26.R1f4 (very much to the point!) when g4 (and perhaps the King as well) dies in flames.

26...bxc3
27.bxc3 Ba6

White's unnecessary Knight move gave Black time to bring this Bishop into play.

28.Rf4 Be2

Black knows that he's busted but he doesn't lose heart. He hangs on for dear life and hopes White goes insane.

29.Kf2 Bd1
30.Nc5??

White saw 30.Ke1 but he wanted to win cleanly and didn't like the look of 30...Ne3. However, a calm look would convince him that 30.Kd2 (or 30.Rxf7) 30...Nxg2 31.Kxd1 Nxf4 32.Bxf4 was hopeless for Black.

The Knight move that White chose gives Black enough time to get his Rooks into the game.

30...Rab8
31.Nd7??

Freaking out. With panic welling up in his chest, White didn't notice that 31.Bxb8 was possible. Notice how White's three unnecessary Knight moves let Black activate his whole army.

Hmmmm, this is actually the "next to last mistake" (actually, White made the last several mistakes) so that earlier rule (the winner is the guy who makes the next to last mistake) appears to be bogus!

31...Rb2+
32.Ke1 Ne3

The worm has turned. Now Black threatens 33...Re2 mate.

33.Rf2 Rb1
34.Rxf7??

Giving in to despair. What if White calmly tried 34.Rh6 (threatening a mate of his own and telling Black to prove his threats)? Then attempts at a slam dunk don't seem to work: 34...Bf3+ 35.Kd2 Nc4+ 36.Kd3 (avoiding 36.Kc2?? Be4 mate) 36...Be4+ 37.Ke2 and Black doesn't have more than a perpetual check with 37...Rb2+.

34...Bf3+
35.Kd2 Nc4+, 0-1. White didn't care what was going on anymore; he'd had enough and just wanted to get away from a bad memory. A sane look at the position would have convinced him that 35.Kd3 Kxf7 (35...Be4+ 36.Ke2) 36.gxf3 was worth playing out.

Did you notice the emotional decline in White's play? Compare it to Black's never-say-die attitude and you will understand why Black ended up winning this game.

Tips

★ The winner is the player who makes the next to last mistake.

★ In chess, never respect anyone! Every player, no matter how high his rating, is waiting to be dragged down and dismembered.

★ If you don't give off an air of confidence, your opponent will sense your weakness and beat you like a drum.

★ Never develop your pieces in the opening with the intention of looking for a plan later. When "later" comes, you are usually on your way down.

★ The side with more space should not exchange pieces.

#3

Goldberg-Schloss (1680-2118), National Open 1998.
KID, Boring Variation.

1.d4 Nf6
2.Nf3 g6
3.Bf4 Bg7
4.e3 0-0
5.Be2

This system, known by some as the reversed London System and by others as the Boring System, is easy to learn and carries quite a bit of sting.

5...d6
6.h3

This allows the f4-Bishop to safely retreat to h2 in case of ...Nh5.

6...b6
7.0-0 Bb7
8.c4 c5
9.Nc3 Nbd7?

Black misses a good opportunity. He had to play 9...cxd4 10.exd4 d5 with the idea of giving White an isolated d-pawn via 11...dxc4. Now White gets an advantage and Black will find it very hard to find active play.

10.d5 Nh5
11.Bh2 Bxc3?
12.bxc3 f5

Problem Position

(144)

White to play.

White's correct plan is far from obvious. Find his next two moves and beyond!

Solution

13.Ng5

The correct plan begins with 13.Ng5!, hitting the weakened e6-square, creating a discovered attack against h5, and preparing to redirect the Knight to f4 (where, if Black has played ...h7-h6, it will hit both e6 and g6) by h3-h4 and Ng5-h3-f4. Most importantly, 13.Ng5 intends to blast open the center (thereby making use of his two Bishops) with f2-f3 followed by e3-e4.

13...Ng7
14.h4

Another fine move. This prevents ...h6 followed by ...g5 and, by doing so, ensures that the White Knight will have access to the f4-square.

14...Nf6
15.f3

Preparing to blast through in the center with e4.

15...h6
16.Nh3 Nd7
17.e4 Bc8
18.Qd2 Kh7
19.Bf4 h5
20.Ng5+ Kg8

So far we've seen a classic case of a higher-rated player trying (in a very incorrect manner) to imbalance the position so that winning chances can be obtained. Unfortunately for Black, his "win at all costs moves" (11...Bxc3? followed by 12...f5 was more wishful thinking than common sense) were really nothing more than suicidal blips on the chessic screen.

Now White, who has played extremely well up to this point, could rout his opponent with 21.Bd3 followed by 22.Rae1 when an eventual e4-e5 or exf5 will break through on the e-file: 21...Ne5 22.Rae1 fxe4 23.Bxe5 and now both 23...dxe5 24.Rxe4 9the weakness on e5 is horrible) and 23...exd3 24.Bxg7 (Black has permanent weaknesses on e7 and e6) are both miserable for the second player.

Note White's correct plan: safe, central play designed to open up the position for his two Bishops.

21.g4??

Groan. With one move, White has weakened his King and activated Black's dormant c8-Bishop.

21...fxg4
22.fxg4 hxg4
23.Bxg4 Nf6
24.Bxc8 Qxc8

Everything's changed! Suddenly Black's Knights have access to the h5-square and Black's Queen, once dead to the world, now threatens to leap into g4.

25.e5 Qg4+
26.Qg2 dxe5
27.Bxe5 Nf5

Black avoids the tempting 27...Qxc4? 28.d6! when he would be in serious trouble.

28.Rf4 Qxg2+
29.Kxg2 b5
30.Bxf6 Rxf6

All right, here we go. Watch White's King turn into a hero!

31.cxb5 Ne3+
32.Kf3 Rxf4+
33.Kxf4 Nxd5+
34.Ke5 Nxc3
35.Rc1 Nxb5
36.Rxc5

Black is a pawn up, but he has no winning chances whatsoever because White's King and Rook are much more active than their Black counterparts.

36...Rf8

Hoping for 37.Rxb5?? Rf5+, picking up the Rook and winning the game. **If your opponent hangs a piece, never just attribute it to stupidity and snap it off. First look at his move and try hard to fathom what nefarious schemes he's creating. If you can't see what's on his mind, THEN snap it off!**

37.Ke6

White's King deserves its royal title.

37...Nd4+
38.Kxe7 Nf5+
39.Ke6 Nxh4
40.Rc7

White's Rook joins the party and snuffs out any thoughts of winning that Black may have entertained.

40...a5
41.Nf7 Kg7
42.Ng5+ Kg8
43.Nf7, ½-½.

#4

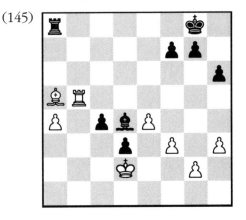

(145)

Goldberg-Faelten (1680-2038), National Open 1998.
White to play.

Black's passed pawns appear to be very dangerous, but White's firm blockade on c3 and d2, combined with the active Rook on b5, allows the first player to more than hold his own.

At the moment, the passed pawns aren't going anywhere because the d3-pawn is firmly blocked by the White King and the c3-square is also under White's domination. To break this down, Black has to achieve a workable ...c4-c3+ at some point, or he must try and achieve a Bishop check along the g5-d2 diagonal (...Bg5+).

40.Rd5

This move not only attacks the Bishop, it also threatens to trade Rooks (with Rd8+) in some situations and prepares to close the Black Bishop out of the attack by an advance of White's central pawns.

40...Bf6
41.f4

This stops Black from playing ...Bg5+ and prepares e4-e5. Notice how White is going out of his way to snuff out the activity of the Black forces.

41...Rb8

Black's Rook now threatens to leaps into a dominant position with ...Rb2+. Naturally, White can't let this happen.

42.Rb5

White's Rook stares down its counterpart! This territorial battle between Rooks is made possible due to the fact that an exchange (via ...Rxb5) favors White due to his passed b-pawn (after axb5), the possibility of creating another passer (via e4-e5, f4-f5 and e5-e6), and the superior position of the White King.

42...Rc8

Threatening to win a piece by 43...c3+ (sacrificing d3 to break the blockade!) 44.Kxd3 c2.

43.e5

Closing the enemy Bishop out and once again laying claim to the blockading square c3.

43...Bh4
44.Bc3 Bg3
45.f5 Bf4+
46.Kd1 Be3

White would be in trouble if Black's Rook could find a way to penetrate into the White position. However, White's pawns (blocking off the a-file and e-file) and White's hard-working Rook combine to keep Black's Rook at bay.

47.a5 Rd8

Problem Position

(146)

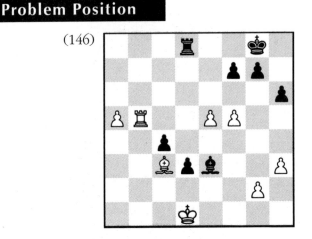

White to play.

Who stands better and what is White's best move?

Solution

48.Rb4

In the actual game, White went berserk and managed to lose. A real shame, considering that he outplayed his opponent up to this point. (Why do marginally higher rated players win so often? Is it really superior strength, or does psychology and consistency play an even greater role in the ultimate result?)

The text is strong because it keeps Black's Rook off the open b-file and ties it down to the defense of the c-pawn. Worse was 48.a6 Ra8 when 49.Rb4 Rxa6 50.Rxc4 leaves White a whole move down on the game, while 49.Ra5 Rb8, threatening mate on b1, would also improve Black's chances.

White's plan in this position is to win the c-pawn for his a-pawn, chase away Black's Bishop and then play to win Black's remaining passed pawn on d3.

48...Rc8
49.a6 Ra8
50.Rxc4 Rxa6
51.Re4

An important move. White's maneuver forces the Black Bishop to give up its hold over the d2-square. This frees the White King and allows it to chop off Black's pawn on d3.

51...Bg5
52.h4

Now White's King gains access to d2 and Black is suddenly the one who will have to play for the draw.

White was saved by his nimble Rook. Always insist that your Rooks perform in the same active manner!

Tips

★ The defending side should always try and trade pawns on one side of the board. This leaves him with a much smaller area to defend and less targets to worry about.

★ Making sure your Rooks stay active is one of the most important concepts in Rook endgames!

★ Passed pawns must be blockaded at all costs!

★ Take away the activity of the enemy forces.

#5

We live in a fast-food nation; everything has to be handed to us quickly and easily. This may explain why so many players are consumed with a desire to know their openings inside and out. So, forget about middlegame study. Forget about the endgame. Memorization is the key for these "sit down, win fast and get up" mentalities.

However, what about old dudes like the author who don't have a memory (youngsters who can't remember anything may also include themselves), think the words "win fast" spring from some other language and actually enjoy playing a long, thoughtful game?

The funny thing about opening study is that all the memorization in the world won't help you if you can't play the other phases in a strong manner; a player who understands middlegame strategy will usually come out on top against an opening expert. Another karmic opening lesson involves this simple truth: you may memorize all the key opening lines, but your opponents don't know these variations—they will *always* step away from the book and leave both of you in the dark! When that happens, isn't knowing how to actually play the game the thing that will ultimately count?

Before I overreach by stepping out of the bounds of opening thought, let's take a glance at a book review by IM John Watson and see what he has to say about opening study:

> "What do most readers look for in an opening book? Unfortunately, something that they won't get. TWIC [Mr. Watson is referring to *The Week In Chess*, a web-site that gives up to the minute chess news] readers, for example, apparently want pretty much what my own students keep asking for: a book which explains all the 'ideas' of an opening, but isn't cluttered up with all sorts of nasty variations which one will never run into over the board anyway.
>
> "I'm sorry to report that this is just a fantasy. Learning an opening by accumulating abstract ideas is a little like learning a language by reading a grammar book. Worse, actually, because generalizations in chess don't apply with nearly the consistency or predictability of grammatical rules.
>
> "If a chess opening could be learned by absorbing the opening's 'ideas' (whatever those might be), the opening phase of the game would be universally mastered and of little interest. The fact is, no verbal description of what squares are important or where the pieces 'usually' go can describe the dynamic interplay of tactics and positional factors in any major opening. Whereas, by contrast, the straightforward study of enough examples will lead to a nuanced and practical knowledge of how to play that opening. In addition, by studying in context, you will automatically get a much better grasp on how those impor-

tant squares and typical maneuvers work than you would have from reading a general description."

What in the world is Mr. Watson talking about? His first paragraph says that the study of opening ideas won't get the job done (which, I am told, enraged many of his readers...hey guys, chill out a bit!), while he later says that learning these abstract concepts by the study of actual games (compared to general descriptions) will indeed give you a good grasp of the system you wish to master.

In other words, he's giving good advice (which he usually does) in a way that managed to confuse many people. Parroting general concepts like a sleep-deprived Moonie is indeed a menu for disaster (but going back to our lazy fast-food mentality, that's what many players yearn for). But learning the correct plans for your particular system (which includes the correct squares for your pieces, the correct middlegame ideas, typical traps and structural problems, and even typical endgames that arise from your opening) is far superior to the soulless memorization that most books seem to insist on.

Up to this point, the main piece of advice is to study master games so you get a feel for the "complete story" of your opening system (opening, middlegame and endgame). Two other bits of chess wisdom, though, will prove useful to the reader:

> **In the opening, middlegame and endgame, your opponents will invariably give you sizable opportunities to knock them for a loop (or, at the very least, to make modest but important gains). To make use of these chances, though, means that you must spot them and pounce when they arise (and they *will* arise!).**

> **While playing the opening (whether you know what you're doing or not), don't allow yourself to get lazy and try to stay flexible (don't make a decision on one move only to realize you want to do something else a short time later. Both laziness and flexibility often go hand in hand). Though vague, these ideas will (hopefully) be clarified in the following examples.**

Makarewicz-Douglas (1700-1800), Los Angeles 1998.
Torre Attack.

1.d4 Nf6
2.Nf3 e6
3.Bg5 Be7

So far we have a very simple position. Now White has to make some basic decisions. Should he place his pawn on e3 or would he like to get that pawn to e4? Does he want to play the game like a normal Queen's Gambit Declined (via c2-c4 and Nc3) or does he prefer the warm confines of a Torre Attack (where the c-pawn usually finds rest on c3)?

4.e3

An innocent looking move, but White not only shows a lack of flexibility, he also demonstrates that he hasn't decided what he wants to do (laziness). If it was White's intention to keep this pawn on e3, then there's nothing wrong with his fourth move. But if he wanted to place it on e4, then 4.Nbd2 (threatening 5.e4 and staying flexible) is obviously superior.

This means that 4.e3 isn't a bad move by itself, but it turns out to be a bad decision when we see what White really had in mind.

4...h6
5.Bxf6?

A really strange decision. Having committed to e2-e3, White should have calmly moved his Bishop back to h4. The only reason one would take on f6 is to gain time for the e4-advance, but White's fourth move has already ruled that out.

5...Bxf6
6.e4

We've now reached a well-known book position with an extra tempo for Black (White should have the free Nbd2 in here). It's clear that White's e2-e3-e4 showed a propensity for laziness that must somehow be eradicated from his chess character.

6...0-0
7.Bd3 Nc6?

Illogical. Black has the two Bishops and should be doing everything in his power to set up a flexible position that can ultimately be opened up (making the Bishops better than the White Knights). Correct was 7...g6 followed by 8...d6, ...Bg7, ...b6, ...Bb7 and ...Nbd7. This formation takes all the advanced squares away from White's Knights (following Steinitz's anti-Knight rule) and prepares the central opening ...c7-c5 advance.

8.c3 e5

This gives Black some kingside chances but it doesn't make the f6-Bishop very happy. The second player seems oblivious to his ownership of the two Bishops.

9.d5 Ne7
10.0-0 d6
11.c4

Though White played c2-c3 a few moves earlier, the c3-c4 advance is a good idea. The reason lies in that often quoted pawn pointing theory: Black's pawns aim at the kingside while White's aim at the queenside. Thus Black will play against White's King with ...f7-f5 (thanks to the closed center) and White will strive to open queenside lines with an eventual c4-c5 advance.

11...Ng6
12.Nc3

I might have been tempted to retain the light-squared Bishop for defensive purposes by 12.Re1 when 12...Nf4 can be met by 13.Bf1.

12...Nf4
13.b4

White could have safely prepared this by 13.Qc2 (allowing the Rooks to defend each other) when 13...Bg4 is answered by 14.Nd2.

13...a5

Suddenly White realized that 14.a3?? loses to 14...axb4 when 15.axb4?? Rxa1 16.Qxa1 Nxd3 leaves Black with an extra piece. However, all is not lost and White begins to play very, very well.

14.Rb1 axb4
15.Rxb4 b6

White's play depends on his ability to eventually toss in c4-c5. Though it appears that Black has stopped this forever, White demonstrates other ways to skin the queenside cat.

16.Qc2 Bg4
17.Nd2 Qc8

A mystery. I suppose that Black was setting up some tactic based on ...Nxg2 and ...Bh3+.

Problem Position

(147)

White to play.

What is White's proper move and what's his proper plan?

Solution

18.Ra1

A great move. White brings the Rook to a safe square, prepares to solidify his kingside with Bf1 and places the Rook behind his a-pawn in anticipation of a2-a4-a5, blasting open the queenside. This mix of defense and attack makes a nice impression.

18...h5
19.Bf1 h4
20.a4

White calmly ignores his opponent's inaccurate kingside demonstration and proceeds with his own plans on the opposite wing. I'm very impressed by White's lack of panic.

20...g5
21.a5 bxa5
22.Rba4 Kg7
23.Rxa5 Rxa5
24.Rxa5 Bh5

White has completely outplayed his opponent and, with 25.c5 (at last!) followed by 26.Nc4, could claim a clear advantage.

25.Nb3?

The Knight doesn't stand well here. Even if White plays c4-c5 (placing pressure against d6), how does this Knight join with the pawn to attack d6? If you place the Knight on c4 (after c4-c5), both the Knight and the pawn work together for one goal (on c4 the Knight can also leap to f5 via e3).

25...g4
26.Be2 Nxe2+
27.Qxe2 Rh8
28.Qd3 Bg5
29.Nd2 Bg6
30.c5 f5

Now White would still stand very well after 31.exf5 Bxf5 32.Nde4 when his Knights are strongly placed and the attack against Black's c7 and d6 pawn chain is in full swing. Unfortunately, he went completely berserk via 31.Qa6?? when he lost a piece and the game after 31...Qxa6 32.Rxa6 Bxd2.

A great pity. He ignored Black's attack beautifully, but in the end, a fear of his opponent's illusory attack prompted a blunder-riddled panicky trade of Queens.

#6

Withgate-Makarewicz (1800-1700), Los Angeles 1998.
Sicilian Defense, Alapin Variation.

1.e4 c5
2.c3 d5
3.e5 Bf5
4.d4 e6
5.Nf3 Nc6
6.Be3 Qb6
7.Qe2

Neither side knows the opening, but one gets the feeling that Black's moves (all directed at the d4-pawn) make sense while White's are, at the very least, suspect (blocking the f1-Bishop with the Queen can't be good). Because of this, Black should look hard for a "vengeful" move here; something that punishes White for the lack of harmony in his game.

Problem Position

(148)

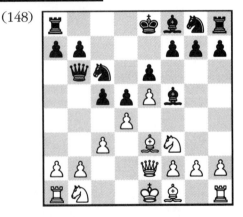

Black to play.

How can Black squeeze the most out of this position?

7...cxd4?

Solution

Forcing White to bring his pieces to good squares. Correct: 7...Bg4!, increasing the pressure against d4. Black would then continue with ...Bxf3 (if it doubled White's pawns) and ...Ng8-e7-f5, with all his guys (a team effort!) hitting d4.

8.Nxd4 Nxd4
9.Bxd4 Qc7

Black's intended 9...Bc5?? loses a piece to 10.Qb5+.

10.Qb5+ now Black played the horrible 10...Kd8?. Though things turned out well for him later in the game, he should have calmly blocked the check with 10...Qd7 when 11.Qa5 (threatening to win by Bb5) again meets with a calm reaction: 11...Ne7 12.Bb5 Nc6 when all is well for Black. Yet another case of a position poisoned by panic!

#7

Makarewicz-Lazarus (1700-1900), Los Angeles 1998.
KID, Boring Variation.

1.d4 Nf6
2.Nf3 g6
3.Bf4 Bg7
4.e3 d5
5.h3 0-0
6.Bd3 c5
7.c3 b6
8.Nbd2 Nc6
9.0-0 Bb7

Both sides have gotten their pieces out in a quiet but reasonable manner. If I was White, I'd probably try 10.Qb1!?, defending the e4-square and preparing to gain queenside space with b2-b4.

10.Ne5?

A pseudo-active move that ends up exchanging pieces and wasting time. If you bring a Knight to an advanced post, make sure it can stay there or be certain that any exchange favors you.

This falls under the category of "lazy move." White tosses his Knight out there without concerning himself with Black's reply.

10...Nd7
11.Nxc6 Bxc6
12.Bh2?

This makes no sense at all. What was attacking the Bishop? Why did the Bishop have to move? Surely a more useful possibility existed? More sensible was 12.Nf3, stopping Black's intended ...e7-e5 for a moment and bringing the Knight to a better square.

12...e5
13.dxe5 Nxe5
14.Bxe5?

This was White's intention all along. Naturally, it also poses a question: why did the Bishop have to be on h2? Couldn't White have done something other than 12.Bh2 and been a whole move ahead? More laziness (we never even asked why White was so fast to give his opponent the two Bishops. Did the obvious attack on d3 bother White so much that he felt obliged to make this huge concession?).

A much calmer (and saner) approach was 14.Be2 followed by 15.Nf3.

14...Bxe5
15.Nf3

Problem Position

(149)

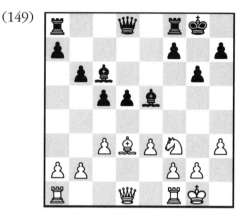

Black to play.

Where should Black park his dark-squared Bishop?

Solution

Black has more space and the two Bishops. Now, instead of his run of the mill 15...Bg7, preferable was 15...Bc7 followed by 16 Qd6 (eyeing both the center and the kingside), ...Rad8 and ...Rfe8. In that case, there wouldn't be any doubt about Black's superiority.

#8

C. Evans-Makarewicz (1950-1700), Los Angeles 1998.
Sicilian Defense, Tal Gambit.

1.e4 c5
2.f4 d5
3.exd5 Nf6
4.c4 e6
5.dxe6 Bxe6
6.Nf3 Nc6
7.Nc3

Problem Position

(150)

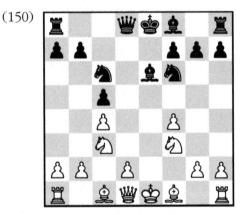

Black to play.

The book move is 7...Be7. Does 7...g6 make any sense here?

Solution

Both sides knew of this gambit (Makarewicz learned it during one of our lessons, while Evans had seen it in an earlier round and was confident that he could do well against it if it appeared again).

At this point, Black forgot the book moves and was on his own. However, not knowing the book wasn't a huge problem because he understood the nature of the position: Black's a pawn down but he has an easy development, pressure on the half-open d-file against White's backward d-pawn, and control over the very nice d4-square.

7...g6!?

The book move is 7...Be7. However, the move played makes good sense: Black prepares to place his Bishop on the fine g7-c3 diagonal. In doing so, he'll gain even greater control over the d4-square.

8.Be2 Bg7
9.0-0 0-0
10.Kh1 Re8
11.d3 h5

I wasn't impressed with this move when I saw it. Nevertheless, when Black explained that he was fighting to control the light squares and, as a result, would increase his control over d4 by the maneuver ...Nf6-g4-h6-f5, I had to heap praise on him. It doesn't really matter if 11...h5 is a good move, any detailed plan of this ilk deserves a hearty stamp of approval.

12.Re1??

Awful. White misses Black's idea and loses a lot of time as a result.

12...Ng4
13.Rf1 Nh6
14.Be3 Bxc4

Black couldn't resist the discovered attack against e3. The confident 14...b6 followed by ...Nf5 would have left White under considerable pressure.

15.Bxc5 Ba6
16.d4

White decides that enough is enough and heads for the safe waters of a draw.

16...Bxe2
17.Nxe2 b6
18.Ba3 Nf5
19.Qd3 Ncxd4, Draw agreed. By knowing the most basic ideas of his opening, Black was able to come up with a novelty and outplay a much higher-rated (and better-prepared!) opponent.

Tips

★ Make sure your "simple developing move" is a part of your plan. If it isn't, you may find that you wasted a move.

★ Panic can destroy the best-laid plans of amateurs and professionals. Have faith in your position and never give the opponent's ideas any respect at all (or at least more than they deserve).

★ If you bring a Knight to an advanced post, make sure it can stay there or be certain that any exchange favors you.

#9

Annotate this game and then go over my notes and see how your ideas and comments measured up.

1.e4 e6 2.d3 d5 3.Nd2 Nc6 4.Nf3 Bd6 5.g3 Ne7 6.Bg2 d4 7.0-0 Ng6 8.Nc4 e5 9.Nxd6 cxd6 10.b3 Bg4 11.Ba3 Qf6 12.h3 Bd7 13.Nd2 b5 14.Rc1 b4 15.Bb2 0-0 16.Nc4 Bc8 17.Qe2 Nce7 18.f4 exf4 19.e5 dxe5 20.Bxa8.

Neuhoff-N.N. (1474-1500), Los Angeles 1998.
French Defense, KIA.

1.e4 e6
2.d3

White began playing this line versus the French when he saw the positions that arose after 2...d5 3.Nd2 Nf6 4.Ngf3 c5 5.g3 Nc6 6.Bg2 Be7 7.0-0 0-0 8.e5 Nd7 9.Re1 b5 10.Nf1 a5 11.h4 b4 12.Bf4 with h5 and Nf1-h2-g4 to follow.

Though acquainted with the general ideas and set-up of the King's Indian Attack, his knowledge proved to be a double-edged sword. He would do well if Black played the moves just given, but if Black varied in some significant manner, White would often repeat the same plan and moves even if it no longer had any point!

This teaches us that basic ideas have value, but if you cling to them, they will turn to poison. Every new move by your opponent, whether it's good or bad, changes everything and must be looked at in a fresh manner.

2...d5
3.Nd2 Nc6

A bit odd. Black usually uses his c-pawn in an aggressive manner by 3...Nf6 and ...c7-c5.

4.Ngf3 Bd6

It's now clear that Black doesn't have anything prepared and is just making things up as he goes. Since Black has wandered so far from the normal path, White should push aside his memorized setups and look for something particularly tasty. Instead, the first player just tosses out his usual moves.

5.g3

Part of his system, but 5.d4! would have punished Black's poorly considered development and given White a clear advantage.

5...Nge7
6.Bg2 d4
7.0-0 Ng6
8.Nc4 e5

(151)

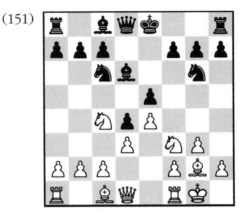

White to play.

Neither side has created anything special during the last few moves. Black has closed up the center while White (with the exception of the aggressive 8.Nc4) has followed his pre-game recipe.

On the eighth move it became clear to White that he wasn't in Kansas anymore. Finally (and, undoubtedly, with a heavy heart) he pushed his hoped-for setup aside (it's hard for White to advance his pawn to e5 when Black's pawn stands there!) and looked for something else to do.

How would one go about making a decision for White? Two things stand out:

1) Black hasn't castled yet.

2) White can grab the two Bishops with Nxd6.

The fact that Black hasn't castled calls for an immediate, aggressive reaction and an opening up of the central position. Gaining the two Bishops is a long-range plan. White would still want to open the position for his Bishops, but he could go about his plans in a calmer manner.

9.Nxd6+

White goes for the Bishops, though at the moment Black's d6-Bishop was hardly a wonderful piece. Personally, I would have preferred 9.c3!, striking at Black's center and initiating a fight while the Black monarch is still a liability.

9...cxd6

An error, but I have to give him credit for not fearing doubled pawns. Black's move actually makes a lot of sense: it firmly defends e5 and opens the c-file for his Rooks (once again proving that doubled pawns are often a very good thing). Unfortunately, White can cast doubt on Black's concept.

10.b3??

Absolutely awful. White is hoping to put pressure on d6 by Ba3, but the price he pays for this is too high. What is that price? A gaping hole on c3 and a backward pawn on c2. Don't create such weaknesses in your own position!

Correct was 10.c3!, letting Black dissolve his doubled pawns. Black could then play either 10...dxc3 11.bxc3 when White's two Bishops and mobile center give him a clear advantage, or 10...Bg4 11.h3 Bxf3, when White possesses two Bishops versus two Knights.

White was caught up in the idea that doubled pawns are bad, and so the idea of letting Black rid himself of them never occurred to him. However, why are those doubled pawns bad? The pawn on d6 is safely defended by the Queen and gives useful support to e5. The pawn on d4 is like a rock, and it gains quite a bit of space.

10...Bg4?!

What does this have to do with the newly created weaknesses on c3 and c2? From this point on, every move Black plays should be aimed at those two targets in the White position.

11.Ba3?

Still barking up the wrong tree. White should play 11.Bb2 followed by 12.c3. If White wanted to insist on his chosen course, then 11.a4 first would have been better, creating an artificial support point on c4 for the Knight (Nf3-d2-c4 is in the air).

11...Qf6?

The real targets lie on the queenside, but Black can't resist staring at the opposite wing. This illogical desire to seek out a mate at all costs is known as "kingside dementia."

12.h3 Bd7
13.Nd2

White heads for the tasty c4-square, but now Black is virtually forced to play a good move.

13...b5
14.Rc1 b4??

Much better was 14...a5 with the idea of 15...a4. Note that 14...a5 15.c3 isn't possible due to 15...dxc3 16.Rxc3 b4, winning material.

Black's actual move ends all thoughts of a c2-c3 advance, but it also gives up c4 to the White Knight. By allowing this, the c-file is neutralized and White is free to seek out kingside play by f2-f4 without fear of a queenside reprisal.

By not making use of his queenside chances (and 14...b4?? kills Black's queenside play), Black allows White to take over the game on the other wing.

15.Bb2 0-0
16.Nc4 Bc8?

I can't comprehend this move.

17.Qe2 Nce7?

Black's last couple of moves seem to be setting up a kind of "help-problem" (Black to play and hang his a8-Rook).

18.f4 exf4??

Completing the picture set up by ...Bc8 and ...Nce7. When you don't follow your correct plan (and Black ignored his queenside chances), you often end up with no plan at all. When this happens, random puttering about, mixed with blunders, often ensues.

19.e5 dxe5
20.Bxa8 and White won.

#10

Problem

Annotate this game and then go over my notes and see how your ideas and comments measured up.

1.d4 Nf6 2.Nf3 c5 3.e3 e6 4.Bd3 Nc6 5.c3 cxd4 6.exd4 d5 7.Nbd2 Bd6 8.0-0 0-0 9.Re1 Qc7 10.Nf1 h6 11.Qe2 Nd7 12.Bc2 Re8 13.Qd3 Nf8 14.h3 Bd7 15.N1h2 a6 16.a4 Rac8 17.Re2 Bxh2+ 18.Nxh2 Na5 19.Nf3 b5 20.Ne5 Nc4 21.Nxd7 Qxd7 22.Qg3 Kh8.

Solution

Suveg-Cota (1700-1800), Los Angeles 1998.
Colle System.

> **1.d4 Nf6**
> **2.Nf3 c5**
> **3.e3 e6**
> **4.Bd3 Nc6**
> **5.c3 cxd4**

What's the hurry? This move exchanges a dynamic c-pawn for White's passive e3-pawn. On top of that, Black lets White open up the e-file for his Rooks and also frees the blocked c1-Bishop.

> **6.exd4 d5**

White can be very satisfied with the result of the opening. His pieces stare ominously at Black's kingside.

Though we can clearly see that White will be playing for a kingside attack, Black's correct plan might be less clear. Kudos for those who noted that the second player should be preparing a minority attack via an eventual ...Rb8, ...b7-b5-b4. Don't forget the pawn-pointing theory here: White's pawns aim at the kingside and Black's point to the opposite wing.

> **7.Nbd2**

Not bad, of course, but a tad inflexible. Why hurry to block your c1-Bishop? And why put off castling, which is a move you know you must make?

7...Bd6
8.0-0 0-0
9.Re1

White later realized that one key plan called for an early Ne5 followed by f2-f4. If this is realized, White would prefer his Rook to stand on f1. Due to this, he could have tried 9.Qe2 with the threat of Ne5 and f4. However, 9.Qe2 Qc7 would have forced 10.Re1, with a likely transposition to the actual game.

9...Qc7
10.Nf1

White tries a different, but good, idea. The Knight gets out of the way and heads for g3 where it will participate in a kingside attack.

10...h6?

This move weakens the kingside and sets up various themes involving tactical explosions on h6. It's clear that Black is worried about his kingside and hasn't begun to consider his own play on the queenside (not hurrying with your own plans is a real recipe for disaster).

11.Qe2

The immediate 11.Bc2 followed by 12.Qd3 made more sense.

11...Nd7

If Black intended to do this, why did he waste time on ...h7-h6?

12.Bc2 Re8
13.Qd3 Nf8

Black led White to believe that he would try ...e6-e5 at some point, but now we see the second player settling in for passive defense. He still hasn't started his queenside counterplay.

(152)

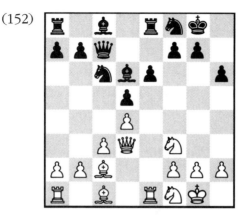

White to play.

14.h3?

Too slow. Why not speed things up with 14.Ne3 (threatening Nxd5) 14...Bd7 15.Ng4 with kingside threats? Note how the Knight on g4 not only eyes the tactically weak squares on f6 and h6, it also keeps tabs on the key e5-square.

14...Bd7
15.N1h2 a6?

What's this? Black has finally figured out that his future lies on the queenside, but he seems happy to go about his business there as slowly as possible. The immediate 15...b5 is much more to the point, since 16.Qxb5? Nxd4 won't be to White's tastes.

16.a4?

White wanted to stop Black's play before continuing with his own. A noble idea, but 16.a4 doesn't stop anything. In general, attacks on opposite wings call for speed and a sense of urgency. Time becomes very important, and one wasted move often makes the difference between a win or a loss.

16...Rac8?

Creating the cheap threat of ...Nb4. However, Black should continue with his queenside expansion with 16...b5 since 17.axb5 axb5 18.Rxa8 Rxa8 (giving Black the a-file) 19.Qxb5? is still very bad due to 19...Nxd4.

17.Re2 Bxh2+?

Giving up the dark squares and the two Bishops. It's hard to guess what prompted this decision.

18.Nxh2 Na5
19.Nf3?

Unfortunate. White wants to place his Knight on e5, but his tunnel vision causes him to miss many key points:

➤ **White should be playing for mate.**

➤ **His Knight is a major attacking piece, trading it more or less dooms White's attack to failure.**

➤ **The f3-square isn't the only way the Knight can reach e5.**

➤ **White would like to place his Bishop on f4 where it eyes both sides of the board.**

➤ **If White can get his Queen to g3 (without allowing a trade of ladies, of course!), his attack would be hard to stop.**

➤ **Playing the Knight to g4 hits h6, f6 and e5. That's a lot more than Nf3 does!**

➤ **White should be willing to make queenside concessions in his desire for a killing kingside blow. The reason for this is based on the fact that White WILL lose on the queenside in the long run. Thus, if he wants to survive, he MUST make his kingside attack work.**

With all this in mind, White's correct course of action was 19.Ng4. One fanciful (but quite possible) line is 19...b5 20.Qf3 bxa4? 21.Bf4 Qb6 22.Qg3 Kh8 23.Nxh6! gxh6 24.Be5+ and mates. Black would have been in terrible trouble after 19.Ng4.

19...b5
20.Ne5

The Knight looks pretty on e5, but it has nothing to do with h6 or f6.

20...Nc4

Now Black is going to exchange Knights and deprive White of a key attacking unit. This makes a lot of sense. Queenside play usually bestows the better endgame on its employer. If you're defending against a kingside attack which requires several attacking units to succeed, an exchange of pieces weakens his attack and brings you closer to that promising endgame.

21.Nxd7

White cashes in for two Bishops versus two Knights. Considering the circumstances, this is a good decision since it gives him something to play for in the long run.

21...Qxd7
22.Qg3 Kh8 and White's time pressure eventually led to a Black victory. In this final position, White should continue to pursue his kingside dreams with 23.Qh4.

Tips

★ You can't find a proper plan if you aren't able to recognize the imbalances in the position.

★ In general, attacks on opposite wings call for speed and a sense of urgency. Time becomes very important, and one wasted move often makes the difference between a win or a loss.

★ Queenside play usually bestows the better endgame on its employer. If you're defending against a kingside attack (which requires several attacking units to succeed), an exchange of pieces weakens his attack and brings you closer to that promising endgame.

#11

In one of the greatest chess books ever written, *The Life and Games of Mikhail Tal* by Tal, the late World Champion discussed a game early in his career in which he was contemplating the sacrifice of a Knight. He tried calculating it from beginning to end but got more and more confused as he studied the position. All of a sudden, he remembered a little ditty by Korney Chukovksy: "Oh, what a difficult job it was to drag out of the marsh the hippopotamus."

At that point, with his clock ticking, Tal began to figure out how one might get a hippo out of a swamp. "I remember how jacks figured in my thoughts, as well as levers, helicopters, and even a rope ladder. After lengthy consideration I admitted defeat as an engineer, and thought spitefully: 'Well, let it drown!'

"Suddenly the hippopotamus disappeared. Straight away the position did not appear to be so complicated. I somehow realized that it was not possible to calculate all the variations, and that the Knight sacrifice was, by its very nature, purely intuitive. Since it promised an interesting game, I could not refrain from making it."

Throughout this book I've discussed various methods of getting your chessic thoughts in order. I must admit that I'd forgotten Tal's Hippo technique, though Alexander Kotov (author of the classic *Think Like a Grandmaster*), upon hearing of its existence, begin to write a book on the subject titled *Think Like a Hippopotamus*. Sadly, Grandmaster Kotov died before completing the work.

Though it's very useful to empty your mind (as the Hippo dictates) when confused by a chess position, taxes or the ravings of the opposite sex, this device isn't sufficient to form a complete system. Due to this, we'll look at the following positions from the point of view of imbalances. I want you to answer three questions about this example (in this order):

1) **What are all the imbalances?**

2) **What side of the board should both you and your opponent play on?**

3) **What is the best move or plan based on the answers to the first two questions?**

Problem Position

(153)

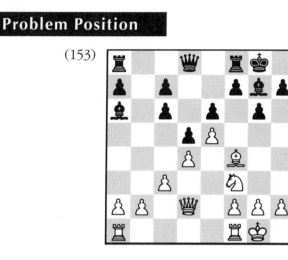

White to play.

What are all the imbalances? What side of the board should both you and your opponent play on? What is the best move or plan based, naturally, on the answers to the first two questions?

Solution

Okay, so you see that the f1-Rook has to be moved. But don't you dare touch it until you have answered those three questions posed earlier! Need a bit of help? All right, let's do them together.

Our first question is: What are all the imbalances? Black has two Bishops, but the g7-Bishop isn't very active. The a6-Bishop looks good at first glance, but it's not working with the rest of it's army to fulfill any goal or plan. Other imbalances are pretty obvious: White has more central space and he also has the better pawn formation.

The next question is: What side of the board should both you and your opponent play on? The center is closed, so neither player can initiate action in that sector of the board. White's pieces are aimed at the kingside, and his e5-pawn hits the weakened f6-square. So kingside play will be a definite part of White's future.

Who is master of the queenside? Black's pawn weaknesses in that area don't inspire confidence for the second player. For example, the hole on c5 might make a nice home for White's Knight someday.

Finally, we're forced to come up with a specific move or plan. Since we have plusses on both wings, wouldn't it be nice to dominate everywhere? Black won't be able to get anything going on the queenside if we can stop him from playing ...c6-c5. So we have to keep an eye out for that (a timely b2-b4 freezes those doubled c-pawns!). The kingside is our domain. Bishop moves like Bf4-g5-f6 are possible, and the simple Bh6 is also in the air.

That only leaves one problem: our threatened Rook! Where to move it? The answer is 1.Rfe1. This innocent-looking move does a couple of very important things! Aside from getting the Rook to a safe square, it overprotects the e5-pawn. Overprotection is a prophylactic maneuver, and its point here is to stop Black from ever getting frisky in the center with ...f7-f6. With our Rook, Bishop, d-pawn and Knight bearing down on e5, we ecstatically answer ...f6 with exf6 when Black has a weak pawn on e6 and a huge hole on e5 (our Knight spends its spare moments dreaming of such a square!).

So, after 1.Rfe1, Black is strategically lost because he doesn't have play anywhere on the board. White will meet something like 1...Qe7 with 2.Bg5, daring Black to play 2...f6. The only difficulty the first player will have is deciding whether to go for a quick kingside kill (Bg5 followed by Qf4-h4 and then Bf6/Bh6 and Ng5), or mixing it with queenside torture with a well-timed Nf3-d2-b3-c5. Also possible is a simple queenside snuff job with b2-b4, ending play there forever. Then White could pursue his kingside aspirations without worry.

#12

Problem Position

(154)

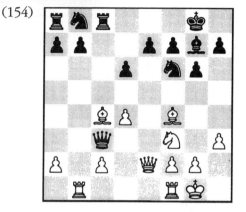

White to play.

Is White doing all right in this position? What would you recommend?

This position arose (White was an 1800 player while Black had a 1900 rating) after **1.d4 Nf6 2.Nf3 g6 3.Bf4** (the Boring Variation of the KID) **3...Bg7 4.e3 d6 5.h3 0-0 6.Bc2 c5 7.0-0 cxd4 8.exd4 Qb6 9.Nbd2 Be6 10.Nc4 Bxc4 11.Bxc4 Qxb2 12.Rb1 Qc3 13.Qe2 Rc8**.

Solution

The imbalances should be pretty easy to read if you make use of the imbalance list in the first chapter. White has two Bishops, active pieces and a nice lead in development. Black is up a pawn and is threatening to chop off our c4-Bishop. Aside from that, the second player has nothing to crow about.

Since the position is so open, and since White's pieces have influence everywhere, White can get something going on the queenside (Rxb7), in the center (Qxe7) and on the kingside.

The most important thing to understand is that White MUST make use of his favorable imbalances. Since he has a lead in time (development), he must play dynamically and try to get the most out of it—once Black gets his own pieces out, White will be in trouble due to his pawn minus.

With this in mind, you should be looking for sharp, forcing continuations that keep your opponent off-balance. In the game, White found the nice:

14.Bxf7+!!

Initiating a powerful attack against a Black army that isn't really ready for a fight.

14...Kxf7
15.Ng5+ Ke8

This wasn't what Black wanted to do, but 15...Kf8 16.Qe6 (also winning is 16.Ne6+ Kf7 17.Nxg7 Kxg7 18.Qxe7+) 16...Qc4 17.d5 also led to a depressing result for the second player (17...Qxd5 allows 18.Qxc8+).

Even worse was 15...Kg8 16.Qe6+ Kh8 17.Nf7+ Kg8 18.Nh6+ Kh8 19.Qg8+ Rxg8 20.Nf7 mate.

16.Rfe1

Not the only move. White could also play 16.Bxd6 Nc6 17.Rxb7 with a quick crush.

16...Nc6
17.Qe6 and White won due to the decisive double threat of 18.Qf7+ and 18.Bxd6.

Yes, some calculation was necessary here, but you certainly didn't need to work things out to the end. Your lead in development and the fact that you could make the enemy King very insecure was all the provocation you needed!

#13

Problem Position

(155)

Row-Cambell (1404-1250), Los Angeles 1997.
White to play.

List the imbalances and find a move that conforms to those differences.

Solution

White has more central space and a lead in development. His position is solid; there are almost no weaknesses in White's camp. Black isn't as fortunate. The c7- and d5-squares must be watched, and the d6-pawn is weak.

Since the center is open, White should try and play right down the middle (always play in the center if you can, it's the most important area of the board).

With no negatives and some long-term plusses in space and superior pawn structure sitting in front of him, White should be patient and just build up his game with 1.Bh2 followed by 2.Re1. If Black tried to advance his e-pawn via ...e5-e4, the h2-Bishop would gain in power and would hit hard at d6.

In the actual game, White felt that he had to do something NOW! Why, I can't say. He played 1.Nb5?? and after 1...exf4 2.Nc7

Qd8 3.Nxa8 his Knight got trapped on a8 (...b6 followed by ...Bb7 is one way to pick up the horse). White ended up losing horribly. A real shame, because he stood better in the initial position.

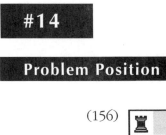

#14

Problem Position

(156)

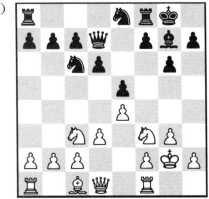

Cambell-Newhoff (1391-1600), Los Angeles 1997.
White to play.

Scan the imbalances and then decide if 1.h4 followed by 2.Rh1 and h5 is justified.

Solution

Not a lot seems to be going on. The pawn structure is symmetrical and no big imbalances exist (though White's Bishop is "good" while Black's is "bad.").

The center is in a static state, and the queenside is also a boring wasteland. That leaves the kingside. Black's last move, ...Ne8, signaled his wish to advance in that sector with ...f7-f5, gaining kingside space and activating his Rook (perhaps both Rooks, if he can double them on the f-file). It's very important to know what your opponent is going to do! Try to figure out his plans before he does!

So, how is White going to get some play, where is it going to be, and how should he deal with Black's upcoming demonstration?

If I was White, I'd look for ways to get some central play (I LOVE to play in the center!). This can be done by 1.Nd5 followed by 2.c3 and 3.d4. Another idea is mixing central play with a kingside block by 1.Ng1 f5 2.f3 with Nge2, Be3 and an eventual d3-d4 to follow. One other plan is 1.Nh4 f5 2.exf5 gxf5 3.f4, starting a hand-to-hand fight in the same basic area.

In the actual game, White showed that he didn't care what Black wanted to do. All he could think of was starting a "mating attack." Thus, the crazy (and completely unjustified) 1.h4? f5 2.Rh1? appeared on the board. At this point Black should probably try 2...h6, keeping White's pieces off of g5 and preparing to meet 3.h5 with 3...g5 (when it finally becomes clear that Black is boss on the kingside!). Nevertheless, White did end up going down in flames. Hopefully he won't set himself on fire in the future.

#15

One thing I insist on when teaching a student is that he/she always plays for a win. This is obvious enough if your rating is 1500 and your opponent is only 900. However, courage starts to deteriorate when you get paired against someone with a 1900 rating! At that moment, you no longer play the opponent, you begin to play the rating and often give the person sitting across from you superhuman capabilities.

The first thing every chessplayer must learn is that human beings make errors. If you go all out to give your opponent problems, an error can easily appear and a big, fat scalp can fall into your lap.

The second key point for the winning player is that all non-titled players (IMs and GMs being the titled guys) are capable of playing very, very badly. Why fear somebody who is quite capable of going berserk at any moment? Simply put, don't give respect to anyone due to rating. Make them earn that respect by waging all-out war!

The third point for the winning player is that you really have nothing to lose! If you go all out every game, you will find that your wins come much more frequently. The worst thing that can happen to you is a defeat, and we all lose games no matter what happens and no matter who we play. A proper attitude gives you results that are far superior to anything you imagined you could achieve. In fact, confidence is worth one to two hundred rating points all by itself!

One more bit of advice: If you are one of those players who plays below his normal standard when you get paired up, stop looking at the opponent's rating until after the game. This circumvents a lot of psychological baggage and allows you to play with maximum confidence at all times.

Let's take a look at the position in diagram #165 and see how the lower-rated player reacts to his much stronger opponent.

Problem Position

(157)

1600-2100.
White to play.

Is White justified in playing 1.h4 in this position?

Solution

This well-known position from the Torre Attack was new territory for the 1600 player and he took a long time here trying to figure out what was going on. Finally he realized that his chances were on the kingside due to his advanced pawn on e5 and chances for a g2-g4 advance—this opens a file for his Rooks and follows the advice: **Always play on the wings with pawns when the center is closed.**

1.h4!

A great move that stops Black from advancing with ...g7-g5 and also gains kingside space. I was proud of him for finding this far from obvious idea.

1...c4

This move attacks the White Bishop, gains queenside space and prepares a general queenside pawn advance (since White is going for the Black King, Black must stake out territory on the other wing). Its only flaw is that it creates a hole on the d4-square. Of course, Black has no intention of taking the h-pawn by 1...Bxh4 since that would only open lines to his own King. 2.Qh5 would make Black extremely unhappy.

2.Bc2

An obvious move that took too much time to play! Instead of just making this simple retreat, White went into a panic about Black's space and sat there for ten minutes before giving in to the inevitable. 1600 often suffers from time pressure and this shows us why—he wastes time on moves that should be made quickly. Why? Because his lack of confidence makes him see ghosts around every corner. As it turns out, this seemingly innocent bit of hesitation was the first step in complete mental surrender!

2...b5

Black grabs more queenside space and prepares to open lines on that side with ...b5-b4. Notice how Black is trying to generate counterplay in the quickest way possible. This does two things:

> ➤ **It gives him a clear plan and his share of the play.**

> ➤ **It can easily disturb White and make him lose confidence in his own plans.**

3.a3?!

The first sign that everything is not right with White. In situations where the play is on opposite wings, it is often fatal to cave in to the opponent's will and begin reacting to his plans to the exclusion of your own. White's fear of ...b5-b4 grabbed his attention so forcefully that his head was permanently turned in the direction of the queenside! Much stronger was 3.g4 (going all out for the Black King) or 3.Nf3. Let's have a look at 3.Nf3 (placing the Knight in a better position and eyeing both g5 and d4 as future homes): 3...b4 4.Ng5 Nc5 5.Qh5 h6 6.Qg6! hxg5 7.hxg5 with the strong threat of 8.Rh8+!! Kxh8 9.Qh5+ Kg8 10.g6 and mates (analysis by Tigran Petrosian). In this analysis, White refused to be stared down by Black and, as a result, his attack crashed through first.

3...Nc5

Brings the Knight up to a great square and eyes the holes on b3, d3 and e4.

4.h5?

A completely useless move that wastes time and actually weakens White's hold on the g5-square (if it doesn't open lines to the Black King it shouldn't be played). 4.h5? was White's one stab at attack but we must wonder why someone would play it if he originally planned g2-g4. The reason is purely psychological: White was so frazzled that any move that got near the Black King made him feel empowered. Thus White becomes another victim of emotion and panic. Naturally, both 4.g4 or 4.Nf3 were superior moves.

4...a5

Prepares to worry White by preparing the ...b5-b4 advance.

5.Nf3

Finally a logical move that actually improves his position. After his first fine move, White has been in a complete nose-dive.

5...Ba6

The immediate 5...b4 failed due to 6.axb4 when the Black a-pawn is pinned to its Rook. Now this pin doesn't exist and White can start to worry about Black's threats again.

6.Nd4

Improving the position of the Knight and eyeing both c6 and e6. Has White gotten back on track?

6...Qb6

This keeps the White Knight out of c6 and prepares to play ...b4.

7.Rb1??

White snaps. Faced with a concrete threat, White goes bonkers and plays a move that actually does nothing at all. He really had to throw caution to the winds and play 7.g4 when Black would be forced to react to White's gestures of aggression on the kingside.

7...b4

Threatens to win a piece by 8...b3 (courtesy of 7.Rb1??). Black's attack is much further advanced than White's so we won't look any further at this rather sad game.

#16

Riese-Carter (1482-1537), Continental Open 1996.
Ruy Lopez.

1.e4 e5
2.Nf3 Nc6
3.Bb5

The venerable Ruy Lopez is one of the oldest known openings.

3...Bc5

A rare line (3...a6 is more common) that prompts White into initiating a tactical flurry.

4.Nxe5

A common tactical device. White knows that he can regain his material after 4...Nxe5 by 5.d4, forking Black's Knight and Bishop.

4...Bxf2+
5.Kxf2 Nxe5
6.Rf1

White prepares to castle by hand with Kg1.

6...Qf6+
7.Kg1 Qb6+

I think White almost had a heart attack when this appeared on the board. After calming down for a moment, he realized that it was not as bad as it originally seemed.

8.d4 Qxb5
9.dxe5 Qxe5

![Problem Position]

(158)

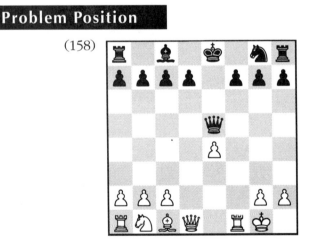

White to play.

Would 1.Bf4 be foolish here?

Solution

In a way, this position was more or less reached by accident. Black got carried away with his material desires while White had no choice after missing ...Qb6+.

Black is a pawn up but things are not all rosy. His King is still in the middle, he will lose time due to the vulnerable location of his Queen and he is considerably behind in development. All these things are dynamic in nature, though, and if Black can get castled and consolidate, his material plus will weigh in his favor.

10.Nc3!?

A logical move that brings a new attacker into position. Also interesting (and most likely strongest) was 10.Bf4!, a move White rejected due to 10...Qxb2 (much worse is 10...Qxe4?? 11.Re1. Safest is 10...Qc5+). However, White should not worry about the loss of another pawn or two, if Black is willing to keep moving his Queen, ignoring the needs of his other pieces. After 11.Nd2, White would be fully mobilized and ready for action.

10...Nf6

The Knight turns out to be vulnerable here. Preferable is 10...Ne7 followed by ...0-0. I don't think Black realized the danger he was in.

11.Bf4

White's final piece comes out and does two things: it attacks the Queen and prepares e4-e5.

11...Qc5+

This gives Black a crucial defensive tempo.

12.Kh1 d6

Black didn't like 12...0-0 13.e5 when the Knight is forced back to the poor e8-square.

Now, after 12...d6, White must find a way to keep his attack alive. If Black is able to castle and develop his Bishop, White's initiative will dissipate.

13.Nd5?

This isn't the right medicine. Much more energetic was 13.e5!, blasting open the center and keeping Black on his toes. After 13...dxe5? (Black has to try 13...Ng4) 14.Bxe5 Black doesn't want to allow 15.Bxf6. If 14...Ng4 (and not 14...Qxe5?? 15.Re1, picking up the Queen) 15.Bxg7 Rg8 (15...Nf2+ 16.Rxf2 Qxf2 17.Bxh8) White wins material with 16.Re1+! Be6 17.Qxg4.

13...Nxe4??

Black goes berserk and opens lines to his own King. Correct was 13...Nxd5 14.exd5 0-0 when the King finds a safe haven.

White now finishes up in a very efficient way:

14.Re1 f5
15.b4

This makes use of the fact that Black's Queen has to keep an eye on the c7-pawn.

15...Qc4
16.Qd3!

Simple but pleasing. White would be quite happy to go into a piece up endgame after 16...Qxd3 17.cxd3.

16...Qc6
17.b5 Qc5
18.Be3

Suddenly the Black Queen is trapped and the game is won. Black resigned in a few more moves.

#17

Problem Position

(159)

Piacenza-Lyles (1713-1650), Continental Open 1996.
White to play.

Don't bother looking for individual moves. Instead, figure out what White's correct plan is. Also, be aware of why you made this decision.

Solution

White is playing for queenside gains and for control over the f5-square. Black is trying to somehow get a kingside attack started. The way White ignores Black's illusory kingside threats and quietly builds up his own plusses is rather impressive.

1.b4

This move gains more queenside space and shows complete disdain for anything that Black may conjure up.

1...h4

Black lashes out on the kingside and tries to put a scare into his opponent. This is the point where most amateurs (as White) would start to defend. To his credit, Piacenza doesn't even blink.

It should be noted that 1...f5 would have turned out very nicely for White after 2.exf5 Bxf5 3.Bd3 when White gets to use the e4-square as a home for his Knight.

2.Be2

This move jumps on the fact that g4 is no longer defended by a pawn. White doesn't mind the doubled g-pawns because he sees that the g3-pawn keeps the enemy Knight out of f4 and h4.

I love White's mentality! Instead of seeing Black's kingside play as a threat, he is looking at it as a weakness!

2...hxg3
3.hxg3 Kh7

Black has opened the h-file in his eternal dreams of mate. White continues to ignore his opponent.

4.Rf1

Clamping down on the f5-square and getting the Rook into a more active position. Also tempting was 4.Qd1.

4...Rh8

Black's Rook hopes to make the acquaintance of the White King. Will this worry his opponent?

5.Nb3

Laughing in Black's face! I'm not sure if the Knight is optimally placed here but White's desire to continue his queenside buildup and ignore his opponent's unsound kingside demonstration is admirable.

Alternatives are 5.a5, 5.Nc4, 5.Qd1 and 5.c4 followed by 6.c5.

5...Bh6

Black exchanges off his bad Bishop for White's good one. This trade was not prompted by positional acumen, though. Instead, Black realized that he could not mate with his Rook alone and, by getting rid of White's dark-squared Bishop, his Queen would have access to the g5-square.

6.Bxh6 Kxh6
7.Qd1

Black has a very bad game due to his inferiority on the queenside and his weak pawns on g4 and f7. The immediate threat against g4 forces Black to either give up the pawn, play the groveling 7...Qd7 or allow a Queen exchange by 7...Qg5 8.Qc1.

7...Kg7
8.Bxg4 Qg5

Black has placed all his hopes in this final attacking gesture. As usual, White just goes about his business and ignores him.

9.Bxc8 Qe3+

Also hopeless was 9...Qh6 (which really doesn't threaten anything at all!) 10.Bh3. Even the scary 9...Qxg3 doesn't give Black enough after the cold-blooded 10.Bf5.

10.Rf2 Raxc8
11.Qf3. Gin! The double threat of 12.Qxe3 and 12.Qxf7+ forces a winning endgame. White went on to score the full point after 11...Qxf3 12.gxf3.

#18

Piacenza-Winston (1713-1265), Continental Open 1996.
Queen's Indian Defense.

1.d4 Nf6
2.Nf3

White avoids the main lines with 2.c4 and instead plays a quiet system known as the Colle.

2...b6
3.e3 Bb7
4.Bd3 e6
5.Nbd2

White eventually intends to advance his pawn to e4, gaining space in the center and preparing for a kingside attack via e4-e5.

5...c5

6.c3 Nc6
7.0-0

So far, Black has handled the opening well. His next move, though, gives us the first hint about his true King-hunting psychosis.

7...Bd6??

Awful. Black is so intent on aiming everything at White's King (I originally thought Black was trying to gain some control over e4 with his ...b6 and ...Bb7. Now I see that he had something much grander in mind!) that he ignores such "minor" things as central play and castling.

8.e4

Threatening a big fork on e5. White doesn't need an invitation to grab the center with gain of time!

8...cxd4
9.cxd4 Be7

Black admits that his first idea wasn't very good. It looks like he's going to settle down and play a real game of chess now.

10.a3

A very useful move. White keeps the Black Knight out of b4 and prepares to gain queenside space with a later b4 advance.

10...h5??

Black unleashes the full fury of his subconscious! Where he got such hatred for royalty is beyond me, but it's clear that only the White King's head will make him happy.

This move demonstrates the desire to attack without any justification whatsoever. In the end, all it really does is weaken the g5-square, waste time and ignore the center.

Problem Position

(160)

White to play.

Black has just pushed his h-pawn from h7 to h5. Is this a good move, and how should White react to it?

Solution

11.b4

After adjusting his glasses to make sure he had seen Black's move properly, White ignores his opponent's berserk play and gains some queenside space.

11...Qc7

Black plays with iron-willed consistency. This move takes aim at the h2-pawn.

12.Bb2

White continues to develop and build in the center and on the queenside. I often see amateurs react to Black's kingside gestures with moves like 12.h3, keeping Black's pieces off of g4. Why waste a tempo on a non-threat and why give Black something to aim at when he advances his pawns by ...g7-g5-g4? Don't give Black's plan more respect than it deserves.

12...Rg8??

Yet another subtle move. I imagine flecks of aggressive foam forming on Black's lips as he looks at his opponent, hoping to see a quiver of terror or eyes wide with fear.

13.Rc1

White yawns and improves his position. Showing such a lack of respect for your opponent's ideas often unnerves him and undermines his confidence.

13...a6

This stops White from winning a piece with b4-b5.

14.Re1?

A nice building move that misses the win of a piece by 14.d5! exd5 15.Bxf6 gxf6 16.exd5.

14...g5??

Black lets out a roar as he jumps into the abyss. He should have played 14...d5, trying to keep the center locked up.

15.g3?

White finally shows some fear and makes an unnecessary defensive move. Far stronger was 15.d5! (meeting an attack on the wing with a counterattack in the center) 15...exd5 16.Bxf6 Bxf6 17.exd5+ when Black should quietly resign before rushing off to lick his wounds.

In the actual game, White went on to win (despite his mistaken 15.g3), but I would like to say that White's attempts to stand fast in the wake of kingside attacks struck a freeing blow for amateurs everywhere.

Problem Position

(161)

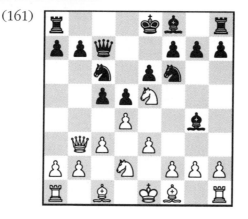

Goldberg-Royal (1700-1800), California 1996.
White to play.

How should White handle this position?

Solution

White is behind in development and will have problems getting his c1-Bishop to a good post. He was not happy here and instead of trying hard to give himself something to play for, he let his poor mood affect his choice of move.

8.Nxc6?

A bad move that exchanges off a good Knight and helps Black strengthen his central position by bringing the side pawn on b7 to the more central c6-square. If White had recognized that this was a key moment of the game (his unhappiness with the position should have clued him in), he might have tried harder and come up with a superior choice. Personally, I would have played 8.Nxg4 Nxg4 9.Be2 Nf6 (9...Nxh2?? 10.g3 traps the greedy Knight) 10.0-0 when the newly acquired two Bishops and the possibility of opening up the position for them by a later e3-e4 would have given White hope for a positive future.

If you chose 8.f4 (laying claim to the e5-square), then you did better than the game's 8.Nxc6 because your move at least does something positive. If your choice was 8.Bb5 (which fights for the initiative), Black will do well with 8...Bd6.

8...bxc6
9.Qa4 cxd4?

This unfortunate and unnecessary move (what compelled Black to make this capture?) gives White a wonderful opportunity which, however, passed over the heads of both participants.

10.exd4?!

White plays the normal capture (he had been taught to always take with the e-pawn in this opening) and, because he wasn't thinking for himself, misses a rare chance to grab the advantage.

The correct idea was 10.cxd4, opening a file toward the weakness on c6. White could then follow up with 11.Nb3, 12.Bd2 and Rc1 with considerable pressure against the Black position. How could he have found this plan? The main sign that something was amiss should have been his feeling that White's game was not very promising after the move actually played.

Why make a move if you don't like the result? Once you see that your intended move lacks panache, place your nose to the grindstone and look for something else! Once you see that you want to turn c6 into a weakness, it shouldn't be too hard to find moves that bring all your pieces to bear on that specific point.

The game continued as follows:

10...Bd6
11.h3 Bf5
12.b3 0-0
13.Ba3

Trying to exchange his bad Bishop for Black's good one. Unfortunately, White continues to fall further and further behind in development.

13...Rfe8
14.Bxd6 Qxd6
15.Qb4 Qc7
16.Nf3

Now it's Black's turn to get excited. He has a huge lead in development and must be feeling the desire to throw some kind of knockout punch. Remember: a development lead is a temporary advantage and must be used before the enemy can catch up. These facts should have told Black that a key moment has arrived; how will he punish his opponent?

The correct move (which Black failed to find) was 16...e5!!, ripping the center open so that the Black pieces can reach the centrally placed White King. Then 17.Nxe5 Rxe5+ 18.dxe5 Qxe5+ gives Black a raging attack since 19.Be2 Re8 picks up material while 19.Kd1 Ne4 creates overwhelming threats against c3 and f2.

Tips

★ You have to keep your eyes open for key moments in the struggle.

★ A key moment has arrived if you are poorly placed and need to find a move that gives you a new lease on life.

★ A key moment has arrived if you are in charge of the game and sense that it's time to search for a knockout blow.

★ The exciting moves that often arise from key positions can only be found if you make a conscious decision to look for them. This means that you must turn off the automatic pilot and try to make the position conform to your will.

#20

Andersson-Flaherty (1588-1707), American Open 1996.
Dutch Defense.

1.d4 f5

The Dutch Defense is an aggressive opening that tends to do better on the amateur level than on the international scene. Black's first move gains kingside space, fights for control over the important e4-square and prepares to place the g8-Knight comfortably behind the f-pawn on f6. Its flaws include a weakening of the a2-g8 diagonal and the blocking of the c8-h3 diagonal (this often leads to difficulties for Black in developing his c8-Bishop).

2.c4

Already a big decision! Aside from popular alternative lines like 2.Nc3 (playing for a quick e2-e4) or 2.Bg5 (with the idea of 2...h6 3.Bh4 g5 4.Bg3 f4? 5.e3! fxg3?? 6.Qh5 mate!), White usually tries the flexible 2.g3 Nf6 3.Bg2 when he can place his Knight on h3 or f3, depending on the system Black chooses. The reason White holds off on c2-c4 until he is castled is simple: this avoids any worry about Black trying ...e6 followed by ...Bb4+.

2...Nf6
3.Nf3 d6

Black shows his interest in a line known as the Leningrad Variation (if he plays 4...g6). White's move order was mainly designed to punish the popular Stonewall Variation, which arises after 3...e6 4.Nc3 d5, with 5.Bf4! followed by 6.e3 when Black will always be a little worse. The flaw in this order is that 3..e6 4.Nc3 can (and should!) be met by 4...Bb4! 5.Qb3 Qe7 with a difficult, more or less equal, game in store.

4.Nc3 c6

All right, now Black's saying that he will play a rare Hort-Antoshin Variation (this line would arise after 5.g3 Qc7). Does he know what he's doing or is he as confused as White is at this point?

5.e3

White avoids main line theory (a wise decision if you don't know the lines!) and decides to develop his pieces in an intelligent and logical fashion.

5...g6

Black decides to go back into Leningrad-type positions. He intends to fianchetto his dark-squared Bishop and then strive for an ...e7-e5 advance with subsequent play on the kingside where he owns more space, or in the center.

6.Bd3

Now the plans for both sides are becoming clear! I've already mentioned that Black intends to play for ...e7-e5. White will strive to get play in the center with e3-e4. If he achieves this, the open e-file will give him good chances to take advantage of the hole on e6 and the backward pawn on e7.

6...Bg7
7.0-0 0-0

It's always a good idea to get your King safe before you open up the center.

8.Re1

White begins to prepare for his dream advance to e4. This is a logical idea, but the immediate 8.e4 also deserved serious consideration (why dream of ice-cream when you can buy some and stuff it in your mouth right away!?).

8...Qc7

Black prepares for his own advance (i.e., ...e7-e5). However, another idea is 8...d5!?, trying to make White's last move look silly. If White had played e4 on this eighth move, Black wouldn't have had this possibility.

The moral here is: **Don't endlessly prepare to actualize a plan when you can just do it and get the ball rolling!**

9.Qc2

White crashes headlong into the pitfall mentioned in the last note! By needlessly making one more unnecessary preparatory move, White gives Black the time to carry out his own plan. Correct would have been 9.e4 when 9...fxe4 10.Nxe4 Bg4 11.Neg5 (threatening both 12.Ne6 and 12.h3) gives White the better game.

9...e5

Problem Position

(162)

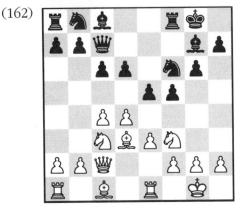

White to play.

Black's center pawns look very threatening. How should White deal with this situation?

Solution

10.dxe5

This is too obliging. Faced with the threat of ...e5-e4, White should have tried hard to come up with some sort of counter-action in the center. Look hard at this position...what would you have played?

If you found 10.c5! you should give yourself a big pat on the back. Now (after 10.c5) 10...dxc5 11.Bc4+ Kh8 12.Nxe5 leaves Black in difficulties, while 10...d5?? Is impossible due to the obvious 11.Nxe5. The real question about the merits of 10.c5 centers around Black playing 10...e4. In that case, White must avoid 11.Bc4+?? due to 11...d5 when Black wins a piece. Instead, 11.cxd6 exd3? (better is 11...Qxd6 12.Bc4+ Be6 though 13.Qb3 is promising for the first player) 12.dxc7 (and not 12.Qb3+?? Qf7 when White remains a piece behind) 12...dxc2 13.cxb8=Q Rxb8 and now 14.Bd2 followed by 15.Rac1 and 16.Rxc2 leads to the win of a pawn for White.

White missed this move because he became overwhelmed by Black's apparent threat of ...e5-e4. If you focus too hard on what your opponent is going to do to you, it is easy to exclude your own possibilities out of panic and blindness. In simple English, I'm saying: always try hard to find something positive for your side to do (actually, you should *insist* on it!). Try to avoid any kind of obsession on enemy threats.

10...dxe5
11.e4 f4

Black has carved out a lot of space on the kingside and will soon launch a kingside attack by ...h7-h6 and ...g6-g5-g4.

12.b4

Realizing that things haven't turned out as he originally planned, White calms down and comes up with an excellent plan. His intention is to follow up with 13.c5 (gaining queenside space) when Bc4+ or Nf3-d2-c4 d6 (making use of the hole on d6) may follow.

By the way, I would probably have preferred the immediate 12.c5 (another case of just doing your plan instead of preparing to do it), since 12...Nbd7 can be met with either 13.b4 or 13.Na4.

12...a5
13.c5

White has suddenly begun to play with great purpose and, as so often happens when you act like you know what you're doing, Black cracks under the strain and just reacts to his opponent's queenside threats.

13...Na6?

This turns out badly. He should have played 13...axb4 14.Qb3+ Kh8 15.Qxb4 when queenside files have been opened (which will make White happy) but Black will get some counter-chances against the potentially weak White pawns on a2 and c5.

14.a3!

A great move. White is now playing with confidence and verve; his control of the queenside is growing with every move while the a6-Knight is no longer taking part in the game.

14...h6

Black doesn't fall for 14...axb4 15.axb4 Nxb4?? 16.Qb3+ Kh8 17.Rxa8.

15.Bc4+

Is this definitely the correct square for this Bishop? I would have voted in favor of 15.Qb3+ Kh7 16.Bb2 when a1 and b4 are both defended and e5 is coming under some pressure.

15...Kh7
16.Rb1 axb4
17.axb4 Qe7
18.h3

At first, this move really disturbed me for three reasons: 1) it wastes time by making a kingside pawn move (don't play in your opponent's area!); 2) this pawn move lets Black rip open kingside lines by a later ...g6-g5-g4; 3) I'm not really sure if this move is necessary (if the f3-Knight intends to go to d6 via Nf3-d2-c4-d6, then it's clearly unnecessary).

A second look shows me that White did have some valid ideas when playing 18.h3. First, he has a space edge and wants to take a square away from the enemy pieces. Second, he has decided to keep his Knight on f3 so that it can place pressure on the e5-pawn. His 18th move allows the Knight to stay in place by stopping ...Bg4.

Does this mean that I like White's move now? No, it still makes me uncomfortable. However, the fact that he had valid ideas to back up his choice goes a long way towards atonement.

18...Nc7?

Black shows that he's mentally beaten. Instead of trying a hopeless defense (he has no chance of survival on the queenside), the second player should have gone all out on the kingside with 18...g5. This would have terrified White and gone a long way towards challenging the wisdom of 18.h3 (after 18...g5, White could try the very interesting 19.Nd5!? when 19...cxd5 20.exd5+ Kh8?? 21.Nxe5 is devastating. However, 20...e4 allows Black to keep fighting).

19.Bb2 Nfe8

Black didn't like the look of 19...Be6 20.Nxe5!.

His 19th move shows that Black has completely given up on his kingside aspirations. His passive play is really nothing more than a form of suicide.

20.Na4

The clamp grows tighter. The Knight is heading for the juicy b6-square.

20...Na6
21.Qc3

This defends b4 and piles up the pressure against e5. I would have preferred 21.Bc3 followed by Nb6 and Qb2 (it's safer to lead with the Bishop, not the Queen). Black's game would then be completely hopeless.

21...Nec7
22.Nb6 Rb8
23.Red1

Announcing his intention to dominate the d-file. Shame on you if you wanted to play 23.Nxc8?. Why trade off your super Knight for a passive Bishop unless you have to?

23...Na8
24.Nxc8

Now this makes sense. White grabs the two Bishops and leaves the Black Knight looking silly on a8.

24...Rbxc8
25.Rd6 N8c7

26.Rad1 Rcd8

(163)

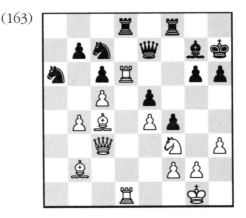

White to play.

27.Rxd8??

Absolutely horrible. Why trade off your super Rooks for Black's pathetic things on d8 and f8? Whenever you are going to make a trade, always ask if your pieces are better than his. If they are, only go through with the exchange if you are making some other kind of major gain. In this case White had several winning continuations, and his willingness to chop off the Rooks demonstrates a flawed mental direction that will eventually lead to his downfall.

Best would have been 27.Qd2! when 27...Rxd6?? 28.cxd6 picks up a piece. Unfortunately for Black, any move of the d8-Rook (27...Rde8, for example) allows 28.Rd7, while 27...Bf6 gets totally wasted by 28.Bxe5!.

So this (27.Rxd8??) is the point where White begins to throw the game away. Why? How did this happen after his fine play during the last several moves? I really don't have any answer because Mr. Andersson was also confused about his motivation and what he was trying to achieve.

Some possibilities are:

1) He was getting tired (poor judgment is common at the end of along, exhausting game);

2) He was getting impatient (he knew he was winning and wanted to get rewarded for his good play as quickly as possible);

3) He suffered a blind spot and thought that Black could trade on d6, not noticing that this would lose to the pawn recapture and the fork that comes with it;

4) He lost his sense of danger and thought that "anything would win" (you always have to concentrate fully until the opponent resigns);

5) He got carried away on the wings of his two Bishops. This means that he felt his two Bishops would grant him a winning endgame so he played directly for that situation;

6) He might have felt that he was winning the e5-pawn and then had misgivings after the exchanges took place.

27...Rxd8
28.Rxd8 Qxd8

All of a sudden the passive Black Rooks are gone and the once-passive Black Queen is sitting on an open file.

29.Qb3?

Feeling disoriented by the change in position (which *he* initiated!), White denies Black the check on d1. Now he's no longer playing against the enemy targets and calling the tune; instead White has sunk back to the unfortunate "reactionary" level.

His last chance to take the game by storm was 29.Nxe5 (at least grabbing some justification for his trades on d8) 29...Qd1+ 30.Kh2 Qa4 (this is what he feared) 31.Qd4 Qxb4 32.Qd8 h5 33.Qg8+ Kh6 34.Nf7 mate.

29...Qe7
30.Bg8+?

White is still much better but now he loses his mind by thinking that Bishops are always better than Knights in an endgame. Though his Bishops are far superior to the enemy Knights at the moment, this is due to the fact that he has taken them out of the game by depriving them of any useful support points. White's unfortunate transition into the endgame lets the horses jump back into the battle and show what they are capable of.

30...Kh8

31.Qf7??

This completes his slide into oblivion. Why exchange the dynamic White Queen for the passive one on e7? Evidently he felt that his Bishops would eat Black alive!

31...Qxf7
32.Bxf7 Nxb4

Reality check! All of a sudden the Black Knights are showing alarming activity and the White pawn on c5 is isolated and weak.

33.Bxe5

White noticed that 33.Bxg6 is met by 33...Nd3 when this horse defends e5, attacks b2 and also attacks c5. Who says that Knights are worse than Bishops?

33...Bxe5
34.Nxe5 Kg7
35.Bb3

Even worse is 35.Bxg6 Kf6 when White loses a piece.

35...Nca6
36.Nd7 Nd3
37.e5 Naxc5 and Black went on to win.

Tips

★ Get your plans in action as fast as you can.

★ By making unnecessary preparatory moves, you will give your opponent time to carry out his plan.

★ If you focus too hard on what your opponent is going to do to you, it is easy to exclude your own possibilities out of panic and blindness. In simple English, I'm saying: always try hard to find something positive for your side to do (actually you should insist on it!) . Try to avoid any kind of obsession on enemy threats.

★ When you play with confidence and purpose, your opponent will often react to your threats and completely crack under the psychological strain.

★ Try not to make moves on your opponent's side of the board. If you do, make sure that you are not needlessly reacting to imaginary threats.

★ Take away as many squares as possible from the enemy pieces when you possess a spatial plus.

★ If you only chance is to play on one side of the board, go all out and do it! Don't waste time trying to wage a hopeless defense.

★ Whenever you are going to make a trade, always ask if your pieces are better than his. If they are, only go through with the exchange if you are making some other kind of major gain.

★ The way to beat Knights is to take all their advanced squares (support points) away from them. The further they advance down the board, the stronger they become!

#21

Problem Position

(164)

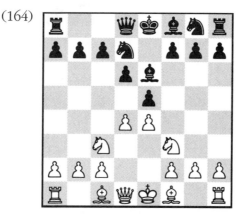

Two unrated players.
White to play.

White has several tempting choices here. What would you do and why would you do it?

This position was arrived at by **1.e4 e5 2.Nf3 d6** (the Philidor Defense) **3.Nc3 Be6?!** 3...Nf6 is better. **4.d4 Nd7**

Solution

To understand this position, we have to break it down in a detailed manner:

Pawn tension: Many of my students have a habit of trading pawns as soon as they come into contact with each other. They have trouble realizing that destroying the pawn tension considerably limits their own possibilities.

In the present situation White would usually refrain from capturing on e5 for the following reasons:

> ➤ **There is no hurry! White is the one with the option to take since a black capture via ...exd4 would only help White bring his Knight to a better post after Nxd4.**

> ➤ **By not rushing to take on e5 White keeps Black off balance by making him worry about both dxe5 and d4-d5.**

> ➤ **Many players think that by taking on e5 they are trading their good d-pawn for Black's good e-pawn. However, this is not really the case! The real trade is d4-pawn for Black's inferior d6-pawn.**

> ➤ **Taking on e5 helps Black by freeing his entombed f8-Bishop. Why do something nice for your opponent?**

Bishop versus Knight: At the moment both sides have two Bishops and two Knights. However, White can try to hunt Black's e6-Bishop down by Ng5 or d4-d5.

Closed center: White must decide whether to close the center by d4-d5, to leave it as it is and just develop a piece, or to open the center completely with dxe5.

Creating a scenario where your imbalance is superior to your opponent's: This is the key to the position! White should take all the information given earlier and mix it together in some palatable form.

Here's the way I would approach this position: I already have a small advantage in space, so quiet development by Be2 and 0-0 is an option (in other words, I can simply nurture the imbalance that I already have). I can also play h2-h3 (a useful move in itself) with the threat of d4-d5, winning Black's Bishop.

More interesting, however, is a plan based on gaining the two Bishops. I could try and hunt Black's Bishop down by d4-d5, but why close the position if I intend to get Bishops? Wouldn't it be more logical to open the position?

With this in mind, the immediate 5.Ng5 comes into consideration (yes, I'm breaking the rule that tells us not to move the same piece twice in the opening!). Another way to do this is 5.dxe5 (didn't I just criticize this move? No, I just pointed out all the things that were wrong with it and said that I normally wouldn't take it into serious consideration. In this case, though, White intends to grab the two Bishops, so opening the position as wide as possible makes a good deal of sense.) 5...dxe5 6.Ng5 when 6...Qf6 7.Nxe6 Qxe5 8.Qd5! (less clear is 8.Nd5 0-0-0 9.Bc4 Qg6 10.Qf3 Nc5) 8...Qxd5 9.Nxd5 0-0-0 10.Bc4 when White has the preferable position thanks to his two Bishops.

White would be doing well if he chose 5.h3, 5.Be2, 5.Ng5 or 5.dxe5 followed by 6.Ng5. Just remember one big thing: don't grab an imbalance if you feel the resulting position (and all the factors that make it up) is at odds with it (e.g., striving for Bishops in a closed position; striving for Knights in an open position. Both these errant plans might prove harmful to your health.).

5.d5?!

White goes for the closed position, not realizing that he is simultaneously making his f1-Bishop a poor piece by placing the center pawns on its color.

5...Bg4
6.h3 Bxf3

Also possible is 6.Bh5 7.g4 Bg6. What's the first thing that strikes you about this position (after 7...Bg6)? How about that hole on f4?

Every student of the game should train himself to salivate whenever a hole appears on the board (of course, you should have an aversion towards creating them in your own position)! Though Black has absolutely no way to make use of that hole at the moment, my eyes would go cloudy and I would fantasize in the following manner: I would dream of trading off my g6-Bishop and one Knight for White's two Knights. I would also dream of exchanging my bad dark-squared Bishop for White's good piece on c1. That would leave me with a good Knight versus White's bad Bishop. Then a quick maneuver like ...Nd7-f8-g6-f4 would give me a winning minor piece.

Naturally, the actualization of this plan might take thirty moves, but the possibility (and the rewards it brings) would never leave my mind.

7.Qxf3 f6??

When I saw this move I almost collapsed in horror! One little pawn push and so much self-destruction. Black has taken the f6-square away from both his Knights, created a hole on e6, made his f8-Bishop even worse than it was, blocked his Queen and thrown a full tempo out the window.

What should Black have done? The answer lies in two areas: 1) the minor piece battle; 2) the closed position and the use of the pawn pointing theory.

When the center is closed you generally play in the direction your pawns point. Since you must attack with pawns in closed positions (compared to piece attacks in open positions), you should usually advance the pawn that is next to your most advanced unit. In this case, Black will play for ...f7-f5 (placing the pawn next to his advanced e-pawn) while White would like to play c2-c4-c5 (something that won't be easy for him to do).

The other key factor in the position is the minor pieces. White has two Bishops and Black would like to follow this rule: **When your opponent has two Bishops, trade one off (for a Bishop or a Knight) and leave him with only one.**

Another rule worth following asks you to trade off your poor pieces for your opponent's good ones. In this case, Black would love to exchange his bad f8-Bishop for White's fine c1-Bishop. This can be done by 7...Be7 followed by 8...Bg5 or by 7...g6 followed by 8...Bh6. Most logical is 7...g6 since it prepares for an eventual ...f7-f5 advance and also prepares to trade the Bishops.

Black's actual move caters to none of these positional demands and, therefore, is an abomination of the worst order.

More of this game follows in problems #22 and #23.

#22

Problem Position

(165)

Two unrated players.
White to play.

This position arose after **1.e4 e5 2.Nf3 d6** (the Philidor Defense) **3.Nc3 Be6?!** 3...Nf6 is better. **4.d4 Nd7 5.d5?! Bg4 6.h3 Bxf3 7.Qxf3 f6**.

List the imbalances and then find a plan that helps White make use of his main plusses. What is White's best move?

Solution

8.Bb5?

White fails to make the most of his opportunities and misses two very interesting plans. The first centers around the move f2-f4. Normally White would not consider this because, after Black takes on f4, the e4-pawn would be backward on an open file and the e5-square would serve as a home for Black's pieces.

Note that the weakening of e6 allows White to dream about placing a Knight there. Unfortunately, White's Knight has no way to reach this oasis in the heart of Black's position. This changes after Black captures on f4 since suddenly the f4- and d4-squares are available to the White Knight and maneuvers like Nc3-e2-d4-e6 are now "on."

This shows us that f2-f4, seemingly a space-gaining idea on the kingside, actually is a well-disguised attempt to infiltrate to e6 with the Knight.

White's second plan is even better. He has the two Bishops and would like to activate the pathetic guy on f1. Since bad Bishops belong outside the pawn chain, the move 8.h4! turns out to be very strong. Please understand that White is not trying to attack Black on the kingside. Instead, he is playing for two goals: 1) the nullification of all Black's kingside play; 2) the activation of the f1-Bishop.

To achieve ...f6-f5, Black will have to play ...g7-g6 at some point (this also allow Black to trade his bad Bishop with ...Bh6). However, after 8.h4 g6, White has the annoying 9.h5. More importantly, White's real intention is to follow up with 9.g3 and 10.Bh3, when the Bishop has turned into a monster!

Once he has stopped Black on the kingside and assured himself of a highly favorable minor piece, White can then turn his attention back to the queenside where he can try to make use of his spatial advantage in that area. Total domination of the board would then be complete, and the game would surely be his.

(166)

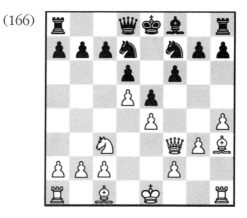

The light-squared Bishop rules!

Putting these ideas into elementary perspective, it is enough to say that when you see a weak square, try to find a way to occupy it. If you have a bad Bishop, fight tooth and nail to get it outside the pawn chain so it can become active.

Both these plans are very advanced, so don't feel bad if you have trouble fully understanding them.

8...a6
9.Bxd7+ Qxd7
10.0-0 0-0-0

Something new has happened. We now have Kings castled on opposite sides of the board. This usually means that both sides will launch attacks against the enemy monarch and seek a knockout. No more subtlety, just brute force and endless aggression.

11.Bd2 Nh6. The rest of this game can be seen in problem #23.

#23

Problem Position

(167)

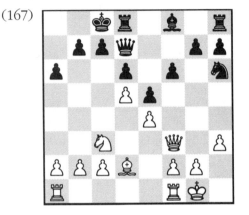

Two unrated players.
White to play.

This position arose after **1.e4 e5 2.Nf3 d6** (the Philidor Defense) **3.Nc3 Be6?!** 3...Nf6 is better. **4.d4 Nd7 5.d5?! Bg4 6.h3 Bxf3 7.Qxf3 f6 8.Bb5 a6 9.Bxd7+ Qxd7 10.0-0 0-0-0 11.Bd2 Nh6**.

A big question comes to mind: should White capture on h6 and open up the g-file for Black's Rooks?

Solution

Should White capture on h6 and open up the g-file for Black's Rooks? The answer is a resounding yes! The reason for this decision doesn't lie with the win of a pawn (which White won't take) or with attacking considerations. Instead, the reason centers around the creation of a hole.

12.Bxh6 gxh6

Frankly speaking, this position is completely hopeless for Black. Normally White would strive to attack the Black King by b2-

b4, a2-a4-a5, Rfb1 and b4-b5 ripping open lines to the enemy monarch (of course, Black would be doubling on the g-file and trying to create his own attack). However, White has a way to kill all enemy counterplay and virtually turn the game into a lock victory.

13.Ne2!

This is it! Instead of eating a pawn by 13.Qxf6 (which gives Black some counterplay with 13...Be7: 14.Qf5 Qxf5 15.exf5 Rdf8 16.g4 h5 17.f3 hxg4 18.fxg4 h5 19.Rf2 hxg4 20.hxg4 Rfg8 21.Rg2 Rh4), White swings his Knight around to the dominating f5-square where it rules the Black Bishop and kills any chances Black may have had for an attack (place the Knight on f5 and White's pawns on h4 and g3. Such a set-up would give Black no hope at all). Once White takes control of the kingside with his super-horse, he can then proceed to play for a queenside attack without fearing any resistance whatsoever.

Several students have asked how to know when it's all right to move a piece several times in a row. "Can't the opponent do something to punish you?"

If the position were open, then long maneuvers would be of doubtful value since development and speed of operations become critical. However, the closed center in our present game means that play will be more ponderous and thus conducive to productive Knight journeys.

13...Be7
14.Ng3 Rdg8
15.Nf5 and White went on to win the game.

Tips

★ Closed positions are conducive to long maneuvers.

★ Open positions call for quick development.

★ Closed centers call for pawn play on the wings to gain space and get the Rooks into the battle.

★ Always be on the lookout for weak squares (holes).

★ If you can exterminate enemy play before proceeding with your own, don't hesitate to do so!

★ Make sure that the imbalance you strive to obtain fits in well with other factors in the position.

#24

Problem Position

(168)

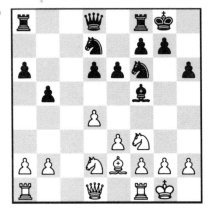

1100-1900
White to play.

Black appears to have an excellent position. Is this true, and what should White do?

Solution

Black appears to have the better game. His Bishop is active and his pawns on e6 and d6 cover key squares on e5, d5 and c5. To make matters even worse for White, Black also possesses a space advantage on the queenside.

In the actual game, White played 1.Rc1 (placing a Rook on an open file; how can such a thing be bad?) and after 1...Nb6 Black was doing well (White quickly realized that his Rook on f1 wasn't taking part in the battle).

White didn't understand the following things:

➤ **His center pawns are pointing towards the queenside while his Bishop also aims in that direc-**

tion. Doesn't this suggest that he seek play in that sector?

➤ Neither player has any aggressively placed troops on the kingside. There are also no weaknesses in that area which tells us that no kingside attacks should be considered for either side.

➤ Both players have solid central positions so active play there is also doubtful.

➤ White's Bishop (it happens to be a *good Bishop*— its central pawns are on the opposite color and thus don't block it) is less active than Black's Bishop. What can be done about this? How can White turn this piece into a useful member of his "society?"

➤ Neither side has any clear weaknesses to attack. This is the key idea in the position! How can White create targets in the enemy camp?

To summarize, you (as White) must ask the following questions and then demand an answer from yourself: 1) how can I make my Bishop stronger? 2) how can I get both my Rooks into the game? 3) how can I initiate queenside play? 4) how can I create weaknesses in Black's queenside fortress? 5) how can I get my Knight's into the action?

Don't forget: each and every piece (other than the King) should play a role in the coming plan. Never leave anyone out!

1.a4!

The only correct decision! Suddenly White is challenging Black for queenside space. He is also hitting the Black b-pawn and, by doing so, is turning his passive Bishop into a strong attacking piece.

Finally, the Rook on a1, which seemed so useless a moment ago, shows that it is actually beautifully placed on its original square.

1...b4

Black doesn't like 1...bxa4 since 2.Rxa4 lets White build up strong pressure against the new target on a6 (White will double

Rooks on the a-file when both Rooks and the Bishop take part in the assault against a6). If 1...Qb6, then 2.axb5 axb5 3.Qb3 shows b5 to be a target.

Note that the advance of the Black b-pawn has given White access to the c4-square.

2.a5!

White had more than one tempting move here. The most obvious is 2.Qb3 (hitting b4 with tempo), but after 2...a5 3.Nc4 Qb8 Black's defenses are tight (though White would obviously have a good position).

White can also consider placing a Knight on b3 since it frees the d2-square for the other horse (which is really doing nothing on f3) and places immediate pressure on a5.

White's actual move, 2.a5, does several things: 1) it takes the b6-square away from Black's pieces; 2) it stops the Black a-pawn from giving support to b4; 3) it fixes the a6-pawn as a target (the best targets are those that can't move); 4) it fixes the a6-pawn on a light-colored square. Now White's Bishop is a very proud piece.

The concept of fixing targets on attackable squares is very, very important. The other idea of turning a rock-solid pawn (on b5) into a target (by a2-a4) is also critical to success at high-level chess.

After 2.a5, Black's position would be quite uncomfortable. Amazing, isn't it? Two moves ago Black appeared to be doing well, and now the picture has changed drastically.

#25

Rau-Melikadamian (1404-1455), Los Angeles 1997.
Torre Attack.

1.d4 Nf6
2.Nf3 e6
3.Bg5

This line, the Torre Attack, is very popular in amateur events. It's easy to learn and carries a lot of sting.

3...Be7

4.Nbd2 d5
5.e3 0-0
6.Bd3 Nbd7
7.0-0

A common mistake. White doesn't want Black to play ...c7-c5 followed by ...Qc7 because then the second player would gain control over the e5-square. To prevent this from happening, White should play 7.c3 when 7...c5 8.Ne5 gives White a grip on e5 and real chances for a kingside attack. For example: 7.c3 c5 8.Ne5 (threatening 9.f4) 8...Nxe5 9.dxe5 Nd7 10.Bf4 (if White had already castled then 10.Bxe7 followed by 11.f4 would be correct. The fact that White is not castled allows him to use his kingside pawns in a more aggressive fashion) 10...f5 11.h4 when a later g2-g4 will give White a strong attack.

7...c5
8.c3

This lets the White Bishop calmly move back to c2 in case of ...c5-c4.

8...h6

Missing his chance to play 8...Qc7! followed by a quick ...e6-e5. Note that 8...Qc7 9.Bf4 would be met by 9...Bd6.

9.Bf4 Nh5
10.Ne5

I was very pleased to see that White wasn't afraid to have his pawns doubled (it doesn't matter if the move is actually good or bad; the fact that he embraced the concept is a very encouraging sign). These doubled guys are not weak at all; in fact, they give White a half-open e-file and firm control over the e5-square.

10...Nxf4
11.exf4 Nxe5
12.fxe5 c4??

Absolutely horrible. What does Black gain by this obvious attack? Yes, he threatens White's Bishop, but is the first player going to leave it there? A bribe might induce him to do so, but aside from that I would guess that any semi-intelligent life form would slide the

Bishop back to c2. So the threat really should not play a part in Black's decision to push to c4. Instead, the gain of queenside space and the closing of the center should be the main points of interest.

In the present position, Black closes the center with 12...c4 and thus forces both sides to play on the wings: Black will play for ...b7-b5-b4, opening queenside files and creating attackable targets in that sector, while White will play for mate with f2-f4-f5. Since White's plan is more threatening than Black's, 12...c4 should be rejected (with a shudder of disgust!) because it takes away Black's chances for central counterplay! Remember: **Central play almost always beats wing play. Place your bets on the center whenever you can and don't get drawn into making useless one-move attacks on enemy pieces.**

By the way, 12...Qb6, attacking pawns on b2 and d4, would have been quite annoying. White would have been so busy trying to hold on to his stuff (the word "how" comes to mind!) that he wouldn't have time to even think about a kingside attack!

13.Bc2

Now White's happy. The d4-pawn has turned into a rock!

13...Bd7
14.f4 f6

Problem Position

(169)

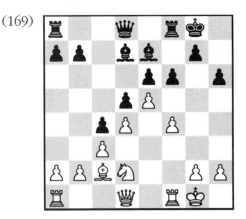

White to play.

In the game White played 15.Bg6. Is this a good move? If you don't like it, what do you think he should have played?

Solution

In this position, White became obsessed with his control over the c2-h7 diagonal and the attacking chances that this brings. Seeing a hole open up on g6, he played 15.Bg6? (all this does is let Black eventually offer a Bishop trade with ...Be8), but didn't have anything after 15...fxe5 16.fxe5 Rxf1+ 17.Qxf1 Qf8 18.Qe2 Qf4 19.Rf1 Qg5 20.Bf7+ (much better would have been 20.Bb1 followed by 21.Nf3 and 22.Qc2) 20...Kh8 and suddenly White realized that his Bishop had gone too far into hostile territory. Bishops are long-range pieces! They don't need to stick their noses in places where they can be cut off.

Going back to the diagram, try to find a way to add new advantages to the ones you already have (kingside space, good light-squared Bishop versus Black's poor Bishop on d7, central space).

15.exf6

A simple move that carries a big punch:

➤ **It opens up the e-file for White's Queen and Rooks.**

➤ **It exposes the e6-pawn as a backward pawn on an open file. In other words, White created an attackable target!**

➤ **It gives the White pieces access to the e5-square.**

➤ **It begins a minor piece fight because now the White Knight will be better than a Bishop once it reaches the juicy e5-square.**

White still possesses those other plusses that he was mesmerized by, but now has a plethora of other blessings also.

15...Bxf6

Even worse is 15...gxf6?? 16.Qg4+ Kh8 17.Qg6 with instant death. On 15...Rxf6, 16.g3 followed by 17.Nf3-e5 would also favor White.

16.Nf3, and White's plan of 17.Qe2 followed by 18.Rae1 (don't forget to get all your pieces into play!), 19.Bb1 and 20.Qc2 leaves Black in sad shape (poor Black is getting killed on the b1-h7 diagonal and is also facing pressure against e5 and e6.

#26

Girlfish-Langer (2071-2279), Reno 1998.
Sicilian Defense, Alapin Variation.

>**1.e4 c5**
>**2.c3**

This move became all the rage in the 1990's.

>**2...e6**
>**3.d4 d5**
>**4.exd5 exd5**
>**5.Nf3 Bd6**
>**6.Be3 c4**
>**7.b3**

This forces Black to part with his space-gaining c4-pawn since 7...b5? 8.a4! is very much in White's favor.

>**7...cxb3**
>**8.axb3 Bg4**

Girlfish admits that pins on g4 (if she's White) or g5 (if she's Black) bring forth a rise of unstoppable panic. Why, isn't clear. Perhaps she was attacked by such a pin when she was just a child or perhaps she saw this kind of pin in a motion picture and was never able to free herself of its horror.

>**9.h3 Bh5**
>**10.Be2**

So far we don't see any ill-effects from hated pin, but her true inner turmoil only shows itself on the twelfth move.

10...Nf6
11.0-0 0-0
12.Nfd2?

What a strange move. Here we see how personal psychosis can make us make moves that other people would never consider trying. Of course, those "other people" tend to have their own hang-ups: the prospect of a doubled pawn could easily send one player into a fit, while another person's inner demons might only come to light if they allow their opponent to gain two Bishops versus Bishop and Knight.

In the present game, Girlfish's pin-fear colors her every decision.

12...Bg6
13.c4

Having dealt with the pseudo-pin (clearly the object of her most primal fears), Girlfish now begins to play aggressively again.

13...Nc6
14.Nc3 Bb4

Black had no interest in giving White mobile center pawns by 14...dxc4 15.bxc4.

15.Nxd5

Not falling for 15.Rc1?? Ba3!, winning the Exchange due to 16.Ra1 Bb2.

15...Nxd5
16.cxd5 Ne7
17.Bf3 Nxd5

A very interesting position has been reached. Black is telling White that the d4-pawn is isolated and weak, while White is saying that the d-pawn is passed and strong.

18.Nc4 Bc3

Black finds a maneuver that hands White two free tempi! One would think that a master wouldn't be vulnerable to such poor decisions. However, they tend to make such errors rather often.

19.Rc1

Now White threatens 20.Bxd5 followed by 21.Rxc3. Black must retreat in shame.

19...Bb4
20.Bd2 Be7
21.Ne5

This looks very natural, but it actually helps Black by chasing the Bishop to f5 and e6, where it finally helps bolster the key blockading d5-square (in other words, it looks good but it has nothing to do with the specific needs of the position). Tempting alternatives are 21.Re1 (simply threatening 22.Bxd5, winning a piece, and keeping her options open) and 21.Ne3! (this conforms to the needs of the position! White forces Black to give up his blockade on d5), forcing Black to abandon his stronghold on d5. After 21.Ne3 Nxe3? (21...Nf4 is much better) 22.Bxe3 Qd7 23.d5 White's d-pawn has turned into a very strong passer, thereby justifying White's earlier view of reality (those two free moves didn't hurt either!).

How many games have been lost when one side tosses out a "natural" move with a song on their lips and hope in their heart.

21...Bf5
22.Re1

White is no longer employing a plan. Instead she places her pieces on nice-looking squares while simultaneously ignoring the need to break the d5-blockade.

22...Re8

Problem Position

(170)

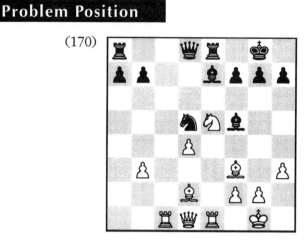

White to play.

In the game, White played 1.Be4. What do you think of this move? Is it a logical choice?

Solution

23.Be4?

This move doesn't make much sense because the light-squared Bishop is White's best piece—it kept Black worried about the d5-square. By exchanging it, all the pressure is off Black and he's finally able to create some threats.

There is also a tactical flaw: White's Rook on e4 is unprotected. This turns out to be very important, and Black tries to take immediate advantage of this fact. Whatever the correct outcome should be, you must be aware of the inherent positional and tactical dangers when playing a move like 23.Be4.

23...Bxe4
24.Rxe4 Ba3!

Threatening both 25...Bxc1 and 25...f6, taking advantage of the unprotected e4-Rook.

25.Ra1 Bb2
26.Ra2 Bc3

The logical continuation, but White can stay alive by using a nice tactical trick that was overlooked by both players. Worthy of attention is 26...f5!?, hoping to create a superior minor piece after 27.Nf7 Qf6 28.Rxe8+ (28.Nh6+!?) 28...Rxe8 29.Rxb2 Qxf7 when the Knight is indeed better than the White Bishop.

27.Qf3?

Missing her big chance. White could have jumped right back into the game with 27.Nxf7! Qf6 (27...Kxf7 28.Rxe8 Kxe8 29.Bxc3 leaves Black in a bad way) 28.Ne5 Qf5 29.Qe2 Bxd4 30.Rxd4 Rxe5 31.Qd3. It seems that Black's attempt to refute White's 23.Be4 tactically was incorrect.

27...Qf6
28.Qg3?

Girlfish snaps. Also bad was 28.Qd3 Nb4 29.Qxc3 Nxa2 30.Qb2 Qa6. However, 28.Be3 Qxf3 29.gxf3 would have allowed White to put up some resistance.

28...Bxd4
29.Nd7?? Qxf2+ and Black won without any difficulty.

GLOSSARY

Active   An aggressive move, line of play, or position. When mentioned in lieu of a player's style, it denotes a preference for sharp, tactical or vibrant types of play.

Advantage   Having a superiority in position based on a particular imbalance or series of imbalances. See _Imbalance._

Analysis   The calculation of a series of moves in a given position. This can be done in actual tournament conditions (in which you are not allowed to touch the pieces) or in a calmer scenario in which the pieces can be moved about (such analysis is often written down for future study or reference). The purpose of analysis is to discover the best move or plan; there is no limit to its length.

Annotation   Written comments (prose, chess symbols or actual moves) about a position or game.

Attack   To make a threat or threats against a specific piece or area of the board.

Backward Pawn   A pawn that has fallen behind its comrades, and thus no longer can be supported or guarded by other pawns of its own persuasion.

In the diagram, Black has backward pawns at d6 and f7. The pawns on h6 and b7 are not backward because they can safely advance.

Bind To have such a vise-like grip on a position that useful moves are difficult for the opponent to find. One often speaks of a crushing space advantage as a bind.

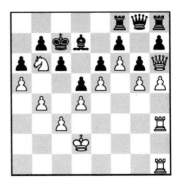

The diagram shows an extreme example of a bind; Black is bound hand and foot and can undertake nothing positive at all.

Bishop Pair To possess two Bishops versus the opponent's Bishop and Knight or two Knights. Two Bishops work extremely well together and are usually an advantage in open positions.

Bishops of Opposite Color A situation in which each player has only one Bishop, each being of a different color, and thus the Bishops can never come into contact. This is usually a good attacking imbalance for the middlegame, since one can't defend what the other attacks. However, these Bishops are known to be rather drawish in the endgame, due to the fact that the defender can place his pawns and King on the opposite color of the enemy Bishop, whereupon they are impervious to harm.

From an attacking point of view, a general rule for Bishops of opposite colors is that they are at their best with other pieces to back them up. On their own, they are often impotent.

Blockade Conceptualized and popularized by Aron Nimzovich (1886-1935), it refers to the tying down (immobilization) of an enemy pawn by placing a piece (in particular a Knight) directly in front of it.

In the diagram, the Knight on d6 is blockading the pawn on d5.

Blunder A horrible mistake that hangs material or makes enormous positional or tactical concessions.

Book Published opening theory. A "book player" is one who relies on memorization of published analysis rather than on his own creative imagination. "Taking someone out of book," refers to sidestepping published analysis by playing a new or unorthodox move. This denies him the chance to make use of a good memory and forces him to find good moves on his own.

Break The gaining of space (and thus more freedom of movement) by the advance of a pawn.

In the diagram, White intends to open lines of attack on the queenside by the break c4-c5 (prepared by b2-b4). Black will strive to attack White on the kingside by an ...f7-f5 break.

Breakthrough A means of penetrating the enemy position. This can be done by a pawn break or by a sacrifice involving pieces or pawns.

In the diagram, both sides are attacking each other's King. At the moment White is safe, since ...gxf3 can be safely answered by Bxf3. So White uses the time given him to effect a breakthrough on the queenside by 1.bxc5 dxc5 2.Nxc5! bxc5. If Black does not capture the Knight, White will simply retreat it to d3 and rip Black open by c4-c5, Qb2 and Black will be mated.

White to play.

Brilliancy A game that contains a very deep strategic concept, a beautiful combination or an original plan.

Calculation The working out of variations without moving the pieces physically. Though this book has taught you to talk or reason your way through a game, there are many positions that have a purely tactical nature. In such situations, the player's ability to calculate variations accurately takes on great importance.

The way to train your combinative (calculative) vision is to study the games of attacking players like Alekhine, Tal, or Kasparov. Follow their opening moves and then cover up the rest of the game score. At this point you should endeavor to figure out all the imbalances, the plans, candidate moves, etc. When this is done, calculate each candidate move as deeply as you can, writing down all this information as you go. All these things must be done without moving the pieces around. When you have done all that's possible (take as much time as you need, we are looking for accuracy; speed will follow with practice), look at the move played, make it on your board and keep repeating the process until the game is complete.

Center Usually considered to be the e4-, d4-, e5-, and d5-squares, though the territory within the c4-, c5-, f4-, and f5-parameters can also be thought of as central.

Centralize The central placing of pieces and pawns so they both control the center and extend their influence over other areas of the board. A piece will usually reach maximum maneuverability and power when centrally placed.

Checkmate See *Mate*.

Classical A style of play (sometimes called a school) that is concerned with forming a full pawn center. The strategic concepts that go with it tend to be viewed as ultimate laws and thus are rather dogmatic. A classical opening is an opening based on these views. See *Hypermodern*.

Closed Game A position locked by pawns. Such a position tends to lessen the strength of Bishops and other long-range pieces simply because the pawns get in their way. Knights, not being long-range pieces, can jump over other pieces and pawns and thus are very useful in such closed situations. A typical series of opening moves that leads to a closed position is 1.d4 Nf6 2.c4 c5 3.d5 e5 4.Nc3 d6 5.e4, etc.

Combination A tactical move or series of moves based on the opponent's weakened King, hanging or undefended pieces or inadequately guarded pieces. Usually involving a sacrifice, it is a calculable series of moves leading to material or positional gains. It is important to note that a combination cannot exist if at least one of the above factors is not present.

Though several players have attempted to create a clear definition throughout the years, the following definition by Silman and Seirawan is the most accurate: A combination is a sacrifice, combined with a forced sequence of moves, that exploits specific peculiarities of the position in the hope of attaining a certain goal.

Compensation An equivalent advantage in one imbalance that balances the opponent's advantage in another. For example: material versus development or space versus a superior minor piece or three pawns versus a Bishop.

Connected Passed Pawns Two or more pawns of the same color on adjacent files. See *Passed Pawn*.

Control To dominate or have the sole use of a file, a square or group of squares, an area of the board, etc. Having the initiative would also put one in "control."

Counterplay When the defending side starts his own aggressive action, he is said to have or be initiating counterplay. However, there are varying degrees of counterplay—some equalizing the chances, some not being quite adequate and some leading to the capture of the initiative and subsequently an advantage.

Cramp A disadvantage in space that leads to a lack of mobility.

Critical Position That point in a position when the evaluation will clearly turn to one side's advantage or stabilize down to equality. In such a position the scales are delicately balanced and the slightest error can lead to disaster.

Defense A move or plan designed to meet an enemy's attack or threats. It is also used in the names of various opening initiated from the Black side. For example: Petroff Defense, Caro-Kann Defense, etc. These Black systems are called defenses since White has the first move and thus Black is considered to be defending. The usual flow from Black's point of view would be: defense leading to equalization followed, only then, by the switch over to a counterattack. This is the classical approach. More modern openings are often designed to create immediate imbalances in an effort to seize the initiative as Black. Strange as it may seem, even these counterattacking openings are usually given the title of defenses: Nimzo-Indian Defense, Sicilian Defense, Grunfeld Defense, King's Indian Defense, etc.

Development The process of moving one's pieces from their starting posts to new positions where their activity and mobility are enhanced. It must be remembered that one's pieces should be developed to squares where they work with the rest of their army towards a particular goal. If an individual piece is providing a useful service on its original square, then there may be no reason to move it.

Doubled Pawns Two pawns of the same color lined up on a file as the result of a capture. Such pawns are generally considered to be weak, though quite often their ability to control certain squares makes them very useful.

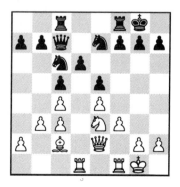

The diagram shows doubled pawns in a favorable light. The doubled pawn on c3 is guarding the critical d4-square, while the other pawn on c4 increases White's control over the important d5-square.

Also note how doubled pawns give their owner an extra file to use. Black's position in the diagram would be considerably improved if he could double his own pawns by placing the d6-pawn on e6.

Dynamic   The word "dynamic" symbolizes the aggressive potential in any given position or move.

Elo Rating   A mathematical system, now used worldwide, devised by Professor Arpad Elo to rank chess players.

En Passant   A French term that literally means "in passing." When a pawn advances two squares (something it can only do if it has not yet moved) and passes an enemy pawn on an adjacent file that has advanced to its fifth rank, it may be captured by that enemy pawn as if the advancing pawn had moved only one square. This optional capture may be made only on the first opportunity, else the right, in that instance, is permanently lost.

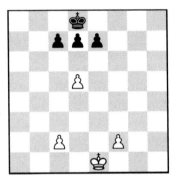

In the diagram, if Black plays 1...c7-c5, White, if he wishes, may capture the pawn as if it had moved to c6. Thus, 2.dxc6. If after 1...c7-c5 White declines to capture and instead plays 2.c4, then after 2...e7-e5 White could no longer capture the c5-pawn. However, he could capture the e5-pawn by dxe6 if he so desired. In chess notation an En Passant capture is labeled by the letter e.p.

En Prise   A French term meaning "in take." It describes a piece or pawn that is unprotected and exposed to capture.

Endgame   When most of the pieces have been exchanged, usually leaving both sides with one to three pieces each (plus any amount of pawns), the game is said to have entered the final phase, known as the endgame.

Equality   A situation in which neither side has an advantage.

Exchange   To trade pieces of equal worth. See *Point Count*. Trading a piece for something of lesser value is called a *Blunder* or a *Sacrifice*.

Exchange, The   A comparison of value between a Rook versus a Bishop or Knight. Thus, if you have won an enemy Rook for your Bishop, you have won the Exchange.

Fianchetto An Italian word meaning "on the flank." Though you will hear many different pronunciations, the correct is fee-an-ket-to. When a Bishop is developed on QN2 or KN2 (b2 or g2 for White and b7 or g7 for Black), it is called a fianchettoed Bishop. This term applies only to Bishops.

FIDE An acronym for Federation Internationale des Echecs, the World Chess Federation.

File A column of eight squares. An open file is a file that is not blocked by either side's pawns.

Fish A derogatory term denoting a weak chess player.

Flank The sides of the board—the kingside and queenside. Flank Openings are openings that deal with flank development. Typical starts for such systems are 1.c4, 1.Nf3, 1.b3, 1.g3, etc.

Force All pieces and pawns are units of force. For example, if White has four attacking units on the kingside to Black's two, White is said to have an advantage in force in that sector of the board.

Forced A move or series of moves that must be played if disaster is to be avoided. Two examples: 1) You face a forced move when your checked King only has one legal move to get out of check. 2) A Knight (or any other piece) is attacked and has only one safe square to go to. Moving it to that safe square is also considered to be forced, even though other moves could legally be played.

Gambit A voluntary sacrifice of a pawn or a piece in the opening with the idea of gaining the initiative, a lead in development or some other compensating factor.

General Principles Basic rules of play designed to serve as guidelines for less advanced players. As one's experience grows, one learns that rules are meant to be broken. For example: the old rule of "always capture with a pawn towards the center," is widely followed, but a good 30% of the time it is correct to capture away from the center. Other rules (such as, avoid doubled pawns, castle as early as possible, develop Knights before Bishops, etc.) are also just as suspect. The simple fact is that every situation must be looked at with an open mind—dogma is not something to be nurtured in life or in chess.

Ghosts Threats that exist only in your own mind. A fear of your opponent or a lack of confidence will often lead to the appearance of ghosts and the cropping up of blunders in your play.

Grandmaster   The highest chess title (aside from World Champion) that one can achieve. Conferred by FIDE, it is awarded to players who meet established performance standards. Other titles (in order of importance) are International Master and FIDE Master. Once earned, these titles cannot be taken away.

Grandmaster Draw   This label, originally used to describe a quick, uninteresting draw between Grandmasters, is now employed to describe a fast draw between virtually any class of players.

Hack   A derogatory chess term meaning a state of chess ineptitude.

Hanging   An unprotected piece or pawn exposed to capture is said to be hanging.

Hanging Pawns   Two adjacent friendly pawns on their fourth rank, separated from other friendly pawns, and subject to frontal attack on one or two half-open files. Though often objects of attack, they also possess a certain dynamic potential. Thus, the battle rages around the question, "are they strong or weak?"

The diagram shows a common hanging pawns situation. The hanging pawns on c5 and d5 give Black an edge in space, good control of the central squares and pressure down the half open b-file. However, they are also exposed to attack.

Hog   See *Pig*.

Hold   A defensive term meaning to "hang on." "Such and such a move would have held out longer," means that the move would have offered tougher resistance, but would most likely have ultimately failed. "Such and such a move would hold," means that the mentioned move would have allowed a successful defense.

Hole   A square that cannot be defended by pawns. Such a square makes an excellent home for enemy pieces (especially Knights). For example, the opening 1.c4 c5 2.Nc3 Nc6 3.e4 is playable, but leaves a hole on d4 that, after 3...g6 and 4...Bg7, can easily be used by a Black piece.

Hutch   A special room set aside for players in a tournament to analyze their games and play *skittles*. Such a room allows various kinds of activity to go on without disturbing the unfinished games in the tournament. Usually used by the non-masters (called Rabbits), the term hutch becomes easily understandable. See *Rabbit* and *Skittles.*

Hypermodern   A school of thought that insists that indirect control of the center is better than direct occupation. In particular, Reti and Nimzovich successfully propagated the idea of central control from the flanks. Unfortunately, they took their ideas to extremes—just as the classicists did. Today it is recognized that both schools of thought are partially correct, and a blending of the two is the only truly balanced method.

Imbalance   Any difference between the White and Black positions. Material advantage, superior pawn structure, superior minor piece, space, development, and the initiative are all typical imbalances.

Initiative   When your opponent is defending and you are attacking or putting pressure on him, it is said that you have the initiative.

Innovation   A new move in an established position or opening.

Intuitive   Usually a sign of experience, it enables a player to choose a move or plan by feel or common sense as opposed to detailed analysis.

Isolated Pawn   A pawn with no friendly pawns on either adjacent file. A common opening that allows an isolated pawn is 1.e4 e6 2.d4 d5 3.Nd2 c5 4.exd5 exd5 5.Ngf3 Nc6 6.Bb5 Bd6 7.dxc5 Bxc5 8.0-0 Nge7 9.Nb3 Bd6 10.Nbd4. The negatives of an isolated pawn are its inability to be guarded by a friendly pawn and the fact that the square directly in front of it usually makes a fine home for an enemy piece since no pawns can chase it away. On the positive side, it offers plenty of space and the use of two half-open or open files on either side of it, with the result that one's pieces usually become active.

Kingside   The half of the board originally occupied by the King, K-Bishop, K-Knight and K-Rook. The kingside is on the right of the player with the White pieces and on the left of the player with the Black pieces.

Liquidation   A series of exchanges that are initiated to quell an enemy attack or to trade off to a drawn or won endgame.

Luft   Literally meaning "air." In chess it describes a pawn move in front of one's King that prevents back rank mate possibilities.

Major Pieces   Also called heavy pieces. The term applies to Queens and Rooks. See *Minor Pieces* and *Pawns.*

Maneuver   A series of quiet moves that aim to favorably reposition one's pieces.

Master   A player becomes a master when he reaches an Elo rating of 2200, though he will lose this title if his rating drops below that point.

Mate   Short for checkmate. It means that you are threatening to capture the enemy King and nothing your opponent can do will prevent its loss. When this happens, you have won the game.

Material   The pieces and pawns, excluding the King. A material advantage is obtained by winning a piece of greater value than the one you gave up. For example, giving up a pawn to win a Rook means that you have an advantage in material.

Mating Attack   An attack on the King that is expected to lead to a checkmate.

Middlegame   The phase of the game that sits between the opening and the endgame. Subtle plans and exciting attacks are generally seen in the confines of the middlegame. Grandmaster Tarrasch once said, "Between the opening and the endgame, the gods have placed the middlegame."

Minor Pieces   The Bishops and the Knights.

Minority Attack   A plan based on the use of two or more pawns (the minority) to act as battering rams against the opponent's three or more pawns (the majority) in order to create a weakness in the opposing camp.

    Here is the most common opening sequence by which a minority attack is reached: 1.d4 d5 2.c4 e6 3.Nc3 Nf6 4.Bg5 Be7 5.cxd5 exd5 6.Nf3 0-0 7.e3 c6 8.Bd3 Nbd7 9.Qc2 Re8 10.0-0 Nf8 11.Bxf6 Bxf6 12.b4 Be7 13.b5 Bd6 14.bxc6 bxc6. White has carried out his minority attack and has left Black with a weak pawn on c6 and a weak square on c5. After a further Rfc1, Rab1 and Na4, White will have great pressure against Black's queenside. This plan is very important to understand, and situations for its use constantly arise.

Mobility   To have freedom of movement for one's pieces.

Mysterious Rook Move   A move with a Rook that seems to have no threat or purpose, but which actually discourages the opponent from a certain type of action (see *Prophylaxis*), or sets up a very deep, well concealed plan.

Occupation   When a Rook or Queen controls a file or rank, that file or rank is said to be occupied. Occupation of a square occurs when a piece is safely placed upon it.

Open   A type of position (see *Open Game*) or file (see *Open File*). This term also refers to a type of tournament in which any class of player can participate. Though a player often ends up with opponents who are much higher (or lower) rated than himself, the prizes are usually structured around classes and, for this reason, opens are attractive to players of every rating. The open tournament is extremely popular in the United States and is beginning to be seen more and more in Europe.

Open File   A column of eight squares that is free of pawns. It is on open files (and ranks) that Rooks come to their maximum potential.

Open Game   A type of position that is characterized by many open lines and few center pawns. A lead in development becomes very important in positions of this type.

Opening   The beginning phase of a game. This usually encompasses the first dozen moves but it can easily go much further. It is often written that the main opening objectives are: 1) develop your pieces in a quick and efficient manner; 2) occupy as much of the center as possible; 3) castle early (King safety).

    While I can say that these objectives are basically correct, the real purpose of the opening is to create an imbalance and develop your pieces in such a way that they all work together in making the imbalance a favorable attribute.

Opposition   In the endgame, a fight between Kings often occurs that ultimately determines which one is stronger. This face-off between the two monarchs is known as the opposition.

Outflanking   An endgame maneuver with Kings which makes forward progress on the board while: 1) Simultaneously preventing your opponent from taking direct opposition; or 2) Temporarily giving up the opposition for a higher goal.

Overextended   When a player tries to gain some advantages by starting a major advance or offensive, and then this offensive fails, he is often left with various weaknesses and nothing to compensate for them. His position is then said to be overextended.

Overprotection A term coined by Nimzovich. It refers to defending a strong point more times than appears necessary. The idea is that a certain pawn or square may be causing the Black (the opponent) considerable problems. By focusing so much energy on it, the Black player would be unwise to break that point because that would unleash the latent energy of the White pieces.

In the diagram, White is overprotecting the e5-pawn. The reason for this is that the e5-pawn spearheads a kingside attack by White.

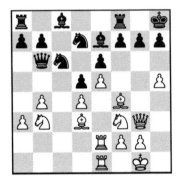

Normally Black might wish to close lines there by ...f7-f5, but now White would answer this and ...f7-f6 with exf6 when all of his pieces have increased their scope and have become extremely active. Thus Black is unable to do anything that would allow White to remove the e5-pawn. As a consequence, his defensive resources are greatly reduced. Also see *Prophylaxis*.

Passed Pawn A pawn that has passed by all enemy pawns capable of capturing it.

In the diagram, White has connected passed pawns on g5 and h6. Black has a passed pawn on a7 and a protected passed pawn on e4.

Passive An inactive move that does nothing to fight for the initiative. A passive position is a position without counterplay or active possibilities.

Patzer A derogatory term that denotes a hopelessly weak player.

Pawn The least valuable unit of force in a chess game. Pawns are not considered to be pieces, they are simply called pawns.

Pawn Center Pawns placed in the center. White pawns on f4, e4 and d4, for example, would constitute a large pawn center. A common opening that allows White to build such a center in the hope of attacking it later is 1.e4 d6 2.d4 Nf6 3.Nc3 g6 4.f4, etc.

Pawn Chain Two or more like-colored pawns linked diagonally. The weakest point of a pawn chain is the base because that is the one pawn in the chain that cannot be defended by another pawn.

Pawn Island A group of connected friendly pawns. In the diagram, Black has three pawn islands to White's two. It is usually considered to be advantageous to have fewer pawn islands than the opponent.

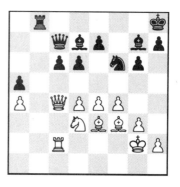

Pawn Structure The positioning of the whole pawn mass. Also referred to as the pawn skeleton. This positioning of the pawns is what usually dictates the types of plans available in a given position due to open files, space, pawn weaknesses, etc.

Pig A slang for Rook. "Pigs on the seventh" is a common term for Rooks doubled on the seventh rank. Also known as "Hogs on the seventh."

Plan A short or long-range goal on which a player bases his moves.

Point Count A system of figuring out the worth of the pieces by giving each of them a numerical value. King = priceless; Queen = 9 points; Rook = 5 points; Bishop = 3 points; Knight = 3 points; pawn = 1 point. The flaw in the system is that it does not take into account other factors (such as position, tactics, etc.) that often drastically change the relative value of an individual piece.

Poisoned Pawn Any pawn that, if captured, would lead to serious disadvantage is considered to be poisoned.

Positional A move, a maneuver or a style of play that is based on an exploitation of small advantages.

Post Mortem A Latin term borrowed from medicine that literally means, "after death." In chess it refers to the sessions that often take place after a tournament game has finished. Both players discuss the game and attempt to find the reason why someone lost—the "cause of death." In particular, those with huge or delicate egos love post mortems because they can show that they saw much more than the opponent (who was undoubtedly lucky to gain the victory). For those of a more open nature, if you have played a stronger player than yourself, you can sit back, ask what you did wrong and hope that the mysteries of the universe will unfold.

Premature A hasty move, maneuver or plan—to take action without sufficient preparation.

Prepared Variation   A deeply researched opening variation that is often strengthened by new moves. It is a common practice to prepare certain lines and new moves for particular opponents, refusing to use it against anyone other than its intended victim.

Problem Child   A reference to a Queen's Bishop that is trapped behind its pawns. For example, the French Defense (1.e4 e6 2.d4 d5) is an attractive opening. Its one flaw is the Queen's Bishop, which is blocked by its own pawns and unable to reach an active square.

Prophylactic Move   See *Prophylaxis.*

Prophylaxis   A strategy explored by Nimzovich. Taken from the Greek word prophylaktikos, meaning to guard or prevent beforehand, prophylaxis (or a prophylactic move) stops the opponent from taking action in a certain area for fear of some type of reprisal. Overprotection is a form of prophylaxis.

Promotion   Also called *Queening.* When a pawn reaches the final rank it's usually turned into a Queen. However, the pawn can be promoted into a Bishop, Knight, or Rook (it cannot be turned into a King). When a pawn is turned into something other than a Queen, the pawn is said to have underpromoted.

Protected Passed Pawn   A passed pawn that is protected by a friendly pawn. See *Passed Pawn.*

Queening   See *Promotion.*

Queenside   That half of the board made up of the four files originally occupied by the Queen, Q-Bishop, Q-Knight and Q-Rook. The queenside stands to White's left and Black's right.

Quiet Move   A move that is neither a capture, a check, nor a direct attack.

Rabbit   A humorous (slightly insulting) term for a non-master.

Rank   A horizontal row of eight squares. The seventh rank in particular is the subject of much activity, especially when a Rook settles there. Control of the seventh rank is considered to be an important advantage.

Rating   See *Elo Rating.*

Refutation   A move or series of moves that demonstrates a flaw in a game, move, variation, analysis, or plan.

Resigns   Realizing the hopeless nature of a position and not wanting to insult the intelligence of the opponent, a player can surrender the game (resign) without having to wait for a checkmate.

Resignation occurs in the vast majority of tournament games, while actual checkmates are quite rare.

Risk   A double-edged sword. A move, plan or opening variation that aims for advantage while carrying the danger of a disadvantage.

Romantic   The romantic era (macho-era) of chess was a time when sacrificing and attacking was considered to be the only manly way to play. If a sacrifice was offered, it was a disgraceful show of cowardice to refuse; thus, many beautiful sacrificial games were recorded simply because proper defensive techniques were not understood. That was in the 1800's. Today, a player who is termed romantic is one who has a proclivity for bold attacks and sacrifices, often throwing caution to the winds.

Sacrifice   The voluntary offer of material for the purpose of gaining a more favorable advantage than the material investment. Unlike a combination, a sacrifice is not a cut-and-dried affair—there is usually an element of uncertainty associated with it. Though a combination always has one or more sacrifices, a sacrifice need not be associated with a combination.

Semi-Open Game   A position with some closed and some open qualities. Typically, 1.e4 e6, 1.e4 c6 and 1.e4 d6 lead to semi-open games. See *Open Games* and *Closed Games*.

Sharp   A bold, aggressive move or position. A sharp player is one who enjoys dynamic, explosive situations.

Shot   A strong move that the opponent didn't expect.

Simplify   An exchange of pieces to reach a won ending, to neutralize an enemy attack or simply to clarify a situation.

Skittles   Chess played in an offhand manner, often at a chess club or after a tournament game.

Sound   An analytically correct move or plan. A safe, solid position.

Space   The territory controlled by each player. Thus, whoever controls the most territory has a spatial advantage.

Speculative   An unclear or risky move or plan.

Strategy   The foundation of a player's moves. The way to achieve a particular plan. See *Plan*.

Style   The preference for certain types of positions and moves. It is typical to have one player who enjoys open, tactical positions while his opponent may cherish semi-closed structures of a positional nature. Thus, the first part of the battle will be to determine who gets the type of position in which he excels.

Support Point   A square that acts as a home for a piece (usually a Knight). A square can only be considered a support point if it cannot be attacked by an enemy pawn or if the enemy pawn advance (attacking the support point) would severely weaken the enemy position.

Swindle   A trick from an inferior position.

Symmetry   A situation in which both armies are identically placed on their respective sides of the board. For example, 1.c4 c5 2.Nc3 Nc6 3.g3 g6 4.Bg2 Bg7 5.Nf3 Nf6 6.0-0 0-0 7.a3 a6 8.Rb1 Rb8 9.b4 cxb4 10.axb4 b5 11.cxb5 axb5 is a well-known symmetrical position that comes from the English Opening.

Tactics   Traps, threats and schemes based on the calculation of variations (at times rather long-winded). A position with many combinative motifs present is considered tactical.

Tempo   The unit of time represented by one move. For example: 1.e4 d5 2.exd5 Qxd5 3.Nc3 gains a tempo, as the Queen must move again if it is to avoid being captured.

Territory   See *Space*.

Theory   Known and practiced opening, middlegame and endgame variations and positions. Opening theory is also referred to as *book*.

Threat   A move or plan that, if allowed, would lead to the immediate depreciation of the enemy position.

Time   Can be used in several contexts. One meaning is the amount of thinking time as measured by special clocks (see *Time Control*) It is also used in reference to the ability to stop a particular action by the opponent, i.e., "Black does not have *time* to coordinate a successful defense against the coming attack." Thus time also measures development (an advantage in time being a lead in development) and the rate at which an attack is pursued or defended.

Time Control The amount of time given to reach a certain number of moves. In international competition this is usually 40 moves in $2^1/_2$ hours (extra time is given after 40 moves have been played). If a player uses up his $2^1/_2$ hour allocation and he has not yet made 40 moves, he will lose the game by forfeit no matter what the position on the board is like.

Time Pressure That period of the game when one or both players have used up most of their time and must make many moves with little deliberation. Naturally, this should be avoided since it often leads to mistakes or game-losing blunders.

Transitions The changing of one phase of the game into another—the opening into the middlegame and the middlegame into the endgame.

Transposition Reaching an identical position by a different sequence of moves. For example, the Dutch Defense (1.d4 f5) can be reached by 1.d4 e6 2.c4 f5 or by 1.c4 f5 2.d4 e6.

Trap A hidden way to lure an opponent into making an error. A trap should only be laid if it is part of the overall strategic plan. This way, it does not matter if your opponent falls for it or not; you will still be improving your position.

Unclear An uncertain situation. Some players never use this assessment, insisting that every position is either equal or favorable for one side or the other. It has even been said that "unclear" is a lazy way to avoid figuring out what's really going on in a position.

Variation The first two to five moves of a game lead to the bare-bones structure of a particular opening. All divergences from that point on are known as variations. Variations also occur in analysis of middlegame and endgame positions.

Weakness Any pawn or square that is difficult or impossible to defend.

Wild Extremely unclear. A sharp situation or move with unfathomable complications.

Zugzwang "Compulsion to move." A German term referring to a situation in which a player would like to do nothing (pass), since any move will damage his game.

Zwischenzug "In-between move." A German term for an often unexpected reply thrown into an expected sequence of moves.